Butcher, Baker, Candlestick maker

SURVIVING *the* GREAT FIRE OF LONDON

Hazel Forsyth

Published in 2016 by

I.B. Tauris & Co. Ltd
London · New York
www.ibtauris.com

Published in association with the Museum of London

ISBN 978 1 78453 748 7

A full CIP record for this book is available from the British Library
A full CIP record is available from the Library of Congress

Library of Congress Catalog Card Number: available

Designed and typeset in 11½ on 16 Garamond by illuminati, Grosmont
Printed and bound by Printer Trento, Italy

(*inside cover*) Shortly after the fire, a large-scale map survey on six sheets
was produced to assess the damage. This reduced version (shown
here in part) was updated and issued in 1669, by John Leake. The map
includes an inset panoramic view of the City on fire and the City arms
with a dedication to Sir William Turner, the Lord Mayor of London for
that year. The key lists the principal buildings destroyed. The location of
livery halls are indicated by their respective coats of arms. Letters identify
individual City wards, with ward boundaries indicated by a pecked line.

(*frontispiece and tailpiece*) *The Great Fire of London* (*detail*), oil on panel,
Anglo-Dutch School, *c.*1666.

Contents

Note *to* readers

No attempt has been made to convert units of currency, weights or measurements to a decimal or metric equivalent. But for ease of use it is perhaps worth stating that there were 12 pence to a shilling and 20 shillings to a pound. Values are generally expressed as £ s d. For convenience, avoirdupois weights have sometimes been rounded up to the nearest pound (16 ounces). The abbreviation 'cwt' is generally used for a hundredweight (112 pounds) but heavier weights have occasionally been converted to tons (2,240 pounds).

Relative values and prices are impossible to convert in any meaningful way, but suffice it to say that wage values were higher in London than anywhere else in the country. The acute labour shortages after the fire forced wages down a little, but it was a volatile market and institutions and employers were keen to shave off as much as possible to keep their costs to a minimum. The most readily accessible wage figures relate to the mass of labourers who were employed to clear and sift the rubble. They were paid on a daily rather than an hourly rate and generally earned 18 pence per day, though a fortunate few received as much as 1s 3d, possibly because they had other skills to offer. Breakfasts were usually provided and these cost between 1d and 2d per person. Craftsmen in the building trades were able to command about 1s 6d per day.

The word 'City' with a capital denotes the area administered by the Corporation of London: largely the area within the walls – the ancient City of London. A lower-case usage and the word 'London' denote the whole of the metropolitan area.

Unless otherwise stated on page 232 all the images and objects illustrated form part of the Museum of London's collection.

The
lamentable FIRE

'the exceeding throng of people &
much bulkey goods pestring ye streets
and lanes … [so all] was burnt and
destroyed.'—*John Kirkham*, citizen &
haberdasher, 13 November 1666

(opposite) Detail from
The Great Fire of London, 1666,
by Jan Griffier I.

(previous spread)
London from Southwark, c.1630. Dutch
school. Oil on panel, not signed or
dated. Panoramic views of cities (or
'prospects') were first commissioned
in the sixteenth century to celebrate
Europe's expanding towns. This rare
view of London is one of the first
painted records of the City before it
was destroyed in the Great Fire of 1666.

In early August 1666 the merchant ship *St Nicholas*, under the
command of Captain Samuel Merryweather, sailed from Barbados
laden with a cargo of sugar. Once the vessel arrived in London,
68 branded casks were unloaded and consigned to John Kirkham,
who placed the larger part in a warehouse in Mincing Lane at the
eastern edge of the City, and the rest in a warehouse in Sabb's
Key just below Harp Lane, a short distance from London Bridge.
Another 31 casks of Barbados sugar were delivered to Kirkham
shortly afterwards and these were also taken to the warehouses. A
few days later, in the early hours of Sunday, 2 September, a baker's
house in Pudding Lane caught fire. By dawn the flames had
reached the warehouses at the bottom of Fish Street Hill; as soon
as Kirkham and his servant Charles Pendleton realized the danger,
they rushed to Mincing Lane and 'used their utmost endeavour'
to remove the sugar to safety. But there was such 'exceeding great
confusion and throng of people and quantitye of gross & bulkey
goods turned out into the streets and lanes' that they were unable
to fight their way through the crowds, and all attempts to save
the sugar failed. In desperation, they turned back into the City
to the warehouse at Sabb's Key, and with 'much cost and paines',
and such help as they could procure, managed to move the sugar
casks into a lighter moored in the dock. But as soon as the casks
were lifted on board, the lighter started to leak and then to sink,
settling slowly into the mud before anyone could remove the casks
to another vessel. Meanwhile the fire had become an inferno. The

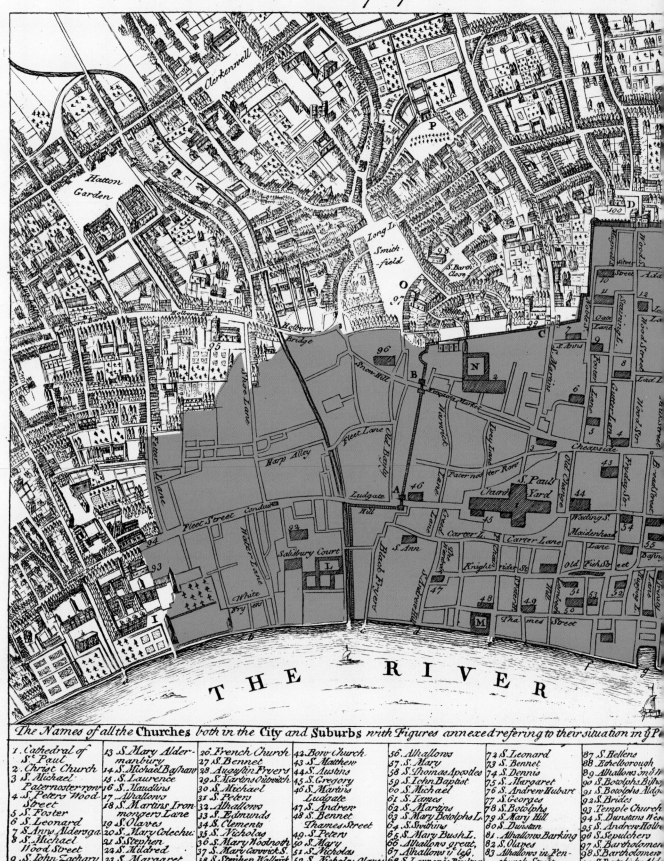

A PLAN of the CITY and LIBERTIES of LON[DON]
The Blank Part whereof represents the Ruins and [&c.]

THE RIVER

The Names of all the Churches both in the City and Suburbs with Figures annexed refering to their situation in ye Pl[an]

1. Cathedral of S.t Paul	13. S. Mary Aldermanbury	26. French Church	42. Bow Church	56. Alhallows	74 S. Leonard	87. S. Hellens
2. Christ Church	14. S. Michael Bassan	27. S. Bennet	43. S. Matthew	57. S. Mary	73. S. Bennet	88. Ethelborough
3. S. Michael Paternoster row	15. S. Laurence	28. Augustin Fryers	44. S. Austins	58. S. Thomas Apostles	74. S. Dennis	89. Alhallows in y.e W.
4. S. Peters Wood Street	16. S. Maudlins	29. S. Martins Outwich	45. S. Gregory	59. S. Iohn Baptist	75. S. Margaret	90. S. Botolphs Bishop
5. S. Foster	17. Alhallows	30. S. Michael	46. S. Martins Ludgate	60. S. Michael	76. S. Andrew Hubart	91. S. Botolphs Aldgate
6. S. Leonard	18. S. Martins Ironmongers Lane	31. S. Peters	47. S. Andrew	61. S. Iames	77. S. Georges	92. S. Brides
7. S. Anns Aldersgate	19. S. Olaves	32. Alhallows	48. S. Bennet Thames Street	62. S. Martins	78. S. Botolphs	93. Temple Church
8. S. Michael Wood Street	20. S. Mary Colechu.	33. S. Edmunds	49. S. Peters	63. S. Mary Botolphs L.	79. S. Mary Hill	94. S. Dunstans West
9. S. Iohn Zachary	21. S. Stephen	34. S. Clements	50. S. Mary	64. S. Swithins	80. S. Dunstan	95. S. Andrew Holbr.
10. S. Olaves	22. S. Mildred	35. S. Nicholas	51. S. Nicholas	65. S. Mary Bush L.	81. Alhallows Barking	96. S. Sepulchers
11. S. Mary Staining	23. S. Margaret	36. S. Mary Woolnoth	52. S. Nicholas Olaves	66. Alhallows great,	82. S. Olaves	97. S. Bartholomew
12.	24. S. Christopher	37. S. Mary Carrwick S.	53. S. Mary Somerset	67. Alhallows ye less	83. Bartholomew	98. S. Bartholomew
	24. S. Bartholomew by the Exchange	38. Stephen Wallbrok	54. S. Iohn Evangelist	68. S. Laurence Poulney	84. S. Catherine Colmans	99. S. Botolphs Alde.
		39. S. Bennet	55. S. Mildred	69. S. Michael Crooked L.	85. S. Catherine Creed C.	100. S. Giles Cripple
		40. S. Pancras		70. S. Magnus	86. S. Andrew Undershaft	* S. Martin Carrwick
		41. S. Antholins		71. S. Margaret		

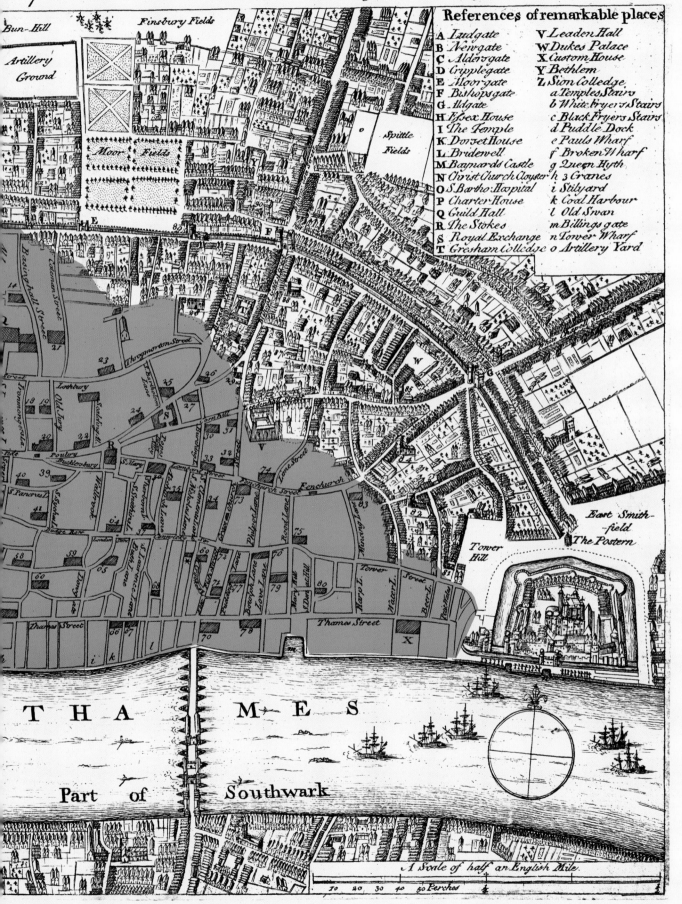

after the *Dreadful Conflagration* in the *Year 1666.*
of the Fire; & the *Perspective that left Standing.*

Bun-Hill

Artillery Ground

Finsbury Fields

Moor Fields

Spittle Fields

References of remarkable places

A	*Ludgate*	V	*Leaden Hall*
B	*Newgate*	W	*Dukes Palace*
C	*Aldersgate*	X	*Custom House*
D	*Cripplegate*	Y	*Bethlem*
E	*Moorgate*	Z	*Sion Colledge*
F	*Bishopsgate*	a	*Temples Stairs*
G	*Aldgate*	b	*White Fryers Stairs*
H	*Essex House*	c	*Black Fryers Stairs*
I	*The Temple*	d	*Puddle Dock*
K	*Dorset House*	e	*Pauls Wharf*
L	*Bridewell*	f	*Broken Wharf*
M	*Baynards Castle*	g	*Queen Hyth*
N	*Christ Church Cloyster*	h	*3 Cranes*
O	*S. Bartho. Hospital*	i	*Stilyard*
P	*Charter House*	k	*Coal Harbour*
Q	*Guild Hall*	l	*Old Swan*
R	*The Stokes*	m	*Billings gate*
S	*Royal Exchange*	n	*Tower Wharf*
T	*Gresham Colledge*	o	*Artillery Yard*

Blackwell Street

Coleman Street

Throgmorton Street

Lothbury

Old Jury

Tronmonger

Poultry

Bucklersbury

Wallbrook

Thames Street

Spittle Fields

East Smith-field
The Postern

Tower Hill

Fenchurch Street

Lime Street

Fenchurch

Mark Lane

Tower Street

Thames Street

THAMES

Part of Southwark

A Scale of half an English Mile.

10   20   30   40   50 *Perches*

piles of timber, hay and coals on the wharves and the stocks of wine, brandy, oil, tar, tallow and other combustible goods in the houses and warehouses along Thames Street and adjacent lanes fuelled the flames. Nothing could check its progress. There were sounds of cracking timbers; sparks rained down on the streets and tongues of flame flickered through the buildings. To John Kirkham's horror, Mr Mortimer's quay next door was set alight; flaming timbers fell down into Sabb's Dock, a burning beam crashed on to the lighter, the sugar casks ignited, and the vessel with everything in it was utterly consumed. In the end, just one of the 99 sugar casks was preserved. A few weeks after the fire, Kirkham was sued by the merchant owners in Barbados for the loss, and the case was brought before the Mayor's Court in London. Kirkham was able to prove that he had done his best to preserve the sugar from the flames and had not been negligent. The case records mention a set of appended accounts detailing the consignment of sugars, with the types, weights, amounts and value of each, but unfortunately these records have not survived.[1]

In five days the 'most destructive fire England has ever seen' consumed a third of the City of London[2] and a small part of the suburbs: a great swathe of land extending from Tower Hill in the east to Whitefriars, Fetter Lane and Holborn Bridge in the west, 'old buildings … all stuffed with ailment for the fire, all in the very heart of the trade and wealth of the City'.[3] As one German correspondent noted shortly afterwards, it is hardly possible with the pen alone to set down an adequate account of 'the pitiful state of things', yet few events in London's history are so well chronicled as the Great Fire of 1666. Several eyewitness accounts provide vivid and graphic descriptions, and extra detail is supplied in sermons, pamphlets, poems, news bulletins, correspondence, legal and administrative records, orders and proclamations. Nor has the subject been neglected since. Over the last hundred years, and especially in the last few decades, the fire has been the focus of a great deal of historical analysis and archaeological investigation. A short bibliography of these secondary sources is supplied at the end of this book. The ashes have been so well sifted that it seems hardly possible to add anything new. Yet there are still areas which deserve greater attention, and one of them concerns the loss of merchandise, commodities and personal effects. Contemporary

(previous spread) Leake's Survey of the City After the Great Fire of 1666, engraved by Wenceslaus Hollar (1607–77). This map, prepared by John Leake, William Leybourne and four others, shows the extent of the area devastated by the Great Fire of 1666. It was first published in 1667.

estimations for these losses make for interesting reading. The first estimate, published in 1667 in *Observations both Historical and Moral*, suggested that the 'goods that every private man lost one with another' was £1,800,000.[4] Almost two decades later, these figures were reissued and expanded by Thomas Delaune in *The Present State of London*, and in this he says that

> It hath been computed by an Ingenious person that the 13,200 Houses burnt, valued one with another at no more than *25 l.* yearly Rent, and at the low rate of 12 years purchase, will amount to *3900000 l*. The 87 Churches, the spacious Cathedral of St Pauls, the 6 Chappels, the Exchange, Custome House, Guild-Hall, the magnificent Halls of Companies, the several principal City Gates, with other publicks Edifices and Colledges, may be well valued above *2000000 l*. The Wares, Household-Goods, Moneys lost, and spoiled by the Fire, or pilfered away by those wicked wretches that made their gain of the Common Calamity, may be modestly be computed above *2000000 l*. The Money spent in a General removing of Goods, during the Fire, and bringing them home afterwards, in the hire of Boats, Carts, or Porters may be reckoned at least *2000000 l*. The total whereof *9900000 l*.[5]

Additional sums of £27,000 were suggested for the loss of wines, tobacco, sugar and plums, which were in abundant supply in the City at that time, and £150,000 worth of printed books and paper in shops and warehouses. These assessments of gross loss have been given a certain amount of credence because they have a degree of precision which suggests reliability, but they must to be taken with a large pinch of salt because there was no reliable mechanism for compiling statistics for civic, corporate or individual loss. There are no continuous sets of customs assessments for London in this period and, although inventories and official documents of one sort and another provide helpful clues, they represent and reflect only a tiny proportion of the population and, to a greater or lesser extent, are both partial and limited. The word 'loss' reoccurs like an echo through the pages of official records, but what did these losses actually mean? People said that they had 'lost everything'; that they were 'utterly undone' by the fire. Did they really lose everything or was the phrase used as a sort of shorthand expression of despair? Documents sometimes provide extra details which suggest that the losses were those of property and not stock or household goods, but in others it is clear that some individuals really did lose all; as one woman said, she had nothing left, 'no clothes but those on her back'.[6] How did people recover from the effects of the fire? What did they have in their homes and businesses? How did they respond? What impact did the fire have on their lives?

This book, written to mark the 350th anniversary of the fire, attempts to address some of these questions. It does not deal with the progress of the fire; neither does it consider the buildings and the rebuilding of the City. Instead it concentrates on material things, household possessions, stock-in-trade and trade practice. The time span of 15 years from 1660 to 1675 is partly determined by the survival of appropriate documents, but is deliberately broad because a rigid adherence to the fire and its immediate aftermath would provide an unbalanced picture of London life and working practice. The first date coincides with the Restoration of Charles II to the throne, and marks the beginning of a period of cultural change, economic reform and technological innovation. But the pre-fire years have also been included because it is simply impossible to appreciate what people stood to lose and hoped to save in the fire without some understanding of what they had before it happened. The last date coincides with the final phase of reconstruction: by 1675 most of the houses, livery company halls and commercial buildings had been rebuilt and were once more open for business.

The book is divided into two main parts. The first deals with aspects of personal loss, evacuation, theft, attempts to salvage goods and the emergency measures put in place by the City authorities to support trade and commercial interests. The second and larger part, arranged in the form of an A–Z by trade, focuses on personal stories and material loss. The evidence is derived entirely from primary sources: household inventories drawn up for the purposes of probate, wills, legal, financial and administrative records for the City and its institutions, government papers, customs accounts, correspondence, sermons, journals and diaries; some of it published here for the first time.

The largest body of source material relates to City institutions: the hospitals of St Bartholomew and Bethlem, Bridewell Prison, Christ's Hospital and the livery companies. These records are held in the Guildhall Library, in the London Metropolitan Archives or by the institutions themselves. Some key groups of records are missing or incomplete for the 1660–75 period, but even those that do survive vary greatly in quality and level of detail. Some are meticulously arranged with fulsome entries and separate sets of minutes and accounts; others are extremely scrappy, little more than bundles of notes with large gaps and random scribblings. But even the best, with a handful of exceptions, seldom refer to trade interests; so it is extremely hard, and sometimes impossible, to gather any real sense of mercantile and commercial activity from these sources alone. It has proved equally difficult to find information about corporate responses to the fire. Some institutions do not mention it all. A few make passing references to the loss of their hall or properties and then turn their attention to other matters such as the next set of appointments for company officers and admissions for freemen and liverymen. Others provide a short statement about the fire and its impact, but even here the focus is never on trade, but rather on the loss of property and rental income. The Clothworkers' Company records are typical. On 13 September the Clerk wrote:

> This day upon consideracon … taken of the greate losse which this company hath susteyned by the late sad and dreadful fire that happened in this Cittie many of their houses being burnt to the ground to the value of £540 odd pounds per annum. And thereby disabled of the performing the charity they were heretofore accustomed and enjoyned to pay out of the rent of the said houses. It is ordered that for the present noe money or Annuitye bee pad to any person whatsoever by the Company without further order of this Court except such money as is here after menconed and expressed.[7]

There are incidental references to monies disbursed for rescuing goods from the fire and payments for labourers to clear the rubble, for temporary lodgings for the company treasures and other matters, but these are relatively few. Just occasionally the somewhat prosaic and matter-of-fact entries include a tantalizing snippet which shows what people really felt, and the word 'fire' is always coupled with an adjectival term such as 'dismal', 'lamentable' or 'disastrous'; it is never 'great'. The lack of sentiment in the records is striking, but there was no need to bewail and belabour personal loss because everyone was in the same situation. What really mattered was the body corporate, and the official accounts are just that – official, formal and very much to the point. The primary concern for the City institutions was to find ways and means to recover their revenues as quickly as possible; to rebuild their property portfolios and to repay their debts.

The rest of the evidence has been drawn from probate inventories for the Archdeaconry Court of London and the Peculiar Court of the Dean and Chapter of St Paul's Cathedral, which alone comprises 1,168 inventories for the 1660–75 period. Just over 900 of these inventories have been used for this book and they relate principally to the precincts and parishes of St Faiths under St Paul, St Giles Cripplegate, St Gregory by St Paul and St Helen Bishopsgate. A few inventories from properties in outlying Middlesex parishes have also been used. The remaining set of inventories were compiled for the Court of Orphans, which was established to look after the estates of citizen freemen who had died leaving children under the age of 21. The executors were obliged to lodge an inventory and a total valuation of the deceased's property with the Court so that a one-third share could be distributed to the widow, one-third to the party nominated in the will, and the remaining one-third to the Chamber of London, which was held in trust for the use of the orphans. The 'nominated' third was more often than not deposited with the City Chamberlain as a sort of gilt-edged investment, and some of this money proved a valuable source of loan collateral to bolster the City's finances after the fire. There are 784 orphans' inventories for the period 1660–75. The quality and level of detail vary enormously, but most of the orphans' inventories follow a formulaic pattern with a preamble citing the name and livery company of the testator, the parish in which his house or shop was situated (not always supplied), the date of inventory, the names and trade affiliations of the appraisers and the name of the Lord Mayor or alderman before whom they were sworn. The inventory usually begins with a room-by-room list of household contents, starting from the garrets at the top of the house and so down, floor by floor, to the cellar; out into a yard and then, if appropriate, to an adjoining shop or warehouse. Lists of stock-in-trade are not always included, but when they are, goods are generally itemized

According to the writer Rege Sincera in 1667, the baker Thomas Farriner had gone to bed with his oven alight, 'leaving his Providence with his Slippers'.

separately or in small, associated groups. Occasionally other rooms in the house were used to store goods and equipment, and when this happened the stock and household items are distinguished with separate valuations. Otherwise, goods are either listed and priced individually or lumped together with one valuation for a group. The inventories end with summary statements of the deceased's household linen, apparel, plate, jewels and any leasehold property. The final entries provide an indication of the 'ready money' in the house or shop at the time of death, which includes the takings of the business between that date and the date of the inventory. Lastly there is a total valuation of the estate; the 'good' and 'bad' debts owed and owing; sometimes a list of debtors and creditors, and disbursements made for the funeral and executors' expenses.

Inventories provide much information about the quality and variety of consumer goods, but it is perhaps worth stating that there are pitfalls and limitations in their use and they can be difficult to interpret. Nomenclature can be challenging: it is not always obvious what the appraiser meant; nor is it always certain if the term had been correctly applied. Spellings were not standardized, all kinds of contractions were used, and there is a good deal of specialist jargon. Panelling, counters, shelves, workbenches and other kinds of fixtures and fittings are seldom mentioned and were only included by appraisers if they had been installed by the deceased and were considered to be 'moveable goods' and not part of the property of the landlord. Even within the same inventory there are often quite stark differences in levels of detail from room to room, and, although some items are described as 'old' or 'worn', the level of new, second-hand and inherited items is impossible to quantify. Some contents are grouped together under a single valuation, while others are listed and valued separately, which makes any kind of comparative analysis within and between inventories extremely difficult. The stock-in-trade sections also vary considerably. In the best, every single item is enumerated, and these can run to hundreds, even thousands, of entries. Otherwise, the goods tend to be bundled together in parcels or subsumed under the catch-all phrase 'other lumber'. Even when the stock is carefully itemized, the tools and equipment are often summarily dismissed with the phrase 'working tooles'. An added difficulty is that probate inventories were produced in a hurry, often in trying and very difficult circumstances, so it cannot be assumed that they give a truly representative or complete picture of the business assets. It is unlikely that consistent stock levels were maintained over the lifetime of the business and it is usually impossible to know if the type of stock listed is exceptional or usual. Does the stock reflect the latest trends or had it been sitting around for a while? How much was manufactured on site? How much had been brought in from other suppliers? Tools and other working equipment are sometimes missing from inventories because they had been already passed on to someone else (usually to a family member, trade associate, business partner), and this was either done because the testator had made the decision to retire or had been obliged through ill health or other reasons to give up his trade. But it is also possible that items were deliberately omitted or poorly described to conceal or disguise the real asset value from creditors and other interested parties. A further complication is that no one could practise a trade or craft within the City unless they were members of a City livery company, but company membership is not necessarily a reliable indicator of occupation. Just because someone described themselves as a citizen haberdasher, it cannot be assumed that they practised the haberdashery trade unless there is other corroborative evidence. Inventories often provide this crucial bit of evidence and it is only by examining the lists of stock-in-trade that one can be certain of the testators' occupation; though it must be said that it was not uncommon for one person to have two or more different occupations, sometimes loosely connected but often, like William Ridges (*see* pp. 86 & 204), quite different.

These fragments of fused pottery and molten window glass were found by archaeologists in Pudding Lane. The pottery has begun to melt, so the fire had reached a scorching temperature in excess of 1,700 degrees Celsius. On 5 September Samuel Pepys picked up a piece of molten glass from Mercers' chapel which he found lying in the street 'where much more was, so melted and buckled with the heat of the fire, like parchment.' He took it home as a souvenir.

Salvaged *or* lost

'I have seen Bells, and Iron Wares melted, Glass and Earthen pots melted together, as it had been by a fire of fusion.'—*Rege Sincera*, 1667[8]

As the wind fanned the flames into ever-greater fury, the fire spread with such speed that nothing could resist. The narrow lanes filled with smoke, sparks rained down into the streets, and the inhabitants awoke to the sound of cracking timbers, falling masonry and the cries and shrieks of their neighbours. Neither thick walls nor open courts and yards could check its progress. Yet many people lingered in their homes 'till the very fire touched them'. Even the pigeons were 'loath to leave their houses, but hovered about the windows and balconies till they were some of them burned, their wings, and fell down'.[9] Paralysed by fear and disbelief, many citizens seemed resigned to their fate. What could they do? Where could their turn? As John Evelyn observed, 'the conflagration was so universal, and the people so astonished, that from the beginning, I know not by what despondency, or fate, they hardly stirred to quench it so that there was nothing heard, or seen, but crying out and lamentation.'[10] Some hurried, some lingered. They ran thither and hither; they fled to the river or to the fields; they obstructed one another; they looked behind and the fire broke out in front; they escaped but found no refuge; the fire blazed in every quarter. Carts and barrows blocked the streets, goods were strewn and trampled underfoot; papers were scattered and lost.

What to take and what to leave behind? This must have been one of the most taxing questions of the moment. The evidence for loss and salvage is covered elsewhere, especially in the A–Z section of this book, so only a few general comments are needed here. Two skeletons which had been suspended on the wall of the Barber-Surgeon's Anatomy Theatre were perhaps among the

strangest items rescued; these, along with rather more obvious 'treasures' from the Company (*see* p. 155), were hurriedly conveyed to Moorfields and thence to a member's house in Holborn Bridge. It would seem from the only surviving set of company records that one, perhaps both, of the skeletons went missing and several payments were made to a 'poore fellow' who received 1 shilling for finding a skeleton; to Peter Smith, the beadle for his charges in 'getting home … a skelliton' and to Jonas Wills 'for the skelliton the Cobler had – 5s'. Whether the 'poor man' and the cobbler were one and the same is unknown; the company records do not provide any further details.[11] Neither is it clear if these were actually embalmed bodies, as is sometimes popularly suggested.

One of the greatest problems was to find a cart and the extra manpower to remove goods, which were both in short supply. At 10 a.m. on 3 September, Lady Anne Hobart in Chancery Lane wrote a hurried letter to her cousin Sir Ralph Verney to explain that

> my hart is not abell to expres the tenth nay the thousen part of it that is all the carts within ten miles round and cars and drays run about night and day and thousen of men, women … carting burdens… I am amost out of my wits. We have packed up all our goods and cannot get a cart for mony, they give 5 and 10 pound for carts. I have sent for carts to my Lady Glascock if I can get them but I fear I shall los all I have and we must run away… I will break open the closet and look to all your things as well as I can…[12]

As John Barker explained in a swift letter on 4 September to Joseph Williamson, under-secretary of state, he had escaped from the Temple with 'little more than the skin of his teeth' and was now staying with a Swedish resident, Lord Lyonberg, until he could get a cart to proceed. As there was not boat, barge, cart or coach to be had, Lord Lyonberg asked for a warrant to 'press four wagons to carry his goods, for at this distance, he is desirous to remove'. Barker took the opportunity to ask for a wagon for his own books and goods too.[13] The time-honoured traffic-flow system was soon abandoned and the convergence of carts and carriages to the City centre caused a massive traffic jam.[14] In an attempt to free up the streets, the authorities prohibited the use of carts in the areas closest to the fire, but this order was soon lifted, and the

This linen curtain, embroidered with blue wool, was reputedly removed out of London at the time of the fire. Although this traditional claim cannot be verified, the curtains date from the mid-to late seventeenth century.

carters and carriers of London had a field day. The prices began to rise day by day, even hour by hour. Instead of the usual rate of 10 or 12 shillings, it was now, as one writer put it, 'five pound for a Cart, another cries out ten pound for a Dray; in one Street one cries out, twenty pound for a Cart, and another in the next Street cries out, thirty pound for a Cart, here one cries forty pound for a Cart, and there another cries out, fifty pound for a Cart.'[15] Dr William Denton, who had fled to Covent Garden, was thankful that he had been able to save his 'moveables but at a vast charge of £4 for every load to Kensington'.[16] Extortionate prices were demanded; Edward Waterhouse claimed that people with great stores had paid £400 to remove their goods to safety, though it is not clear how much they had and whether one or several carts were employed. There were, he continued, many honest carters and labourers, but people lacked the cash to pay them: 'men paying out all on Saturdays their pay day; and those who had thus drayned themselves were certainly put to great straits, being either forced to give one part to carry away the rest, or to leave all to the fire…'[17] All the streets were jammed with goods. Horses driven mad with fright ran amok and broke their traces; and many carts laden with salvaged goods were abandoned in the streets to burn.[18]

To make matters worse, many people found that they had to remove their goods not just once, but several times. The Tallow Chandlers' Company silver plate, a little nut 'garnished with scriptures', their books, accounts and linen were first removed to Golden Lane and then, before the flames reached them there, on again, to the master's family home in Pinner.[19] The churchwardens of St Mary Woolnoth were able to procure a cart to remove the vestments, plate, 'bookes and cushings in the tyme of the Fyre to severall places in the country', and for this and for 'bringing them in London again, and then removing them to severall places to secure them and carriage about the same', they spent £5 6s.[20] A fortunate few (*see* p. 126) had the resources and connections to enable them to remove everything well out of harm's way. The goldsmith-jeweller Sir Robert Vyner wisely removed all of his money, jewels and valuables out of London to Windsor Castle, where they were kept under strict guard until he was able to make arrangements for their return.[21]

Apprentices, journeymen, company beadles, porters and clerks offered valuable support and assistance in the emergency. But a few abandoned their posts or were tempted away by the offer of a financial reward. One such was Richard Field, apprenticed to Thomas Graves, citizen and haberdasher, who when his help was most needed 'did neglect to pack up severall goods' belonging to his master, so they were utterly consumed. Then, to rub salt in the wounds, Field 'went and helped another person ... for above an hour who gave him half crowne for the same'.[22] Another apprentice (*see* p. 92) abandoned his heavily pregnant mistress and left his master's goods to burn. Notwithstanding the cowardly and selfish few, there were many more who neglected their own affairs to help others. On 21 November 1667, William Foster of the Skinners' Company handed over the key of the trunk which held the Company's plate and confirmed that he still had in his custody a 'carpett of arris, a Clock and three cushions belonging to the Company which goods hee promised to deliver when hee should be required thereunto'. The goods were eventually returned, and in 1668 Foster asked that he might receive some compensation for the 'great losses' he had sustained in the fire in order to save items belonging to the Company. The Court ordered that he should first pay all the arrears due upon his account for the time that he had served as Renter Warden, and only then would they consider his losses. A few months later, Foster paid his fine of 40 shillings and submitted a paper, which was read out to the Court. It was decided that monies could not be paid until it was clear what Foster had actually lost, so he was asked to provide a written statement for the next meeting the following month. The account was duly presented and a witness appeared on Foster's behalf who informed the Court that he had indeed lost several goods, namely a kettle, a table, some pewter and some skins (both unspecified). The witness affirmed that Foster had been instrumental in saving some of the Company's goods and she knew this because he had lodged them in her house and had given her £6 by way of thanks.[23]

Dr Merrett, the librarian of the Royal College of Physicians, managed to save 140 of the 'chiefe books' and charters from the fire, spending, he claimed, £10 of his own money and losing many of his own books and goods to the value of £50.[24] Merrett

In 1665 this iron chest was discovered open and robbed of its contents (£700 and silver plate) following a break-in to the College during the Great Plague. It is believed to have been subsequently used for the admission fees of Honorary Fellows. It was rescued from the College in the Great Fire.

asked the College to reimburse him for his salary arrears and for the losses he had sustained in the fire, but when the matter was discussed in committee the president and officers felt that Merrett had been rather liberal with the truth: they were not sure how many books and goods he had actually saved; they also felt that he had 'sufficient time and warning' to remove his own possessions to safety.[25] The dispute rumbled on for years.

In the early 1940s a huge hoard of glass was discovered in a cellar near All Hallows Church, on the corner of Lombard and Gracechurch Street. The cellar was covered by a layer of charred beams and the contents were filled with Great Fire debris: pottery, tobacco pipes dating to the 1660s, 125 wineglasses, 77 beakers, ale-glasses and flutes, 114 bottles and miscellaneous items including four retorts. John Stracey, Master of the Glass Sellers Company in 1679, lived in the vicinity and it is just possible that the discarded material represents part of his stock-in-trade.

The Merchant Taylors' Company faced a rather different challenge. Two years after the fire, the stack of books rescued from the Company library at St Lawrence Poultney, which been taken to the house of the former master, Nathaniel Withers, 'at the time of the late dreadfull fire in London', together with various other goods belonging both to the Company and to Mr Coad, the schoolmaster, had not been returned. All attempts to claim them were thwarted and Withers seemed determined to 'keepe & deteyne the said Bookes & other goods to the great prejudice of the Companie'. There was a heated exchange. When Withers still refused to relinquish the Company's property, the wardens decided that they would obtain a search warrant from the Lord Chief Justice or the Lord Mayor of London and go to his house in Seething Lane and 'demand all the said bookes & all other goods whatsever that are in his custody or that he hath knowledge of & belonging to the Company'.[26]

The Goldsmiths' Company had a different problem. When their accounts were audited in March 1667, there was an outstanding sum of £24 15s 9d which they were unable to explain. The accountants were questioned; Mr Mason said that the ledger book in which he had entered all his receipts and payments had been locked up in a cupboard in the Company's great parlour and 'was there burnt by the late fire', so he was unable to supply the detailed information required. But he affirmed that 'hee had not one penny in his hands of the Companies money and that the money now resting upon the foot of the accompt hee was well assured was laid out in the Companyes service'. He asked that the account be discharged and agreed to pay a proportionate sum in 'lieu thereof'.[27]

Escape & evacuation

'Sir Philip [Frowde] and his lady fled from the [letter] office at midnight for safety; [Hicks] stayed ... till 1 a.m., till his wife and childrens' patience could stay no longer, fearing lest they should be quite stopped up; the passage was so tedious, they had much ado to get where they are ... is sending his wife and children to Barnet.'—*James Hicks*, postmaster, 3 September 1666[28]

As the fire approached the Letter Office in Threadneedle Street,[29] the acting postmaster, James Hicks, was forced to flee. He managed to save some of the most important official letters and papers from the recently arrived Chester and Irish mails, and set up a temporary office at the Golden Lion inn in Red Cross Street, Cripplegate. The following day he followed his wife and children to Barnet, and from there issued a circular letter to the provincial postmasters to inform them of the disaster, with the command that all 'letters from Ministers of State are to be sent hither to me, that I may convey them to the Court. When the violence of the fire is over, some place will be fixed upon for the general correspondence.'[30]

The same day, and in the nick of time, a procession of 200 children from Christ's Hospital in Newgate, which had been set up in the former Franciscan house of the Grey Friars to provide education for the orphaned children of poor Londoners, were marshalled out of the City to Islington, to the safety of the Nagg's Head inn, where they camped overnight. The inn belonged to the Hospital and was fortuitously empty, but it was hardly suitable, and after what must have been a very troublesome and

(*opposite*) Letter, dated 4 September 1666, from James Hicks, postmaster of London 'To my good friends ye Postmasters betwixt London and Chester and so to Holly head.'

(*previous spread*) *The Great Fire of London*, 1666, after Jan Griffier the Elder (*c.*1645/52-1718). Oil on canvas, not signed or dated. This dramatic view of the burning City shows citizens fleeing through Newgate. Flames billow from the roof of St Paul's Cathedral beyond.

To my good ffriends ye Postmasters betwixt London
& Chester & so to Holly head.

Gentlemen

    it hath pleased Alm: God to visit this famous City of L:don with most
raging fire wch began on Sunday morning last about 2 a clock in Pudding lane,
in a bakers house behind the Kgs head taverne in new ffish streete & though all
the meanes possible was vsed yet it could not bee obstructed but before night
it had burnt most part of ye City wth S^t magnus church & part of ye Bridge
to Q. Hith to the water side, Canon streete, Dowgate, & vpon munday struck
vp to Gratious streete, Lumbard street, Cornhill, Poultry Bartholomew
lane, ffrogmorton street, Loathbury & the last night & this day rages
through all parts of the city as far as Temple Barr, Holburne bridge
Smithfeild, & by all conjecture is not by any meanes to bee stopped
fro vs further ruine except god in his infinite wisdome prevent it
I am at ye Red Lyon in Barnet wth my family & blesse god in reason
able good health, notwithstanding great losse & suffcrings by the
distractions of o^r office yet I am Comanded to let y^{ou} know y^t what
letters come to yo hands fro any ministers of state yt you give them
all quicke & speedy dispatch to mee hither yt I may convey y^m hence
to Court or such places as I may receiue direction for, & I am also
to intimate to you y^t w^t letters are sent to y^{ou} fro Court I shall here
them here forwards fro hence to you with speedy Care & conveyance
& so soone as pleaseth god to put an end to ye violence of this fire
some place will bee pitcht on for y^e generall Correspondence as
formerly of wch you shall god willing haue aduice at p^rsent this
is all

                                 yor sorrowfull friend
                                 James Hicks.

Barnet sep. 4. 11 at night.

uncomfortable night the children were moved to better accommodation in Clerkenwell, where they remained for four days. Each child received a ration of 5d per day for food and drink. The Hospital precinct was virtually consumed by the fire, apart from the cloisters, which were undamaged, three of the 'sickwards', the wardrobe and a few small rooms, so the children could not return; consequently a week later 62 children were sent to Ware in Hertfordshire to 'be nursed there att 16d per weeke besides schooleing', and three days later another 50 were taken to the town of Hertford.[31]

The forced evacuation of some 100,000 people caused major problems.[32] The City institutions faced particular difficulties in managing their affairs. On 3 October, the wardens of the Spectacle Makers' Company complained that so many of their members had dispersed 'into severall remote parts as yet unknown' that they were unable to hold a Court meeting.[33] A month later, the master of the Grocers' Company announced that important matters had been neglected because members had to travel great distances to reach the City and many were put off from making the attempt as it was too dangerous to scramble over the ruins on dark evenings. It would be better, he suggested, to hold business meetings on Friday afternoons in the hope that more people would make the effort to come.[34] The dwindling membership was so serious that many companies had to find ways to bring in new people to maintain business and bolster their revenues. The Carpenters' Company wardens appointed more assistants to 'cover their losses' but were also troubled that 'the livery of this Company now growth thinne & few in number by reason of the late Mortality and other casualties & impediments.'[35] Attracting new people to fill these posts proved a challenging task. Many members had settled elsewhere or were so reduced by their losses in the fire that they were unable to make the necessary financial contributions. But there were other issues too. Thomas Gallaley, a member of the Clothworkers' Company, had been constrained, he said, to remove a hundred miles into the country; as he had no intention of returning, he suggested that the annuity monies which had accrued from his gift to the Company of £3,000 should now go to someone else who he would appoint, and he asked the wardens if he might surrender his position and withdraw his membership.[36]

Before the fire, Robert Hayes, had a coffee house called The Turk's Head in Panier Alley (a passage running from Paternoster Row near St Paul's Cathedral to Newgate Street) from which he issued his first trade token: 'AT YE COFFEE HOUSE IN PANIER ALLEY'. This property was destroyed in the fire so Hayes was forced to relocate. He issued another token to advertise his new business address for his customers, which was carefully worded to drive the point home: 'IN BARBICAN FORMERLY IN PANNYER ALLY'.

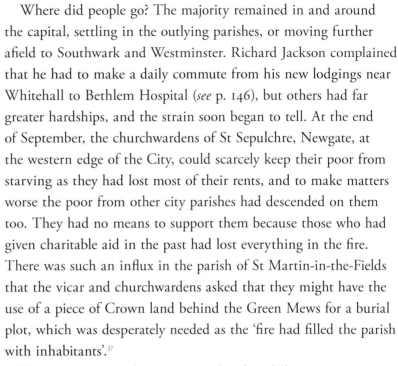

Where did people go? The majority remained in and around the capital, settling in the outlying parishes, or moving further afield to Southwark and Westminster. Richard Jackson complained that he had to make a daily commute from his new lodgings near Whitehall to Bethlem Hospital (*see* p. 146), but others had far greater hardships, and the strain soon began to tell. At the end of September, the churchwardens of St Sepulchre, Newgate, at the western edge of the City, could scarcely keep their poor from starving as they had lost most of their rents, and to make matters worse the poor from other city parishes had descended on them too. They had no means to support them because those who had given charitable aid in the past had lost everything in the fire. There was such an influx in the parish of St Martin-in-the-Fields that the vicar and churchwardens asked that they might have the use of a piece of Crown land behind the Green Mews for a burial plot, which was desperately needed as the 'fire had filled the parish with inhabitants'.[37]

Many migrants and non-natives abandoned the city to return to their birthplace. The pewterer John Fryer said that his mother Suzanna, who had come to London to make her living as a servant and had worked for Mr Stoner in Bow Church Yard before the fire, had to leave the capital because her employer lost everything and could no longer support her. Suzanna returned to her home county and was taken in by a relative in High Wickham.[38] The draper Joseph Stockle was also forced to leave London, returning to his birthplace in Banbury, from where eight years later he petitioned the King, asking that he might be granted the freedom of the town, which had hitherto been denied, to the detriment of his trade and well-being.[39] The large immigrant community in London were particularly vulnerable and there was a great deal of xenophobia. 'Owing to the great fire which has taken place here I have not dared to go out' wrote one Dutchman to his compatriots in The Hague. He continued:

> the people believed that the Dutch and French had set fire to the city. They said that the conflagration was begun by a Dutch baker, who was bribed to do this work, and the French went about scattering fireballs in the houses. All foreigners alike were held to be guilty, no discrimination being shown, and many who were well-known to be of good character, and upon whom no suspicion could rest, were cast into prison …

Mr Germinus, who has the appearance of a Frenchman, … was grossly ill-treated. A poor woman walking in Moorfields, who had chickens in her apron, was seized by the mob, who declared that she carried fire-balls, and not only did they violently abuse her, but they beat her with sticks and cut off her breasts. A Dutch baker in Westminster, Riedtveldt, heated his oven to bake bread. The people, seeing smoke issuing from the chimney, cried out that the rogue was setting the town on fire at that end, and they dragged him into the street, severely wounding him, and then beat him nearly to death. The Duke of York happened to pass the house just in time to save the man from being murdered. The mob plundered his house, and the baker is completely ruined … It will be a long time before the people of London forget their wild rage against foreigners.[40]

Little wonder, then, that Jacob Huisman hastened out of town and then wrote to the secretary of state to ask for a safe-conduct letter as 'foreigners were ill accepted', pointing out that as a native of Antwerp and therefore a subject of Spain he was an entirely innocent party and still wished to continue to serve king and country as best he could.[41] But when John Bonneau, a French Protestant, lost his job as a sugar refiner because his master's property and goods had been destroyed in the fire, he decided that it was time to return home and was granted a special certificate which enabled him to do so.[42]

One of the greatest challenges was to discover where people had gone. Pepys joined a throng of people in Gresham College (*see* p. 53) who had gone there to satisfy their curiosity to see the 'new place' which had been set up to house the merchants and traders from the Royal Exchange and the City officers, and partly to 'find out and hear what is become one man of another'. Here, Pepys noted, 'I met with many people undone, and more that have extraordinary great losses.'[43] The problem was so serious that those inhabitants whose houses had been burned and who had settled in other parts of the city and suburbs were encouraged to put their names and new addresses down in a register so that their customers would know where to find them. Every effort was made to maintain trade, and the King appointed officers to set up an 'office of intelligence' whereby letters, goods and other items could be directed and forwarded on to those who had entered their names in the record book. The office location was to be advertised in the weekly *News-book*, and every week a new sheet would be issued with the names of those who had applied.[44] Three months later it was still proving difficult to trace people, so in some exasperation one merchant petitioned the King for leave to set up his own address office where merchants and traders, inhabitants and strangers alike could leave their names. This kind of voluntary service was commonplace on the Continent, he claimed, and the want of it was keenly felt in London after the fire as people were arriving in the capital from so many parts of the kingdom in the hope of finding their friends and relations. Such a scheme, he argued, would prove of great benefit to all and would serve to promote trade rather than hinder it.[45]

The need to keep track of people was a pressing concern. On 5 October the governors at Bridewell, a house of correction for poor children, orphans, vagrants, beggars, idle youths, run-away servants and petty criminals, were particularly worried. The precinct was destroyed in the fire, and the children who were put to work under the guidance of 'artsmasters' who taught craft and trade skills, such as weaving, glove making, comb making, shoemaking, felt making, pin making and spinning, were now living all over the city (*see* p. 146). The artsmasters were asked to leave a note at Bethlem Hospital in Bishopsgate, with their name and those of their apprentices and their new addresses, so that clothes, food and other items could be delivered at the appointed time.[46]

This hastily compiled 'Book of views', using scraps of paper with scribbled notes and rough plans, was compiled to record the losses sustained by the tenants of St Bartholomew's Hospital. This page refers to three houses in Knight Rider Street, to the south of St Paul's Cathedral.

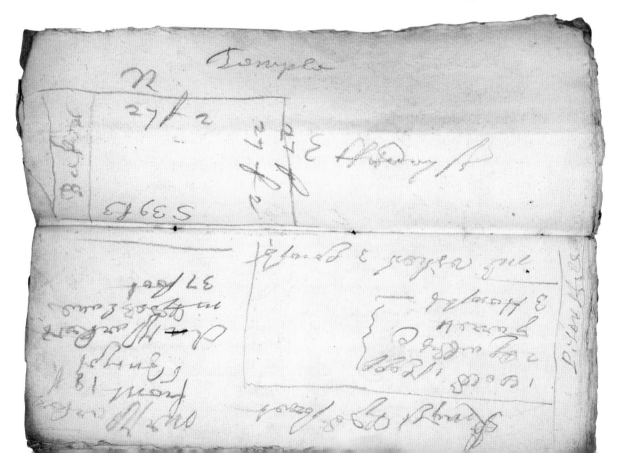

Sheds, booths & tents: a *makeshift City*

'the poore Inhabitans dispersd all
about St Georges, Morre filds, as far as
higate, & severall miles in Circle, Some
under tents, others under miserab[l]e
Hutts and Hovells, without a rag, or
any necessary utinsils, bed or board,
who from delicatnesse, riches & easy
accommodations in stately & well
furnished houses, were now reduc'd to
extreamest misery & poverty.'
—*John Evelyn*, 4 September 1666[47]

By 6 September the fire was almost spent. Flames continued to
belch from bitumen and oil-filled cellars, plumes of smoke arose
from the embers, and people stepped gingerly over mounds of
smouldering rubble that was so hot in places that it scorched the
soles of their shoes.[48] It was a scene of utter desolation. Many of
the streets and alleys had all but disappeared under piles of debris,
and when Pepys travelled down river to his home by the Tower he
was saddened 'to see how the River looks – no houses nor church
near it to the Temple – where it stopped'.[49] Just one great void of
ash and rubble, punctured here and there by blackened chimneys,
tottering steeples and tumbling towers, and a few shacks which
had already started to appear among the ruins serving beer and
other refreshments to the labourers 'who walk from the suburbs
into the City'.[50] The Court of Aldermen held a crisis meeting and
emergency measures were speedily introduced. The bridgemasters
were ordered to make a clear path across London Bridge and to
remove all obstructions impeding traffic from Southwark. Next,
provisions were made for the freemen of the City who were 'destitute of habitacons' so they could erect sheds on any of the void

places on either side of the Bridge to resume their trades. Other patches of void ground at the foot of the Bridge were identified as suitable spots for sheds so long as permission was obtained from the tenants and taken upon 'such termes as they thinke fit'. If no one wished to avail themselves of this offer, then the bridgemasters were to enclose the ground with rails for the security of passengers. Finally, an urgent dispatch was sent to the King for tents to be delivered to Finsbury Fields for the poor people who had lost their homes and were unable to find alternative accommodation.[51]

Two days later, the Court of Aldermen decreed that any citizen who wished to erect a tent or shed for their trade and employment could now move into the Artillery Ground; into Moorfields just to the north of London Wall; to an area marked out from Moor Gate to the Postern Gate near Broad Street; and, within the wall, on a vacant patch along Coleman Street. A further zone was set aside in Smithfield. The City surveyor, Mr Mills, was ordered to set out the grounds and apportion the space 'as bee most convenient'.[52] There was an immediate scramble for places. Sheds and booths started to go up everywhere. But this makeshift cityscape was not entirely welcome. The influx of sheds in and around the Artillery Ground was a particular concern to the Honourable Artillery Company, which protested that people had started to encroach upon their grounds, and so on 24 September the Company officers demanded that all sheds and structures which had been put up without their consent would be immediately pulled down and the occupants proceeded against as trespassers. To bolster their claim to the grounds, the clerk was told to obtain copies of the lease to prove their title to the Artillery Garden, as well as copies of the draft assignments from the old trustees to those currently in office. And because the wall around the grounds had been breached during the fire, urgent repairs were made to repel further incursions.[53]

Sheds started to pop up across the City. In October, Widow Warde, a tenant of the Stationers' Company, sought permission to build a shed on the site of her old tenement called the 'Darke-house' for the 'driving on of some trade there for the present'. Permission was granted, and she was asked to build a substantial structure over the entire plot, partly to give her as much room as possible but also to prevent anyone else encroaching on the land.

(*overleaf*) Moorfields and the fields to the north of the City are clearly shown on the 'Copperplate Map' *c*.1588, the earliest known map of the capital.

The Stationers' Company carpenter and two wardens visited the site to view the ground and agree the terms and conditions of her rent. They concluded that the cost of the shed would be borne by the Company.[54] The Corporation received applications from all quarters. Tom Bowles, a turner, Edward Brown, cutler, William Hope, bookseller, and Moses Browne, miller, asked to build sheds in the churchyard of St Martin's Outwich at the southern end of Bishopsgate. Thomas Randall and Robert Knight, grocers, wished to put up two booths each measuring 16 foot at the south-west corner of Chiswell Street near the Artillery Ground; James Windus asked to build an 8 by 4 foot shed in the yard of Gresham House under Dr Goddard's window (*see* p. 52), and Thomas Parsons wanted to set up a little booth to 'draw drink' at the lower end of Cornhill.[55]

By the end of October the City Chamberlain, with the assistance of the surveyor and others, imposed a more structured scheme for shed building across four main sites which were distributed in a wide arc around the northern edge of the City: Smithfield, Moorfields, Broad Street and Leadenhall; a few isolated spots near the Cripplegate conduit; against the walls of various city churches and beside some private houses such as Lady Vincent's house in Bishopsgate Street; and adjoining Richard Tucker's 'new dwelling house in Winchester Street'.[56] A little more information is known about these sheds because 'An Account Book of money received and paid for sheds erected in Moorfields, Smithfield, and other places' has survived and provides all kinds of detail. It covers the period from 23 February 1667 to 7 May 1670, and includes the names of the 310 licensees, their occupations (not always supplied), the terms of the lease, rental values, fines, and the locations of the sheds and stalls.[57] There were at least 54 in Smithfield, 75 or more in Moorfields, and 16 in Leadenhall, but it is difficult to be exact because some names were entered more than once; some people had several shops and stalls; and it is not always apparent from the accounts if a shed was a new-build or simply had a new occupant. Neither is it certain, in the absence of corroborative evidence, if the trades listed were actually practised by the shed owners. Thirty-three separate occupations are specified for 90 people; from this evidence it is clear that there was a degree of occupational clustering between one site and

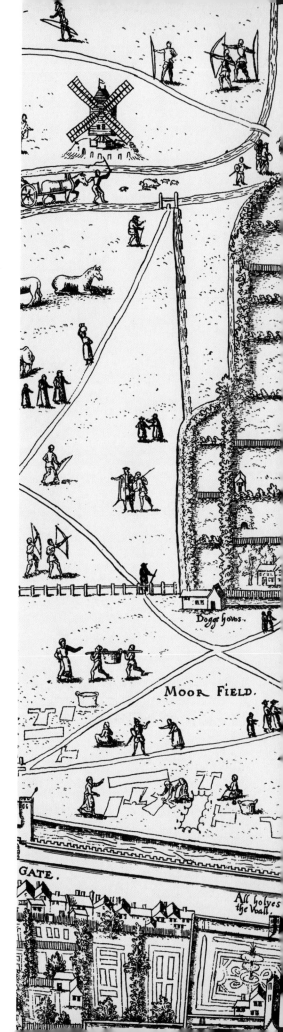

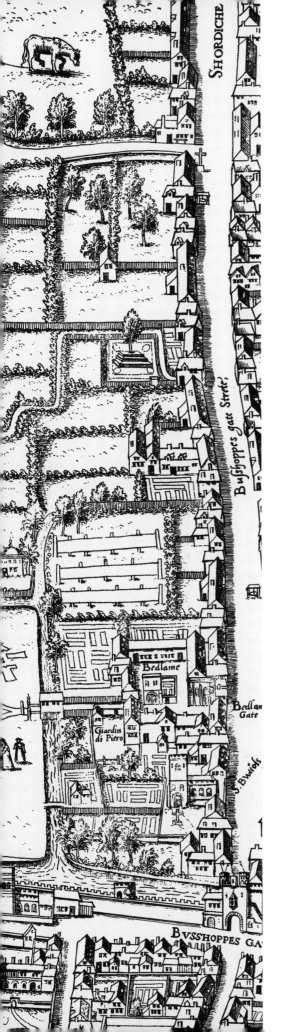

another. The fishmongers were based in West Smithfield, beside the Cripplegate conduit or within the Green Yard in Leadenhall. The poulterers and butchers were in Leadenhall or Smithfield. The drapers, mercers and grocers tended to favour Moorfields. The largest occupational group were the 16 fishmongers, closely followed by 13 grocers, 10 ironmongers, 9 haberdashers, 6 joiners and 5 coopers. The remaining trades are represented by just one or two artificers.

Moorfields was unquestionably the most important of the main sites set aside for shed-building. It was also the largest and the most convenient, lying to the immediate north of the City wall between Moorgate and Bishopsgate, partially enclosed on its eastern edge by private gardens and summer houses, and to the north and west lying open to Mallow Fields and Finsbury Fields in Shoreditch. For centuries this marshy/quaggy ground, criss-crossed by watercourses and rough paths, had remained largely untouched because the ground was ill-suited for building. Tenter-grounds for stretching and drying cloth ran along the northern edge of City Ditch towards Cripplegate; some of the ground had been divided up into smaller fields enclosed by scrubby hedges; but the largest tract of land, the Moor Field, was open fallow ground, with tussocky pastures for grazing, for drying clothes, and for all sorts of pastimes and entertainments. For many years the fields and ditches had also been used as a dumping ground for rubbish and all kinds of filth and dung. By 1605 the area had become such an eyesore that the City decided that it should be cleaned up, drained and levelled. Elm trees were planted around the perimeter, and raised walks bisecting the grounds offered a 'pleasurable place of sweet ayres for Cittizens to walk in'.[58]

Moorfields became a place of sanctuary for Londoners in the fire. The neatly laid out paths soon turned into a quagmire, the grass was strewn with possessions, and the fields were covered by a sprawling encampment. All sorts of ramshackle structures started to go up; makeshift tents fabricated from remnants of canvas or cloth were hurriedly hoisted over boxes and meagre piles of belongings, and 'miserable huts and hovels' sprung up across the site. There were people and goods everywhere. The same situation was replicated across the City, and it was only with the utmost difficulty that some kind of order was imposed on the chaos.

The Moorfields encampment comprised four key areas: Moorfields itself; Little Moorfields to the west; the Moor Ditch, running along the length of the wall; and the Mallow Fields, adjoining Finsbury Fields, just to the north. Even the tiny patch of 'waste ground' between the City wall and the Postern Gate was used.[59] In November 1666 the new inhabitants of the lower Mallow Fields drew up a petition asking permission to install a turnpike across the road so that they could bring in and remove their goods from their dwellings by cart as and when required. The Court of Aldermen pondered for a while because they were unsure whether this would cause greater inconvenience to the citizens and further damage the fields.[60] A site inspection was made and a report written and presented to the Lord Mayor, and it was decided that a turnpike could be installed at the south-west corner of the field so long as the carts followed a particular route: along the walks by the wall and then across the four main avenues quartering the plot, and so along to the petitioners' 'houses' on the east side; not on any other 'walks' or parts of the field. And because it was expected that the heavy traffic would churn up the pathways into a rutted morass, the ground was to be prepared with gravel and other materials to provide a level and firm surface. The costs of this work would be borne by the petitioners. A toll fee of 4 pence would be levied for every cart passing through the turnpike; 3 pence of which would go to the 'use of the Citty' and the remaining penny to the field keeper, who would be responsible for opening and shutting the gate. And just to make sure that there was no cheating, the field keeper was to provide quarterly accounts and pay the monies directly to the City Chamberlain so the funds could be used to cover the costs of maintaining the walks and other parts of the fields for the next few years. Finally it was agreed that none of the field keepers should 'intermeedle' with the toll duties until they were bound with sureties and were 'liked and approved by [the] Court'.[61] It would seem that neither Thomas Exton nor Symon Bone, who had worked as keepers or groundsmen in Moorfields before the fire, was considered suitable, because on 26 March 1667 they complained of 'ye decay of their said places by occasion of ye late dismall fire [and asked] for some reliefe in recompense of their said losses'.[62]

Ann Smith, widow, applied for a stall or shop space adjoining the wall of Gresham House, and Samuell Willson set up five stalls in Bishopsgate Street nearby.[63] Sheds were erected in the 'Green Yard' on the Leadenhall site, but warehouse space was commandeered too, and in February and March 1667 four ironmongers – Nicholas Roberts, William Hamon, William Pate and David Urrey – were granted licences to move into warehouses to carry on their trade, possibly working together as a syndicate. The sheds in Smithfield were rather more tightly packed in an area known as the 'Round' on the western part of the site, which had been created in 1615 as part of a local improvement scheme to turn the area into 'faire and comely order'. The main part was paved, sewers and underground watercourses were installed, and 'strong rayles' were set up to turn the central area into a 'very faire and civill walk ... and to defend the place from annoyance and danger, as well from carts as manner of cattell, because it was intended hereafter that in time it might prove a faire and peaceable market-place'.[64] It was to this west Smithfield location that people who had lost their homes in Newgate, Aldersgate and Ludgate flocked, and it was here that many remained for weeks, months, even years. It was here, too, that Samuel Pepys's cousin Thomas was forced to move.[65] The goldsmith Evodius Inman also had a booth in Smithfield Rounds (see p. 125).

The next set of rules governing the sheds was introduced by the Court of Common Council on 14 November. A diligent search was to be undertaken of all of the sheds and booths which had been put up after the fire to find out by whom they had been built, by whom they were occupied and to what use they were employed; a written report would be compiled for the future welfare and good government of the City.[66] As a result of this survey and other inspections, new sheds were set up in serried lines in a grid pattern with streets and passageways between. Nineteen shed licences were granted in February 1667; in March there were 122. There was considerable variation in the rents both within one district and between one site and another: the variation presumably reflecting the size of the plot, the type of shed structure on it and the relative advantage of its location. The cheapest at £2 10s were for the booths in the City churchyards. The shed rents in West Smithfield varied from £3 to £36, though most were

The Great Fire of London, Anglo-Dutch school, *c.*1666. Oil on canvas, not signed or dated. A view of the burning City from the west, with Essex Stairs and Temple Stairs stretching out into the river on the left.

between £6 and £15. The Leadenhall rents varied from £22 to £30; and the Moorfields shed rentals ranged between £7 and £36. The most expensive spot by far was the Moor Ditch and here rents averaged £32 per shed, with some at £40 and one, belonging to Peter Hublon a wealthy merchant, at £88. And it was perhaps for this reason that in February 1667 'divers citizens (some whereof are of this Court) … with sheds in Moorfields and Mooreditch' submitted a petition to the Court of Common Council, asking that they could 'enjoy their sheds without paying any rent or fines'. Their plea fell on deaf ears.[67]

When Pepys visited Moorfields on 7 April 1667 he was astonished to see 'houses built two stories high, and like to stand, and must become a place of great trade till the City be built; and the street is already paved as London Streets used to be – which is a strange, and to me an unpleasing sight.'[68] Some of the sheds were evidently very large because Joseph Titcombe, a carpenter, paid £20 8s for 'a parcel of ground conteining in length 140 foote' for five years from September 1668 in Little Moorfields. Pepys's reference to paving is particularly interesting because the central thoroughfare within the Moorfields shed-city rapidly acquired the sobriquet 'New Cheapside', which suggests that it had become the premier market and shopping street for the City, selling all kinds of luxury goods: a crude counterpart of the old Cheapside, which for centuries had been a jewel in London's commercial crown. New Cheapside even began to feature as a new 'search location' for the Goldsmiths' Company, and in 1668, under the heading '[i]n the buildings in Morefields called New Cheapside', the wardens entered Samuel Boulton's shed and found various small wares including a wine cup and two dram cups. They were denied entry to the sheds of the goldsmiths James Shaller and Samuel Hawks nearby (*see* p. 125).[69]

In January 1667, another review was made of the sheds in Smithfield, Moorfields, Queenhithe, Duke's Place and 'all other places' on the City's lands, so that the terms of the leases could be settled and any rental arrears paid. In an effort to help people, the committee appointed to this task decided that the citizens could continue to build and live in a shed for seven years. After this time the buildings would be dismantled and the rents would cease. The shed owners could carry away any of the materials, and anyone wishing to cut the lease term short would be obliged to pay a fine.[70] The seven-year lease term seems to have been remarkably prescient because by 1672 most people had managed to rebuild or find alternative accommodation elsewhere. Perhaps the lease term simply spurred people into action because they knew that the clock was ticking.

Although the sheds were temporary structures, ownership and title were taken very seriously indeed. On 23 April 1668 a case about the transference of a shed lease in Moorfields was brought before the Lord Mayor. Thomas Pownsett, a scrivener (notary), appeared on behalf of John Whittler, grocer, in a complaint against John Proffitt, a druggist. Pownsett testified that he knew both parties and had done so for about 12 months. He was shown a copy of the lease and confirmed that this was indeed the document that he had drawn up between Whittler and Proffitt, 'touching a Booth' called the Woolpack in New Cheapside, Moorfields, in which Proffitt kept his shop. He was actually present when the document had been signed and sealed, and he had entered his own name as a witness. He had prepared the indentures of lease for his client and had left a blank for the day and month, which should have been dated before Michaelmas (29 September). Unfortunately the document was mistakenly dated 12 October 1667, and in consequence Proffitt had taken advantage; had kept all kinds of goods in his booth and had not paid the extra month's rent. Whittler did not realize the mistake until it was too late and the indenture had been sealed.[71]

By 1670 some of the sheds were rather tumbledown and were becoming a nuisance. The churchwardens of St Stephen Walbrook ordered that the sheds cluttering up their churchyard should be pulled down,[72] and in April 1673 the Lord Mayor and the Court of Aldermen received additional powers from Parliament to enforce the demolition of the sheds. One year's grace was given: citizens were told that by 29 September 1674 all 'sheds, shop and other Buildings shall be punctually taken down and removed'. But those who had put up sheds and booths without grant or licence from the City or had in some way infringed the rules and regulations or taken up more ground than was first allowed them were given less time and were told to pull down their structures by 24 June 1674; otherwise it would be done for them. A timely reminder was printed and distributed to all shed owners on 17 March 1674, and people were told that they should remove all of their goods and materials in proper time; otherwise, they would be seized by the City.[73] By 1669 the income from the shed licences was £4,198 19s 6d. Some of this 'Shed Cash' was used towards the costs of rebuilding the ship *Loyal London*, and for other administrative costs incurred by the town clerk and aldermen.

Extra sets of keys and locks were needed to replace those lost or destroyed in the fire, and all sorts of trunks and strong boxes were used to store valuables.

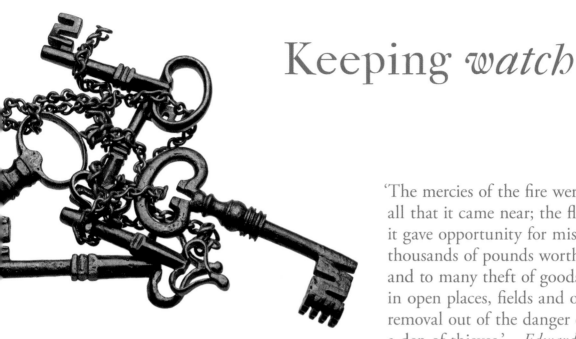

Keeping *watch*

'The mercies of the fire were cruel to all that it came near; the flight from it gave opportunity for miscarriage of thousands of pounds worth of goods, and to many theft of goods lodged in open places, fields and others … a removal out of the danger of fire into a den of thieves.'—*Edward Waterhouse,* 1667[74]

In the midst of turmoil, where 'all men's minds are full of care to protect themselves and save their goods', Pepys noted that the 'Militia is in armes everywhere'.[75] The Duke of York assumed command and on Monday, 3 September, a disaster-contingency plan was implemented. Designated fire posts were set up in front-line positions in Cripplegate, Aldersgate and Coleman Street, and five more were established at the western fringe of the City at Temple Bar, Clifford's Inn Gardens, Fetter Lane, Shoe Lane and Cow Lane in Smithfield, as a further bastion of defence. Each post was placed under the charge of a privy councillor or noble, with three Justices of the Peace, 30 foot soldiers under the command of a 'good careful officer', the parish constables and a muster of a hundred local men. Fortunately, just three months before the fire the Lord Mayor had issued a precept to the City companies that they should equip themselves with arms and ammunition for the service and safety of the City.[76] Supplies of bread, cheese and beer were allotted to each post and any man who proved diligent in fighting the fire was rewarded with a shilling. Orders were sent to the Lords Lieutenant of the surrounding counties to rally their militias for the capital's aid and, over the following days, fresh contingents from the country arrived to relieve the troops guarding the fire posts.[77]

John Evelyn was assigned 'to look after the quenching of Fetter-land end, to preserve (if possible) that part of Holborn', but he did not receive his commission until 5 September, and noted that 'while the rest of the gentlemen took their several posts, some at one part, and some at another', many were apathetic and indolent, standing around, he noted, cross-armed in a posture of resignation. Only gradually did people accept that the only way to check the progress of the fire was to blow up buildings to create a firebreak, and Evelyn was keen to adopt this method in his own patch to prevent the flames reaching St Bartholomew's Hospital, which was full of wounded soldiers and sailors.[78] A further order was issued to two companies of trained bands who were deployed to guard people's goods which had been abandoned in the open spaces of Lincoln's Inn Fields, Gray's Inn Fields, Hatton Garden and St Giles-in-the-Fields. A senior officer was assigned to inspect these sites to make sure that the orders had been properly executed. On 6 September, after the Earl of Oxford had done his rounds, he discovered that out of the eight posts, only the constables at St Giles-in-the-Fields had done their duty. The Holborn Bridge and Smithfield contingent had been kept up to the mark by the vigilance of Mayor Wheeler, but there were no gentlemen at all on duty at Cripplegate near the Barber-Surgeons' Hall.[79]

A national proclamation was issued for the supply of the 'distressed people left destitute by the late dreadful and dismal fire', and the King ordered that all of the churches, chapels, schools and public buildings should be kept open to receive the goods of 'those who know not how to dispose of them', and that the towns and villages around the capital should welcome the refugees and 'permit them to exercise their trades 'on promise that they shall afterwards be no burthen to them'.[80] By 4 September the people were so exhausted that Lord Fanshaw of Hertfordshire was ordered to send 200 foot soldiers to the City with enough food and provisions to keep them for 48 hours with supply wagons of pickaxes, ropes, buckets, spades, and all sorts of tools and fire equipment 'lest the want thereof add to the calamity'. The troops were to muster at Kingsland near Bishopsgate to await further orders from the Justices of the Peace and deputy Lieutenants. Similar orders were dispatched to the other county Lieutenants:

These carved figures of a wounded soldier and sailor were probably used as a sign outside a ward or over the entrance to St Bartholomew's Hospital. How they came into the Hospital's possession is unknown, but on 1 June 1657 they were ordered to be 'painted in oil whatever colour the governors order.' John Evelyn was one of the commissioners appointed to look after prisoners of war and wounded soldiers and sailors.

the Kent troops were to assemble in Southwark, the Middlesex contingent at the Temple and the Surrey group in Lambeth.[81]

On 7 September the fire was over. The Middlesex troops were sent home but the Lord Lieutenant of the county was commanded to send in as many tools and supplies as he could spare; similar notes were sent to his counterparts in Kent, Surrey and Hertfordshire. But the task of keeping watch and providing aid to the destitute proved an immense challenge. There were all sorts of difficulties. Some people were immensely kind and generous (*see* p. 118). Others, however, refused to help even when asked to do so. Thomas Gaddesby, a wheelwright in Islington, used 'opprobrious words' to the gentleman appointed by a special warrant to 'keep watch and ward … and induce the inhabitants to give what Christian relief and reception they could to those who took refuge there'.[82]

The most pressing need was to find shelter and protection for salvaged goods and possessions. People *were* vulnerable and they *felt* vulnerable. There were increasing reports of robberies across the City; as one correspondent rather uncharitably remarked, the 'first rank … minded only for their own preservation; the middle sort so distracted and amazed that they did not know what they did; the poorer, they minded nothing but pilfering'.[83] The schoolboy William Taswell recorded that some people came to his home under the pretence of being porters and had offered their assistance to his family to move their goods to safety. His father gratefully accepted their help, but unfortunately they 'so far availed themselves of our service as to steal goods to the value of forty pounds'.[84] The Taswells were not alone, and over the following weeks several people were indicted for stealing: Anne Hamper sued Francis Lane for 'defrauding her of certain goods' which she had delivered to him at the time of the fire; Mary Fisher was indicted on suspicion of stealing 'several quantities' of Virginia tobacco from John Martin's property on the corner of Mincing Lane and Fenchurch Street; and Richard Robinson of St James, Clerkenwell, brewer, was summoned before the Middlesex magistrates 'to answere for the taking away a cloath coate from the late great fire'.[85]

Twelve wherries manned by Richard Pyke and 23 of his fellow watermen were employed to patrol and 'row diligently' on the

Thames to prevent 'the embezzlement of the goods of merchants and others'. And makeshift security hoardings went up all over the City. Precarious wobbling structures were put together from odds and ends, with fixtures and fittings salvaged from the ruins, so hastily assembled that they began to tumble down almost at once; the wardens of the Grocers' Company were immensely frustrated when their hoardings, buffeted by strong winds, collapsed time after time over the following winter. Carpenters, bricklayers and labourers strove to enclose vulnerable sites from prying eyes, and most of the livery companies erected all kinds of defensive structures around their halls.[86] The Cutlers gathered salvageable materials from the ruins and stashed them in a damaged cellar, which was bricked up for security.[87] The rubble in Drapers' Hall was sifted and thrown into the cellar of the Porters' old lodging for safe keeping.[88] The Clothworkers' carpenter put deal boards around the exposed 'open to the Ayre' end of Lambs Chapel in Cripplegate, with a door through the hoarding which could be locked for 'better security', which was fortunate because a few months later thieves climbed up on to the roof and stripped it of lead (*see* p. 173).[89] The hoarding mercifully protected the interior. Iron bars were stolen from the ruins of the Apothecaries' Hall in Blackfriars Lane,[90] and the Barber-Surgeons were obliged to issue a warrant for 'severall persons suspected to have some of the Companyes goods'.[91] Security guards kept watch over the ruins, and after the theft at Lambs Chapel the constable of Cripplegate Ward provided a watchmen to protect the site for three nights.[92] The Clothworkers had six men working on 24-hour shifts for ten days at the site of the ruined Hall and the grounds were patrolled by huge mastiff dogs, which were kept at the Hall for 42 weeks at a cost of 12d per week. The Company accounts include payments for their food, collars and chains.[93]

As word of the disaster spread to the provinces, felons gathered like vultures to prey on weak and defenceless citizens. Lawrence Powison of Stoke-on-Trent in Staffordshire and Thomas Road of Kilburne in Middlesex tried to make off with a great parcel of lead but were apprehended by an attentive constable. Another man was committed to a temporary prison in Bishopsgate for stealing old iron and lead.[94] One of the most notorious crime spots was the fields and houses in and around Islington, where 'a very great

number of distressed persons [had] taken refuge, with the goods which they have with difficulty saved from the fire'. For some reason the parish was without a Justice of the Peace or a deputy Lieutenant, and so refugees and inhabitants alike were in 'danger of being deprived of what they have'.[95] Everyone was ordered to keep a strict watch, but still items were taken. Henry Griffiths had to relay the sad information to one of his relations in Shrewsbury that 'somethings of yours that were at Mr Strings are saved, viz. a little red trunke and some satten, and some other things which I saw there. But for your trunke at our name sakes at Lothbury, it was then lost, being carried into the fields, whence it was stole.' Griffiths explained that he had been in great hope of tracking it down, and had made several enquiries, but he was worried that the 'party will not return till 'twill be too late to send you word, and hoping they have writ to you before now'.[96]

Foreign correspondents and diplomats sent home scurrilous reports about the general breakdown of law and order in the capital, and the Venetian ambassador claimed that one of the most serious and disturbing issues of the moment, which he rather enthusiastically suggested might result in great dissensions and quarrels, concerned the enormous quantity of plate, money and other valuables which had been taken to Whitehall for safety. The owners could not be identified. There were claims and counter-claims, and no gentleman could stand judge since there was too much conflict of interest. With some relish, the ambassador added that the King and the Duke of York had washed their hands of the matter, because it was 'too perilous and likely to draw on them the discontent and anger of the people'.[97]

But the King did not disregard the needs of his subjects so lightly; two days after the fire, Sir Richard Ford, Sir Robert Vyner and other members of the Court of Aldermen were asked to draft an order for the 'discovery and restoration of goods imbezilled in the confusions during the late dismall fire'.[98] The proclamation was issued on 19 September under the King's name. It is an interesting document because it is clear that the many people were so amazed by the speed and destructive force of the fire that they were overtaken by the flames before they had time to remove their goods, and in their haste and confusion left behind very great quantities of 'plate money Jewells household stuffe goods

and merchandize' as well as valuable building materials. All sorts of goods had been found amid the ruins and seized by 'diverse persons [who] still dayly presume to take … and carry away whatsoever they can finde or lay hands upon which may be of any value'. It was understood that some people had taken goods with every intention of restoring them to their rightful owners as 'soon as they shall bee knowne'; but others, either wilfully or in ignorance, had succumbed to temptation, neither fully understanding the nature of the crime nor aware of the dangerous consequences of their offence. So to remove all doubt and to prevent anyone

Broadside entitled: *A true Pourtraict with a Brief Description of that deplorable Fire of London Befallen the 12, 13, 14, 15 and 16 Sept. 1666* (sic), published by Marcus Willemsz Doornick in Amsterdam, between 1666 and 1670, with descriptions in Dutch, French and English. A key to the major landmarks is provided in Dutch. Mention is made of the arrests of some Dutch and French in London on suspicion of arson.

making excuses or pleading ignorance of the law, a number of measures were introduced. First, it was ordered that anyone in possession of someone else's goods should take them to the Artillery Ground in Finsbury Fields, within eight days. Second, the goods were to be inventoried by a specially appointed officer and the items kept under his control and safe keeping until such time as the owners reclaimed them. Third, the goods could only be reclaimed upon certain proofs of ownership and payment of a small fee. Fourth, part of the reclaim fee would be set aside as a reward for the finder, but the level of reward would be judged on a case-by-case basis, at the discretion of the Court of Aldermen. Finally, anyone who was discovered to have 'broken ye peace and possessed themselves by Rapine and spoyle of other mens goods' after the eight-day period had elapsed would be prosecuted with the utmost severity of the law, even to death. A further order was issued to all the bailiffs in Southwark, Westminster and adjacent liberties to take all the items which they had seized or had been delivered to them after the fire to the Artillery Ground. And to avoid any future misunderstandings, none of the goods at the Artillery Ground would be handed over to a claimant without an express order from the Court of Alderman, Lord Mayor and Sheriffs.[99]

Despite this ruling, crimes of larceny became ever more frequent. On 3 November 1666 the City authorities were alarmed by the rising numbers of vagrants, 'sturdy beggars and idle persons' who were wandering among the ruins, and ordered that whipping posts be set up with a 'substantiall paire of stocks' in convenient locations in each ward both to punish offenders and to serve as a deterrent.[100] By February 1667 the situation was so bad that Gilbert Thomas, provost marshal of Middlesex, complained that after the fire Westminster and its immediate environs had become a great resort for criminals. The volume of work had increased so much that he could no longer cope on his own, so he asked for ten men 'well mounted and armed' at a rate of 3 shillings per day to apprehend thieves and rogues in Middlesex, Westminster and adjacent counties. He also asked for a salary rise by way of compensation, which was granted on the understanding that he paid the money back, and obtained his future salary from commissions and incident fees.[101]

Shopping emporiums

'There is a great necessitye … for Shopps to manage theire Trades for the support of themselves and famalyes … and alsoe for supply of persons that wants Commodityes.'—*St Bartholomew's Hospital*, 15 September 1666[102]

On 3 September 1666 the governors of St Bartholomew's Hospital held an emergency meeting 'upon the sad disaster of the Terrible and unmercifull fire all over this Cittye'. The discussion was brief and to the point. How could they preserve the cash and the ledgers, writings and accounts which dealt with the hospital affairs and where should they send them? They decided to keep the cash reserves in the Treasurers' Compting House where it was currently stored, and only such 'writeings and Books … that were most usefull' were packed in a trunk and sent to Governor Squire Ridges' home in Hornsey (*see* p. 87) until such time as it was convenient to return them.[103]

In the event, the main hospital site was untouched, though the fire came terrifyingly close to the boundary and the hospital fire engines were badly damaged in a desperate effort to quench the flames (*see* p. 110). The greater calamity was the almost complete destruction of hospital property in other parts of the City; some 190 messuages, tenements and shops across 30 separate sites, some close at hand but others as far afield as Tower Street in the east.[104] This was a grievous loss to the occupants but also to the hospital, since the rental income, estimated at £2,000 per annum, was used to support sick and wounded seamen and soldiers, whose maintenance depended 'chiefly upon those revenues'. There was an urgent need to provide accommodation for tenants who had lost their homes and for the many tradesmen among them

Plan of St Bartholomew's Hospital, 1617.

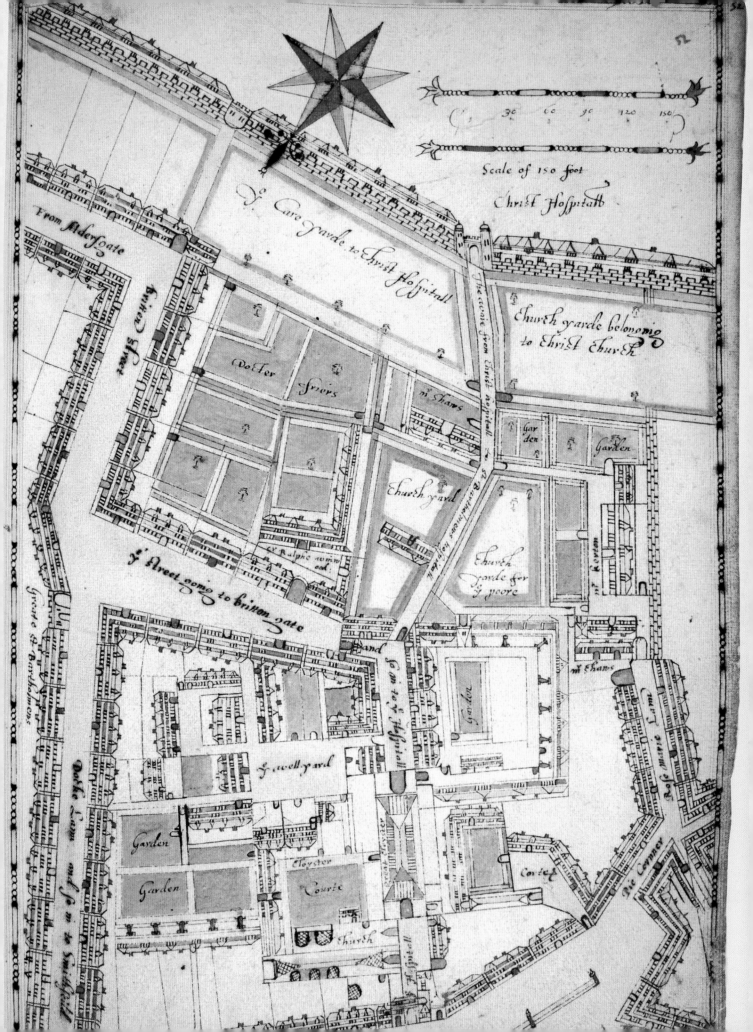

52

Scale of 150 foot

Christ Hospitall

Yͤ Care yarde to Christ Hospitall

The weie from Christ Hospitall to Sͭ Bartholomews Hospitall

Church yarde belonging to Christ Church

From Aldersgate

Briting Streete

Docter Priors

Mͬ Shaws

Church yarde

Church yarde for yͤ poore

Garden

Garden

Mͬ Gorton

Sͭ Ralphe winwod

Yͤ Streete going to britten gate

From the Hospitall

Hand

Garden

Mͬ Shaws

Sͭ Bartholomews

Rose Marie Lane

Greate Sͭ Bartholomews

Docter Lane

Swellyard

Garden

Garden

The Cloyster

Cloyster Courte

Church

Hospitall

Cortet

Pie Corner

who needed 'Shopps to manage theire Trades for the support of themselves and famalyes … and alsoe for supply of persons that wants Commodityes.' The governors wished to alleviate suffering and find innovative ways to raise money, so on 15 September, the first meeting after the fire, they set up a committee to consider the 'speedy erection of shops' within the hospital precincts, including the Great Cloister and the three churchyards nearby, beside the 'Long Walk' or common passage leading south towards Christ Church, and any other convenient space. The committee had to decide upon the number, location and size of the shops and were charged with the task of measuring out the ground and contracting with the workmen for the materials and building. Once the works were complete, the committee was empowered to let or sell them to tradesmen at such rents as they 'deemed mette and reasonable' for a lease term of seven years.[105] The costs of the work would be covered by the hospital.

After an inspection, the committee decided that the black, white and gold painted pillars running along the length of the Cloister should serve as demarcation posts, effectively defining the breadth, height and depth of each shop.[106] Other shops could be squeezed into the east side of the Cloister, with a side extension into the apothecary's shop, and beyond into the series of low rooms currently occupied by the hospitaller and cook in Well Yard. Twelve shops each 10 foot square were to be erected in the Great Church Yard; four were to be ranged along the wall of the churchyard adjoining the Vicar's house and three more in the little churchyard behind. Some were to have a supporting wall 7–8 foot high with a tiled pentice or canopy to protect them from the elements. For this scheme to work, new accommodation had to be found for the store of coals, for Mr Moulson the cook and for Michael North the apothecary, who had just spent a lot of time, money and effort in 'raiseing and altering' his tenement to suit his needs.[107]

On 19 September the governors asked the carpenters and bricklayers to start work on the 19 shops in the Long Walk, and when these were done to begin work in the Cloisters. The apothecary's shop and three chambers above it were converted into one shop with a dwelling house, and the cook's house was divided into two shops and two dwelling houses. Peter Mills, bricklayer and City

Surveyor, informed his fellow governors that he had acquainted the Lord Mayor with the proposed plans to make shops in the Cloisters and Long Walk, and that his lordship had given consent, with some cautionary advice that they should be 'let upon reasonable tearmes and not in an exacting way'.[108]

A week later the committee decided that there was a better way to maximize the available space for shops, which included utilizing the cellars of the houses on the west side of the Cloister and the conversion of the adjoining King's Ward into a shopping precinct on two levels. In the end, 5 of the 15 wards were closed because of the 'late losses happening to this howse in theire Revenues lately by the fire'. Most of the medical staff were reassigned to other wards; one was admitted as a patient, the others discharged.[109] Dr John Tearne was asked to leave because it was felt that the 'business of the docters will bee much lessened hereafter occasioned by the said late great losses in the hospital revenues', but a few weeks later Tearne asked permission to continue his work among the hospital poor 'and now gratis and without expectation of any salary or other compensation from this hospital, it being so pious a work'. His offer was gratefully accepted, and it was not until 20 January 1669 that the governors ordered that his salary should be restored to him. Tearne remained in post until his retirement on 24 March 1670.[110]

On 28 September 1666 the first 16 occupants of the new shops arrived. Into the King's Ward came Matthew Proter, citizen weaver, who took a space at the north end; Mary Vintner, widow, took on the lease of the adjoining two spaces on condition that she fitted out the shops herself (her trade is unknown). Fraunces Draydon, a spinster, was given a space in the lower King's Ward close to the door; while Edward Swinton, salter, was to have the lease of the 'fourth shop and the room and yard behind it towards the west, [as well as] the little room over the back roome as it is now divided from the upper King's Ward'. Richard Johnson, cutler, took over the tiny shop next to Matron's entry between the King's Ward and the Queen's Ward. Outside in the Cloister were spaces for Richard Melling, leatherseller, and, at the south-east end, the stationer Richard Royston, who took over the apothecary's shop and rooms so that he could 'sett his Bookes in the Corner … between his shop and the gate'. He was given permission on the understanding that he did not obscure the 'Poores Box' set up on the adjoining wall. Richard Heviside, merchant taylor, was to have a shop underneath the hospitaller's house; the former cook's house was partly occupied by Thomas Hill, haberdasher, and the yard adjoining and five other rooms were taken by William Smith, fishmonger. Job Hancock, iron-monger, moved next door and Philip Knifton, haberdasher, oc-cupied a space under the steward's house. Ferdinando Lockwood, also a haberdasher, moved into the corner shop by the hospital gate and Gilbert Shephard, goldsmith (p. 122), took the 'little shop att the north end of the east corner of the hospital between the gate and the pillar' measuring just 7 foot 8 by 5 foot 8. He was subsequently commended for making it 'soe handsome' and was given 40 shillings as a reward for his extraordinary charges.[111]

Eventually the new shops were given longer lease terms of 21 years, but the fines and rents were calculated on an individual basis to take account of the type, size and position of the shop and the needs of the occupant. The governors expressed the hope that the shops would soon yield a yearly income to support the poor,[112]

Plan of properties along the Hospital's cloisters, compiled by Edward Jermyn. Gilbert Shephard's tiny shop is shown at the north-eastern end of the row of cloister shops.

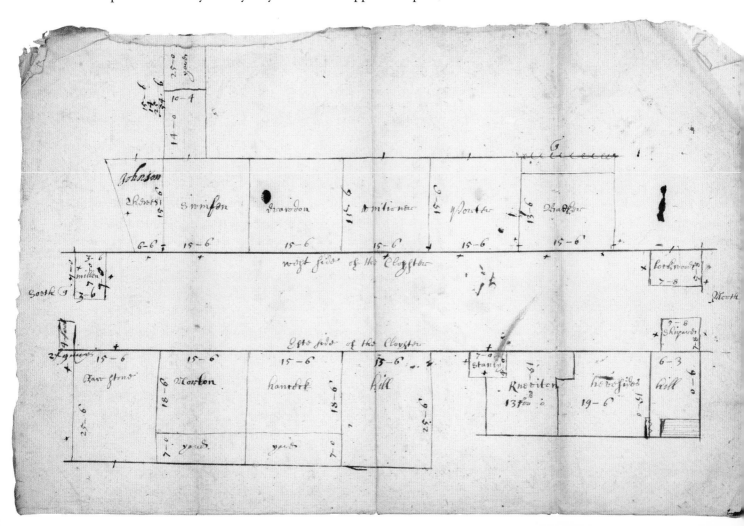

and in 1667 they noted with some satisfaction that the revenue in lease fines had already reached £412, producing an annual rental yield of £240.

As more of the shop spaces were taken up, the leaseholders started to complain. Mary Baker bemoaned the fact that her shop near King's Ward could only be reached via a short flight of steps from the Cloister, and was 'soe darke and inconvenient' that it was proving a great hindrance to her trade. Mary asked for the removal of an adjoining wall to make more space; although this proved impossible, she did receive an abatement in rent and was allowed to extend her stall beyond the pillars. Richard Royston submitted an earnest request for the use of one small dark room in the 'long darke entry neare his shopp', which was granted on condition that he occupied the space during daylight hours only. Others asked for shop extensions. The shopkeepers in the Cloisters were so frustrated by the lack of space that they submitted a petition requesting that each unit should be enlarged by 1 foot in breadth and that their several stalls should be folded up every night against the windows to widen the passageway and protect their stock.[113]

'When the Fire [entered the Royal Exchange] how quickly did it run around the galleries, filling them with flames, then descending the stairs compasseth the walks, giving forth flaming vollies, and filling the court with sheets of fire!'— *Thomas Vincent*, 3 September 1666[114]

As the governors of St Bartholomew's Hospital met in emergency session, the fire had already started to engulf London's great trading bourse, the Royal Exchange, in Cornhill. The noise, wrote Thomas Vincent, was so great that it was as if 'there had been a thousand iron chariots beating upon the stones'. By the late afternoon, the flames swept along Throgmorton Street, moving swiftly towards the northern edge of the City, until suddenly checked, veering away to the west and stopping just short of the southern end of Broad Street and Bishopsgate. Barely a block to the north, and unscathed, stood Gresham College. Founded as an educational institute by Sir Thomas Gresham in 1597 and left jointly to the Corporation of London and the Mercers' Company the main College buildings ranged around a central quadrangle,

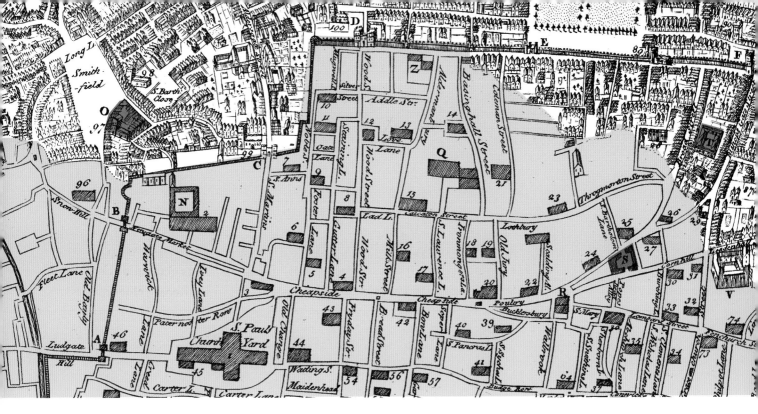

with a small yard facing Bishopsgate Street to the east, and a smaller 'back yard' adjoining Broad Street to the west. Covered and colonnaded walkways ran around the central court and the stairwells tucked beneath the main gate arches led to the Reading Room, Long Gallery, White Gallery, and to private lodgings for the Gresham Professors of Logic, Civil Law, Rhetoric, Physic, Geometry, Astronomy and Divinity. The precinct included a small garden, two stables, a hayloft, sheds, cellars and warehouses, and against the Broad Street boundary wall were a small cluster of almshouses belonging to the Mercers' Company.

The College, or House as it was known, proved to be a tremendous asset for the Corporation in its hour of need, and an emergency session was held within its walls on 6 September. The Lord Mayor, Sheriffs, Town Clerk, Chamberlain, Notary Public and other officers who had lost their dwellings in the fire decided to move in. Thomas Bludworth, Lord Mayor, took over part of the Divinity Lecturer's lodgings; the Chamberlain of London installed himself in the rooms of Dr Goddard, the Gresham Professor of Physic; the Mercers were initially promised space for their records either in the four chambers occupied by the Civil Law Lecturer or in the three rooms occupied by Dr Croone, the Rhetoric Reader, but Dr Croone asked that he might stay 'in regard of his great necessity', having nowhere else to go. Dr Horton, Gresham

Wenceslaus Hollar's engraving of London after the fire shows just how perilously close the flames came to destroying Gresham College, indicated by the letter T, and St Bartholomew's Hospital, indicated by an O. The Royal Exchange is marked by the letter S.

Professor of Divinity, was loath to give up part of his lodgings to the Deputy Town Clerk and the City Swordbearer, but on 8 September he was told in no uncertain terms to clear out, 'and in case of any contempt or neglect … the City Artificers [would] break open the Doors and see it executed accordingly'. The officers of the Assurance Office and the Aldermen who had passed the Chair had to make shift in what had been Dr Goddard's kitchen and two adjoining privies, with the promise of more salubrious accommodation later on. Special dispensation was granted to Dr Walter Pope, Professor of Astronomy, and to Dr Robert Hooke, 'in regard to the many curiositiyes which remaine [in their lodgings] and that the Royal Society may have accommodacion there for theire meetings'.[115]

The East India Company were ordered to remove their stocks of pepper from the warehouses (*see* p. 155) with all convenient speed so that the shopkeepers and merchants from the burnt-out Royal Exchange in Cornhill could use this space and the adjoining walks and gardens to store their goods.[116] But before the exodus could begin, the Joint Committee, which had responsibility for the administration of the building and welfare of the Gresham Professors and other tenants, decided that it would prudent to put some rules in place. A subcommittee was formed to consider the 'choice of places', the number of shop-room for the new tenants, and the terms and fines of the rents. Another troubling matter was that many of the Royal Exchange traders had sublet their shops before the fire, so the Committee was unsure whether new leases should be granted to the principal tenants or their under-tenants. In the end it was decided to 'prefer' the lessees since they had suffered the greater loss and it was felt that the under-tenants, who had paid high rents before the fire, 'are like to bee Ganiers by paying very small considerations for these [new] shops'. The next decision was where to put people. To avoid squabbles, the Committee decided to arrange the shop spaces according to seniority and to give each shopkeeper an area equivalent to the one they had previously enjoyed in the Exchange; the under-tenants 'in like manner after them'.

At first the shopkeepers from the shopping arcade known as the Pawn (*see* p. 53) in the Royal Exchange were granted permission to erect temporary sheds no more than 4 foot in extent up against the College walls and in one of the inner quadrangles, which was to be paved over to accommodate them.[117] But it was soon obvious that the open spaces within the College precincts were not going to be enough, so on 25 September several other likely spots were inspected and surveyed. The Long Gallery was 151 foot in length, and the walk below 1 foot less; the gallery next to the Astronomy lodgings occupied by Alderman Morpells measured 85 foot; other walks and spaces were variously measured at 96, 124 and 30 foot, giving an overall figure of 636 foot, which the Committee estimated would accommodate 106 shops.[118] The long covered walk on the Bishopsgate side of the Great Yard was split into seven units, each occupying a space between one set of columns and the next, were given to the most senior tenants of the Royal Exchange. Ralph Small, a bookseller, and Henry Mosse, Notary Public, were given shop space for the annual rent of £10. Next in line came Robert Briquett, John Webb, milliner, and Robert Horne, bookseller, with shop spaces set at a yearly rent of £20. Thomas Culling Esq. occupied the corner plot, where 'he have liberty to build a shop for the accommodation of himself and his friends' for the annual rent of £25, and the final spot was given to Rowland Worsopp, citizen Mercer, but a goldsmith by trade (*see* p. 122) for £10 per annum. The lease terms were all set for one year.[119]

The Joint Committee was soon overwhelmed by demands for shop space and not just from former Exchangemen. John Hamersley, a sword cutler, who had lived in Bartholomew Lane before the fire, took over a 6 by 4 foot shed against the College wall in Broad Street; Edward Cox, a milliner, asked that they 'take the best care they can' to find him room as his house and shop had been burned in Cheapside and he needed a convenient shop for his trade; and Mrs Oliver, a widow with eight children to support, who had 'long kept a linen shop' near the Great Conduit in Cheapside, asked the Committee to 'gratify her with a shop if any be left undisposed.' The Geometry Lodgings, Common Rooms, warehouses and cellars were soon commandeered for public use, and within weeks every nook and cranny was filled with stalls, booths and other makeshift structures. Robert Swift, a spurrier, squeezed into a tiny room 13 foot by 4¼ foot under the great stairs on the north side towards Broad Street at an annual rent of £5; and John Cade, stationer (*see* p. 182), moved into the stables adjoining the Civil Law lodgings for the annual rent of £12, on the understanding that he 'leave itt in the same condition hee finds itt'. Soon the 'general want of roome for tradesmen' was so great that the poor almsmen in Broad Street were asked to vacate their rooms so that the Joint Committee could let them 'to the best Advantage which may yield'. The almsmen were given £3 6s 8d apiece in addition to their salaries of £6 13s 4d to 'provide themselves lodgings'.[120]

In view of the great hustle and bustle, no public lectures could be held or teaching done in the College and, because more space was needed for tradesmen, another survey was undertaken to make sure that the galleries were structurally sound and able to support the added weight of the Exchange shops and the great 'concourse of people like to frequent it'.[121] Some of the floorboards were repaired and renewed as an added precaution, but the general view was that the structure was strong enough to 'beare the Burthen'. The great stable and hayloft were divided into four equal parts valued at £50, and a codicil was added to the leases that whoever takes them 'bee obliged to leave the whole in the like condition as itt now is and to bring noe Carts within the Colledge Gates'. Sheds popped up across the site. Mr Curry, a periwig-maker, moved into one of the smallest – just 4 foot square – under the window of Dr Goddard's lodgings. William Lightfoote, stationer, erected a shed in the cellar passage between the quadrangle and Bishopsgate. The five sheds nestling against the wall by the stable door on a plot 46 foot long, were taken at a combined rent of £30 per annum. There were four sheds under the gateway, and seven more up against the College wall in Broad Street; some 12 foot long at £7 per annum and some 6 foot long at £3 10s.[122] The rents calculated for three-quarters of the year ranged from as

little as 10 shillings to just over £10; the fine reflecting the shop
location and its size. Most of the 130 tenants rented one shop
space, but a fair number had a 'three-quarter space' or a 'shop and
a half'. Five tenants had two shops and one had a large part of the
warehouse. There were shops in nine principal locations: the White
Gallery held 11; the Long Gallery 21; the 'Walk under the Anatomy
Lodgings' had 23, and the 'Walk below the Great Shed' or Warehouse 17; the Stone Walk had 25, the Reading Room 4, the yard
next to Bishopsgate 12; the Inner Yard 4 and the 'Back yard next
Broad Street' held 13.[123] There were probably a good many more
traders operating in these shops than the official registers suggest,
since the annual accounts list only the primary tenants. In reality
the working population within the College was extremely fluid,
with people moving in and out over the years. Henry and James
Bayles do not feature in the Joint Committee accounts, but in
the Goldsmiths' records they are both listed among the Gresham
College traders. Henry had nine 'curralls' (or bells) set in silver,
which the wardens wished to assay, but they were denied access to
the glass showcases and Henry's 'man' claimed not to have a key.
Eventually the offending items were removed and were discovered
to have copper wire with clappers worse than standard, for which
he was fined 17s 4d.[124]

A month after the fire, the subcommittee was struggling to
satisfy the various interests of the tenants in Gresham College,
so they decided that it was time to introduce a few rules and
regulations. The allocation of shop spaces was assigned to the
subcommittee and no one could start to build a shed or shop until
they received permission. The costs for each shop or shed were to
be borne by the tenant, and the amount of the rent was calculated
on an individual basis according to the 'proportion of shop roome
which they respectively enjoy'. The Exchangemen had to prove
that they were entitled to a space by showing a copy of their Royal
Exchange lease or some other proof of title. A handbell was purchased, which was to be rung every night at eight o'clock to signal
end of trading for the day, and by nine the doors of the College
were to be locked 'for the security of the house'. The Exchangemen asked permission to convert the stables and hayloft for some
alternative use, partly because they were considered a fire risk, but
also because of the great 'noysomenesses of the dunghill', which

had become an intolerable nuisance. The clattering and rumble of carts into the yard from the gentlemen and merchants was another source of contention; new sets of stairs were needed at both ends of the cellar leading into the quadrangle so that 'passengers may goe with more safety', and more lights were needed to illuminate the darkest recesses of the cellar passage. A clock was installed in the quadrangle so that the merchants and traders may 'better know when to leave the Exchange', and the porters were asked to shine a candle and lanthorn along the cellar passage and other dark areas and to ring a bell at one o'clock so that the merchants would know that the trading time had ceased. And a new set of locks were ordered for the great gates, as the old ones were defective and too many of the keys had been issued to strangers, who had begun to open the doors at 'unreasonable' times.[125]

For the next five years the College doubled up as a shopping emporium and a town hall and so the pressure on space was immense. Four attorneys from the Lord Mayor's Court asked for 'little places' in the Reading Room 'where people who come about business may know to finde them', but although the door keepers tried to direct customers to the right part of the building they often got lost. When the Exchange keepers opened the doors in the mornings there was such a press of people through the narrow passageways that no one could move. Everyone tried to get in and out through the same gates and the throng was so great that a one-way system was introduced. The shopkeepers tried to find a more advantageous spot to promote their business, and soon there were all kinds of complaints about the higgledy-piggledy arrangement of sheds and shops and neighbourly disputes. The Committee decided that the tenants with shop spaces around the quadrangle should install partitions between them, each placed up against the middle of the columns, and when Mr Port and Mr Maddox moaned about the lack of light reaching their shops in the cellar, floorboards were cut away to provide extra light through the cellar window. Others protested that the blocked passage at the end of the Long Gallery had almost 'wholly destroyed' their trade. Shops sites were swapped or extended, and Samuel Joyce asked to move out of his single shop in the Long Gallery 'to the shop and Quarter next to him' which had become vacant, 'in regard hee hath not roome enough for his accommodation'.

And some of the Exchangemen lobbied to prevent one man from letting his shop in the Long Gallery to someone else, which would cause the trades to be 'ill sorted' to everyone's discontent.[126] There was even a complaint from Nathaniell Brooke, stationer, against his neighbour, Mr Horne, who had set up his shop in Gresham House under the sign of the Angel. It transpired that this device had been used by Brooke in his former dwelling house in Cornhill, which had burnt down, and he was naturally trading under the same from his shed in the College 'where hee was settled and had fixed his signe many moneths, before the said Hornes coming thither'. As this was very much to the disadvantage of Brooke and infringed the customs of the City, Horne's sign was taken down and 'demolished' (*see* p. 52).[127]

By the summer of 1669 the Joint Committee had begun to turn their attention to the eventual return of the shopkeepers to the newly rebuilt Royal Exchange. They were of the opinion that whereas before the fire the shops in the Pawn were variously let at £20, £18 and £15 per annum, 'upon this Emergency' they might be reasonably raised to £22, £20 and £18 per annum; which amounted to £22 for single shops on the south side facing Cornhill, £20 for single shops on either the east or the west side, and £18 for those on the north. This was agreed on condition that each one may bear a small share of the 'great losse by the fyre'.[128] The shopkeepers were finally able to return in 1671.

Troubled times

'I to church, where our parson made a melancholy but good sermon – and many, and most, in the church cried, especially the women.'—*Samuel Pepys*, 9 September 1666[129]

This detail from the frontispiece to *Pyrotechnica Loyolana, Ignatian fire-works, or, The fiery Jesuits temper and behaviour being an historical compendium of the rise, increase, doctrines, and deeds of the Jesuits*, printed in 1667, suggests that the Jesuits were responsible for the Great Fire of London. Robert Hubert, the simple-minded, innocent French Protestant who was hanged for starting the fire, holds a fireball. With him is a Jesuit labelled 'Pa.H' – possibly Harcourt, an alias used by William Waring, who was one of the Jesuits hanged at Tyburn on 20 June 1679.

Although the fire did not destroy the entire metropolis, the loss of so many buildings of cultural and commercial significance – symbols of municipal identity and corporate pride – had such a profound psychological impact that it was if the whole of London was engulfed by the conflagration. It was a local calamity with national consequences: a stab in the heart to national pride and economic prosperity. For what 'city, county or Town in England was there', exclaimed one writer, 'that was not one way or another, refreshed and advantaged, if not enriched with the silver streams of London.'[130] As word of the disaster spread across the country, there were many expressions of sympathy and offers of help. City councils sent their condolences and sums of money were raised for the destitute.

A letter from the mayor and council of Londonderry to 'the deare mother citty' arrived with the promise of £250 and regrets that, owing to their great proverty, they could spare no more. The Council of Ireland offered to send 200 head of cattle in lieu of cash.[131] Reports and letters were despatched to the Continent. The French King Louis XIV asked his citizens to put aside thoughts of egocentric nationalism and all rejoicings at England's misfortune, it 'being such a deplorable accident involving injury to so many people', and generously offered to send food and other necessaries to aid the refugees.[132] The Venetians were shocked to receive letters from compatriots which described all kinds of unspeakable horrors of 'persons burned to death and calcined limbs … the old, tender children and many sick and helpless persons … all burned in their beds and served as fuel for the flames'.[133] Even worse was to follow:

on 24 September the Dutch circulated a weekly news bulletin in Italy to suggest that England was teetering on the brink of ruin. This once 'proud theatre of universe', the author crowed, has been reduced to 'an incinerated corpse'; this nation, which once 'presumed to rule not merely over the earth, but over the winds and waters as well', has been utterly reduced. Now the English know that 'God is the only Master of the elements … [she has been punished] with the torments of fire … thereby showing her, as in a mirror, how human calamities may proceed from vain ambition.'[134]

The financial cost of the war with France and the Netherlands proved too much for national coffers and a temporary truce was arranged with both countries within the year. But if the Dutch, with whom England was at war, thought that the fire had effectively snuffed out England's economic strength and will, and that she would capitulate and sue for peace, they were wrong. Londoners were not so easily cowed. Alongside the raw emotions of despair and grief were those of anger and fortitude. There was a sense of urgency and common purpose and, although individual

The small village of Cowfold, in Sussex, contributed £2 13s 9d towards the Lord Mayor's fund for those who had lost their homes in the fire.

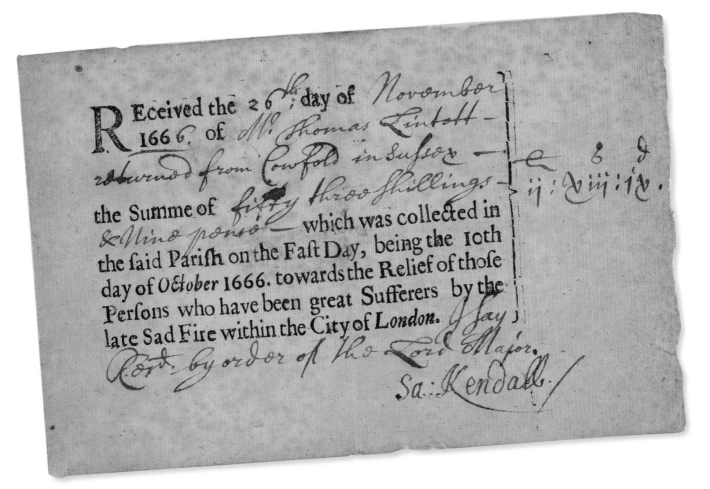

circumstances and reactions were infinitely various, the overriding motivation was to recover; to re-build shattered lives, homes and businesses and to return to some kind of normality as soon as possible. This at least was the intention, and it is certainly the case that many people endured privations and losses with remarkable stoicism and resignation. But what of the sufferings? What did people actually lose? How did they deal with the loss of their homes and business? Did they actually recover?

These questions are easy to ask but are generally impossible to answer in any meaningful way because everyone's situation was different and no two individuals' experiences were alike. Losses of this type and magnitude cannot be measured in purely economic terms. Houses and business can be rebuilt, but it is not easy to recover from trauma and shock. Consider, wrote one commentator, the 'greatness of it, the destructiveness of it. Oh the many thousand families that were destroyed and impoverished in four days time!' Rich and poor alike were reduced to the basic elements of their nature. Wealth and position were rendered meaningless. It was, wrote one commentator, a 'universal judgement ... [and] of many it might have been said the day before the fire, who so rich as these? And the very next day it might have been said of the same persons, who so poor as these?'[135] People who had been entirely self-reliant before the fire suddenly found themselves dependent. A month afterwards, William Ridges Esq (*see* pp. 86 & 204) appealed to the Court of Common Council, asking to be excused from the office of alderman to which he had been sworn the previous year, upon payment of a fine, because he had eight indisposed children and had lost £8,000 of his estate. His request was granted on the understanding that he paid the fine within six days.[136] Sarah Crafts was also affected, having lost £5,000 worth of property in the fire, so that she was reduced with her children 'from a plentiful condition to turn servants, and work hard for a poor livelihood'.[137] Though wealth and status did provide opportunities for escape, the means to pay for porters and carts to carry belongings to safety, and the funds to relocate in some measure of comfort, some wealthy citizens were slow to avail themselves of the opportunity and left it too late. They could have escaped with their possessions and commodities, but flattered themselves that the fire would not reach them; they thought they would be

safe and secure, but then, wrote Thomas Brooks, the rector of St Margaret's New Fish Street, in 1670,

> when the flames broke upon them, O then any money for a Cart, a Coach, A Dray. To save some of their Richests and Choicest goods! O what fear were many Parents now in, that their Children would either be now trod down in the press, or lost in the crowd, or be destroyed by the flames! And what feat were many Husbands now in, concerning their Wives, who were either weak or sick, or aged, or newly delivered! Words are too weak to express that distraction that all men were under, when the fire went on raging and devouring all before it.[138]

While the fire raged, it was survival pure and simple. Everyone struggled. It was only afterwards, when the first phase of shock had past, that people had time to take stock. Dr William Denton wrote to his nephew that 'my wife's houses were £86 per annum [all burnt] and now she hath had a little time to recollect herself she cries all day long.'[139] Pepys conveys something of the emotional toll in his diary entry for 9 September, the first Sunday after the

The cylindrical alms box has a coin slot at the top and the lock has two keys. The padlocked strongbox, painted on the front with the arms of the Barber-Surgeons' Company, was used to collect monies for the poor. It was acquired from Widow Lucas for 20 shillings in 1636, and was preserved from the fire with the other treasures from the Hall.

fire. The church was packed and Pepys noticed that there were 'few of fashion and most strangers'. The sense of loss which Pepys eloquently describes is palpable: a great outpouring of communal grief. It is possible that this shared loss, directly or indirectly felt, helped to ameliorate or deaden the most acute pangs because so many people were in a similar or worse predicament. Some were clearly crushed by the enormity of the situation and were unable to think for themselves. Others just got on with life as best they could. Sir James Bunce, alderman and linen-draper, wrote to the King asking for the monies due to him from the customs of £5,776, as the fire had consumed almost all he had left. The court musicians found themselves in particularly straitened circumstances because they were owed 4¾ years of arrears in salary and had lost all their houses and goods in the fire. John Gamble, a member of one of His Majesty's wind-instrument consorts, was in dire need

because, as a result of the money he was owed, he had contracted a debt of £120 and one of his 'securities' had been sent to Newgate Prison for debt. Gamble asked for £221 10s 4½d for his arrears of salary; otherwise, he commented sadly, ruin awaited them all.[140]

The fire certainly did force people to reconsider, to question their ideas, aspirations and beliefs; even to ponder the very meaning of charity. When the Pewterers' Company wardens met in temporary accommodation in the Blackamoor's Head on Pye Corner a few months after the fire, they concluded that because the Company had suffered such great losses and the 'generalitie of ye poore sort of people hath been in some measure gainers' nothing should be given to the poor at that time.[141] It was harsh pragmatism. And the Pewterers were not alone. Many of the City institutions felt that they simply did not have enough resources to help everyone as they would have liked, and there was so much need that it was difficult to know who to help and how to do it. Recognizing the difficulty, the Lord Mayor and Aldermen ordered the Companies to 'take care … of their respective poore during the present extremity';[142] only when their means allowed would they offer wider benevolence.

The records of the City companies are full of pitiful complaints from needy members who had lost everything in the fire. The worst affected were widows with children. On 29 August 1667 the Carpenters' Company received a petition from Amy Smith, 'a poore distressed widow' who had lost her husband William when he fell from the upper storey of their house in Pudding Lane (*see* p. 79) – probably, though it is a little ambiguous, during the fire. Apart from her children, Amy had lost everything she had. When character witnesses testified on her behalf, she was given 5 shillings from the poor box to tide her over for the next few days, and her name was entered in a register to receive quarterly payments for the rest of her life.[143] The Corporation of London also received direct applications. On 10 December 1667 Francis (*sic*) Ashley, a 69-year-old spinster, presented a 'humble petition' for help. She had spent her entire life in the parish of St Dunstan-in-the-West, living with her parents, and then, after their death, on her own. Her parents had left her some money, but her principal income, and latterly her sole means of support, had come from the rental of a house in Fetter Lane which had yielded an annual income of £23. This property had been completely consumed in the fire, and because she was in poor health and had been blind for some years, and was, she said, both 'friendless and helpless', she could not support herself or find any means of employment. The poor woman's plight was so desperate that she was given 40 shillings out of the monies set aside for charitable contributions to 'ye poore distressed by the ... fire', and was also recommended to the care and protection of the ward of Farringdon Without.[144]

The shock of loss proved too much for some and resulted in untimely death. Anthony Joyce committed suicide (*see* p. 187); Richard Howell collapsed (*see* p. 198); William Merrell died with 'noe estate his habitacon being burnt in the late Dreadfull fier', the ground worth just £7; and Peter Garretson, gentleman, passed away with nothing to his name apart from a feather bed, bolster and some 'odd thinges' valued at 40 shillings, his clothes worth £3 and the 'lease of a piece of ground whereon the deceased built a boothe' at £30.[145] Some poor souls were driven completely mad (*see* p. 182). In November 1666 Joseph Matthewes, the Porter of Bethlem Hospital, and his wife Millicent, who worked as a matron, reported there had been a huge influx of patients after the fire. The work had become 'very dangerous in regard of the great number of lunatickes', and, because of the high prices and the drop in their income as a result of the fire, the porter, matron and other staff could not afford to buy clothes and other necessaries for their work, so they asked the Hospital governors to provide them with shoes, stockings and working clothes for their 'shifts'.[146]

Provision for the mentally frail became a particular worry for the City because most of the patients were supported by relations or parish contributions. The loss of homes and property in the fire caused extra hardships. In April 1667 Mary Hey wrote to the governors at Bethlem in great anxiety. Before the fire, the monies used to support her 'lunatike' brother John had come from rental income for which their father had made provision in his will. But these houses in the parish of All Hallows Barking had been destroyed, so the governors decided that, if Mary could find two friends to stand as guarantors to help her pay the weekly charge of 2 shillings towards her brother's care, they would continue to keep him. At the same time, the governors made provision for shoes, shirts, stockings and other items for nine of the poorest inmates who had neither money nor friends to provide for them.[147] Richard Young appealed to the governors of Christ's Hospital for aid for his 'deare and most deserving wife', mother to their two children, for monies to sustain her in her old age because she was 'very crasey' and unable to earn any money herself. They had sustained such losses in the fire that he had nothing to leave her and feared that she would be 'constrayned to begg'.[148]

However, the fire also brought new opportunities. Active profiteering was forbidden, but many people living outside the burnt area or arriving in the City to help with the reconstruction were able to capitalize on the misfortunes of others. As one man sardonically remarked to a correspondent on 8 September, 'want promotes trade more than plenty', and he went on to say that he had overheard a gentleman demand £100 for an item for which he would gladly have taken £50 a mere eight days earlier, because he is now 'almost master of the commodity'. Only by trade would the city recover from ruin.[149]

(*opposite*) Fifteen years before the fire, the astrologer William Lilly published *Monarchy or no monarchy in England… which foretold the Great Plague, the Great Fire and various other events for the reign of 'Charles, son of Charles'*. This image, one of two woodcut hieroglyphics relating to the fire, aroused suspicion, and on 22 October 1666 Lilly was questioned by the Parliamentary Committee investigating the causes of the fire.

'all orders, ranks and degrees of men suffered
alike, and were abased alike: the furious flames
made no difference, they put no distinction
between the Russet Coat and the Scarlet Gown,
the Leather Jacket and the Golden Chain, the
Merchant and the Tradesmen, the Landlord and
the Tenant, the Giver and the Receiver –

There is no difference, Fire hath made,
Equal the Scepter and the Spade.'[150]

'Our trades do meet in Companies, our Companies at halls, and our halls become monopolies of freedom, tied to London: where all our Crafts and Mysteries are so laid up together … by means whereof, all our creeks seek to one river, all our rivers run to one port, all our ports join to one town, all our towns make but one city, and all our cities but suburbs to one vast, unwieldy and disorderly Babel of buildings, which the world calls London.'—*Thomas Milles, 1608*

A–Z *of* TRADES

'people ... are at their wits' end, not
knowing how to carry on trade by
reason of the great fire in London.'—
Robert Scrivener, 17 September 1666[2]

This section is arranged in alphabetical order by trade. It is a
fairly even distribution, though some letters are better represented
than others: there are no trades with the initial letters *Q, X* or
Z; the letters *K* and *R* are problematic; and it just so happens
that a number of trades have the initial letters *C, P, S* and *T* in
common. Only those crafts and trades that have a link to the fire
have been included, and the surviving evidence has determined
the final selection. Sometimes the connection to the fire is
obvious; in others it is a little more tenuous. There are 31 trade
headings, but some trades have been grouped together or subsumed for convenience, either because they have a natural affinity
or because the trades were more or less indivisible in practice: so
booksellers are included with stationers; mercers with silkmen;
drapers with clothworkers; water-pipe borers with plumbers;
brickmakers with tilemakers. The term 'upholsterer' has been used
rather than the contemporary 'upholder', and the various tobacco
trades – tobacco-cutter, tobacco-presser, tobacco pipe-maker
and tobacco seller – which were sometimes separate specialisms,
but more often than not combined, have been grouped together
under the heading 'tobacconist'. Wax chandlers are incorporated
with tallow chandlers because most of the relevant evidence is
balanced towards the tallow-chandlery side of the trade. It is
necessarily something of a patchwork pattern, but taken together
the sample does convey something of the occupational diversity of
London in the pre- and post-fire period and provides a snapshot
of Londoners' responses and reactions to the fire, and the kinds
of goods and possessions lost and recovered.

*These Tradesmen are Preachers in the
City of London or A Discovery of the
most dangerous and damnable tenets
that have been spread within this few
years; by many erroneous, heretical and
mechanic spirits* (London, 1647). This
satirical broadside lampoons the idea
of untrained artisans preaching in the
capital.

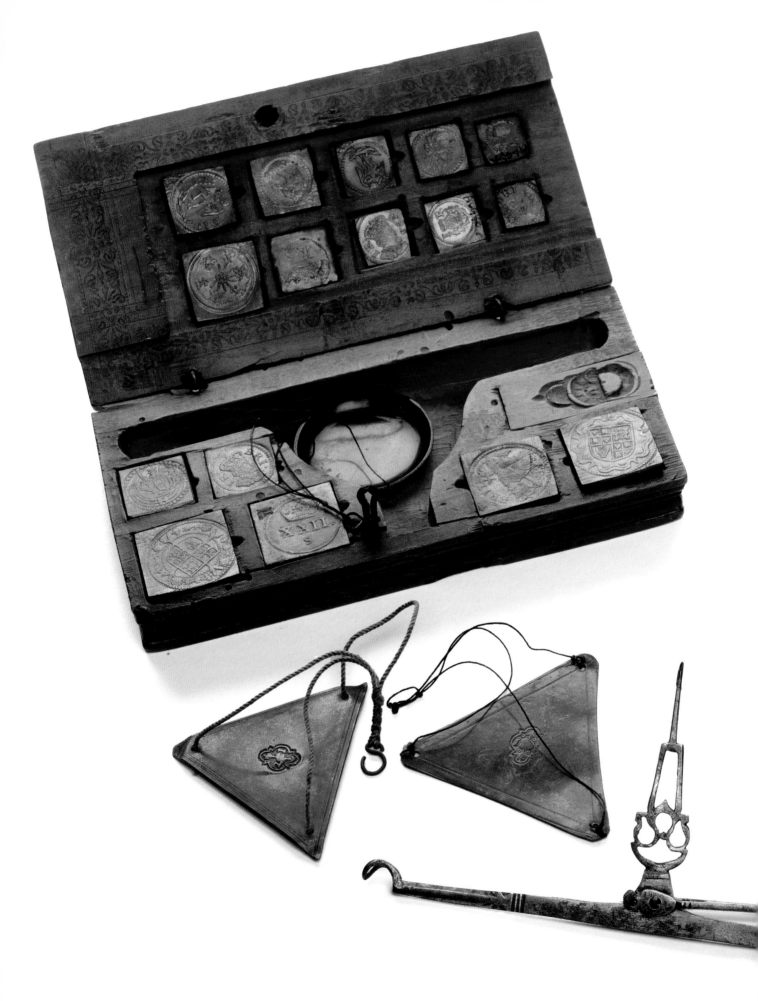

Apothecary

'[Valerian,] an excellent medicine …
against nervous affections … trembling,
palpitations, vapours and hysteric
complaints.'—Nicholas Culpeper,
The Complete Herball, 1653

The slow process of recovery from the shock and horror of the fire
must have sparked a brisk trade in soothing simples, salves and
drugs for burns and nervous complaints. References to injuries
are few, but one commentator mentioned those 'burnt, starved
and disabled to make and follow theire trades', and the Barber-
Surgeons' Company gave 10 shillings to a seaman who was injured
when he climbed onto the roof of their Anatomy Theatre to
quench the flames.[3] Specialist manuals such as *De combustionibus*,
the first book devoted to burns and their treatment, published
in Basle in 1607, were perhaps avidly read, and the apothecaries
would have drawn upon their vast knowledge of herbs and simples
to relieve pain and discomfort. The apothecary Nicholas Culpeper
recommended the bruised leaves of St Peter's wort and alkanet
to ease 'burnings by common fire'; and fresh ivy leaves boiled
in wine and applied as a plaster, he suggested, were 'effectual to
cure all burns and scalds, and all kinds of exulcerations coming
thereby'.[4]

The sheer range of pills, potions and lotions sold in
mid-seventeenth-century London was staggering.[5] Therapeutic
preparations of all kinds are described in herbals and pharma-
copeias, but detailed evidence for trade practice is comparatively
slight. The records of the Society of Apothecaries mention the
'herbarizing' excursions to the fields around the City to gather
plants for drugs and cosmetics; they refer to periodic inspections
of apothecaries' and druggists' shops, and, more rarely, to an
improper use of ingredients. In 1664, one man (unnamed) was
fined 10 shillings for 'haveing ruberb & sirop of Violetts bad' and

(*above*) Amber was considered to have
great therapeutic benefit. (*left*) The
sheer quantity and variety of foreign
coins in London created confusion for
legitimate traders and opportunities
for the unscrupulous. Scale balances
with an accompanying box of stamped
brass coin weights, for both foreign
and domestic issues, were used by
merchants, tradesmen, physicians and
apothecaries to ensure that they were
not short-changed.

for making and selling London treacle (used as a preventative against plague) without permission.[6] But the best evidence comes from inventories which provide detailed lists of the drugs and other wares in apothecaries' shops. When Theophilus Dyer's stock was appraised for probate in 1663, for instance, he had an old still for distillation, a lead 'bottom' used as a base for the still, and a boiling pan in his kitchen, along with other household goods. The yard held an 'old stone mortar' with his 'signe and signe post', and the shop stock comprised several purging electuaries made from dried, sieved and finely powdered herbs, flower petals, seeds and roots mixed with warm clarified honey; various drug ingredients in nests of small, medium and large boxes; drugs and several kinds of seeds in barrels; several sorts of 'old syrupps', conserves, oils, unguents and 'divers masses of Pills'. The working tools included a brass mortar and pestle, and three more 'mortars blacke', as well as an old iron furnace. There was a 'short ladder' to reach items stored on the highest shelves, several 'old bookes' and a desk in an adjoining closet. Apart from wooden boxes, there were flasks and pharmaceutical glasses and several kinds of earthenware 'galley pots' or drug jars.[7] The sizes of these jars are not specified, but surviving examples range in size from minute pots little bigger than a thimble, designed perhaps for a special compound or a single dose of a prescription drug, to large containers holding a quart or more of dry or wet ingredients. Many of the vessels were made in standard sizes with a slightly waisted girth to enable the pot to be handled and easily removed from a stacked shelf. Some were plain white, some had polychrome banding and chevron patterns, others were marked with the proprietary name of the product.

The apothecary Peter Culley, who died two months before the fire, either manufactured drugs on-site or stocked supplies for others, because he had a warehouse full of drugs behind his shop in the parish of St Andrew Undershaft. The shop itself, subdivided into a retail, storage and working space, was filled with parcels of 'simple and compound' waters and syrups, all sorts of conserves and electuaries, oils, cordials, powders, pills and plaisters, spices and 'chemical preparations', as well as several

packets of drugs stacked on shelves and in assorted cupboards nearby. There were glasses, gallipots, a mortar, stills, and various other utensils, and behind the counter in the 'back shop' were other boxes, barrels and a still pot. The warehouse drugs were piled onto shelves and one of the garrets above, doubled up as a store for five tubs, 12 old boxes, odd items of lubber and some 'bladders' which were used to cover the rim of drug jars and distillation vessels to protect the contents from drying out. The bladders were often punctured so that 'excrementitius and fiery vapours may exhale', but they were not considered suitable for glass or stone syrup pots 'unless you would have the glass break and the syrup lost'.[8] The combined value of Culley's shop and warehouse stock came to £253 7d.[9]

Evidence for the fire's impact on trade and the lives and businesses of individual apothecaries is rather harder to find. There is a terse but rather telling entry in the probate inventory for the apothecary Michael Markland, which reads: 'Item. Paid for the charges of removing the Testators household goods plate ready money & other things in the tyme of the late dredfull fire – £5.' This odd scrap of evidence conveys so much and yet so little. Where did he live? Was he able to resume his trade? Did the fire mark the end of his career and destroy his life? The absence of detail is all the more remarkable since it was written two and half years after the fire on 11 March 1669.

Some of the most intriguing evidence for the apothecaries' trade in the immediate pre- and post-fire period comes from two rather surprising sources. The first occurs in a case brought before the Mayor's Court in London on 29 September 1668. The deponent was Daniel Van Mildert, a 25-year-old Dutch merchant based in Homerton in Hackney, who testified that he had sold two cases of drug ingredients to Thomas Watson, an apothecary in the City, on 25 May 1664. Both cases had come from John Cloppenburg in Amsterdam, for whom Van Mildert acted as an agent. The first contained 17¾ lb of 'trimed-agric' (possibly some kind of fungus) at 8s 6d per pound, and the second, delivered in June, held 119 lb of Antimonium preparatum (powdered antimony sulfide or elemental antimony) at 11½d per pound.[10] Once the goods were delivered, Van Mildert naturally expected to be paid, but nothing came. Then Watson unfortunately disappeared, leaving Van

(*above*) Decorative slabs were used by apothecaries as a shop sign and for rolling out pills and ointment pastes. (*left*) The inscription 'S: TVSSIL' for *Syrupus Tussilago* or Syrup of Colt's Foot appears in pharmacopoeias between 1618 and 1677. It was reputed to be good for a dry cough. The unicorn head motif is rare; this jar might have contained plague water with ground hart's horn to prevent 'swoonings, faints, fevers and convulsions'.

Mildert at a loss to know how to proceed and to whom to turn for help.

But this was not all. At about the same time, John Cloppenburg had sent several other parcels of drug ingredients to his London agent, including 'one Barrell with fine amber conteining (according to ye said Cloppenburgs advice) £138, and … one case marked DM. 1 by Jacob Hendrix conteining by the same Advice £95 of trimed-agric.' These two parcels were left unsold in Van Mildert's house in the City. On 2 September he was 'enforced through the great violence & fierceness of ye said fire' to abandon these goods, in addition to 'divers of his owne in the place where they stood'.[11] The document does not say where the goods were kept, but the reference to fine amber is particularly significant because this natural resin, worn in the form of beads or ground to a powder mixed with wine or broth, was believed to have great therapeutic value and amuletic power. It was considered so efficacious that it was used to treat a whole host of different afflictions. As the physician Thomas Nichols wrote in 1659, the white 'oderiferous Amber is esteemed best for Physick … against the Vertigo and Asthmatick Paroxysmes, against Catharres, and Arthriticall pains, against diseases of the stomach, and to free it from stuffings and putrefactions, and against diseases of the heart, against plagues, venoms and contagions'.[12] In short, it was a panacea for all ills.

The second reference also comes from the Mayor's Court. On this occasion, Nathaniel Crassey, who was apprenticed to Edward Rich, an apothecary in Houndsditch, complained that he had received inadequate instruction from his master; that stocks were low and bought in from other druggists; and because there was hardly any trade he had been unable to learn all that he should to complete his training. John Falde of London, an apothecary aged 62, was summoned to testify on Rich's behalf: on 6 September 1669 he explained that he had served his apprenticeship with Rich; though at first the shop was 'sufficiently furnished with druggistery wares', trade was generally indifferent. By the end of his apprenticeship, however, Rich had a thriving business, and for many years afterwards had continued to prosper. Falde eventually left to

(*below*) This cup, fashioned from the toxic element antimony, was probably made by the Welsh-born quack and astrologer John Evans (*c.*1594–1659), who specialized in making and selling antimony cups from his shop in Gunpowder Alley near Fleet Street. In extolling the 'virtues of antimoniall cups' he suggested that the user should fill the cup with wine flavoured with a little mace and cloves, leave it to stand overnight and then drink it the following day.

(*left*) Larger mortars were needed to grind herbs and drugs in bulk so that, as Dr Willis observed in 1666, 'when many people are sick, and there is not leisure to compound every Dose of these Medicines severally, there should be a large mixture of each kind made up together.'[14]

set up on his own account, but in the course of his work and for social reasons he had visited Rich on several occasions, and had seen his apprentice Nathaniel Crassey 'playing with ye boys in ye street & neglecting his masters shop & business'. Falde said that it was common practice among the 'best & greatest of Druggists in London' to buy goods from one another because of the vast number and types of commodities that they sold, and that after the fire Rich had been 'constrained to live where he doth & therefore hath not the trading as he had before ye fire nor can it be expected in regard of ye situacon of his house [and that his] customers are much dispersed'.[13] The case against Rich was dropped.

Baker

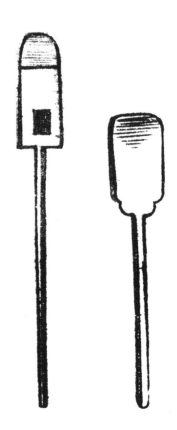

'Good bakers, make good bread! …
Hot bread is unwholesome for any
man for it doth lay in the stomach
like a sponge … yet the smell of new
bread is comfortable to the head and to
the heart. Soden bread, as simnel and
cracknels and bread baked upon a stone,
or upon iron … is not laudable. Burnt
bread, and hard crusts and pastry crusts
doth engender colour, and just and
melancholy humours; wherefore chip
the upper crust of your bread.'
—*Andrew Boorde*, 1542[15]

On 7 June 1665, at the height of the plague in London, the
wardens and assistants of the Corporation of Bakers gathered
in their company hall in Harp Lane near the Tower of London
because it had come to their attention that several of their
members were burning too much fuel and had been firing up their
ovens to make extra batches of 'peck loafe or housewifes bread' for
their customers, 'especially in these calamitous times and the great
decease of people in and near to London'. So they issued a direc-
tive to all the bakers in the City that from 12 August none was
permitted to fire their ovens or make any kind of bread apart from
on Tuesdays, Thursdays and Saturdays, 'which was formerly and
antciently the only dayes wherein such kind of bread were baked'.
Fines were imposed for infringements.[16]

Bread was a staple food: used as an accompaniment to cheese,
fish and meat, as a thickener in pottage (a simple broth of pulses
and milk), for frumenty (a sweetened glutinous porridge) and
for puddings. And, as one writer remarked in 1587, it was made
'of such graine as the soil yeeldeth … the gentilitie commonlie
provide themselves sufficientlie of wheate for their owne tables,

whilst their household and poore neighbours … are inforced to content themselves with rie, or barlie, yea, and in time of derth, mannie with bread made either of beans, peason or otes, or of altogether.'[17] The London bakers supplied fresh white rolls or manchets made with fine-quality white flour, weighing 6 ounces; the housewives' loaf or 'cheat' bread, a robust wholemeal or brown bread; and the coarse 'maslin' made from a mixture of grains and pulses, typically barley, wheat, rye, pease and malt, ground to a meal and, according to Gervase Markham in 1615, mixed with hot water in a large wooden kneading trough.[18] There was much regional diversity, and the London bakers probably made a much wider variety of breads than the official lists suggest, including fancy breads for special occasions, jumbals or spice breads, cakes and biscuits. They also baked 'pyes puddens and other ovenmeates' for local residents, taverns and cookshops, though this sideline activity was frowned upon by the wardens of the Bakers'

This type of oven was set directly on top of a brick stand and either heated from below or fired from within – the kindling set alight and then raked out prior to baking. The opening was covered by a wooden door sealed with dough. Similar ovens have been found in excavations in colonial America.

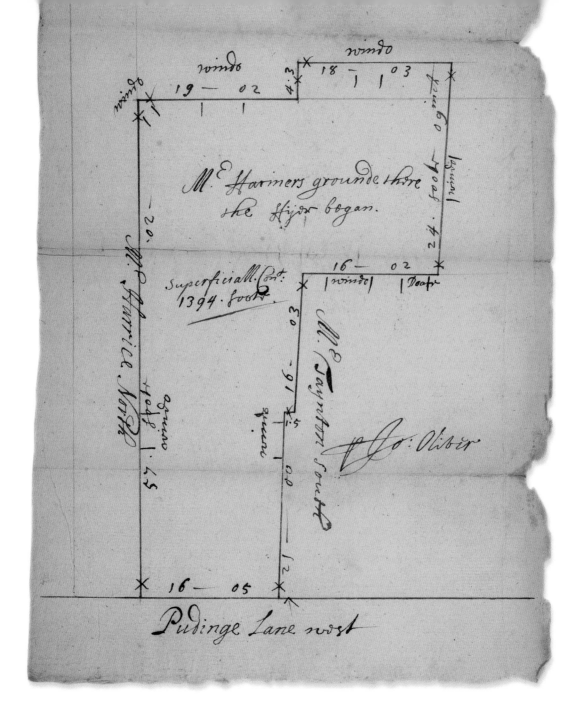

On the plan (handwritten annotations):

windo
windo
19 — 02
3
4
18 — 1 | 03

Mr Fariners grounde there the ffyer began.

Superficiall M Cont:
1394. foott

16 — 02
windo
Doore

Mr Taynton South

Jo: Olivier

Mr Harrice North

16 — 05

Pudinge Lane west

Company as properly belonging to the cook's trade. The bakers made several batches of bread a day, each announced by a blast on a horn, a ringing bell or the 'cryes of their boyes or other servants about the streets'.[19]

The Bakers' Company records provide little information about their trade and nothing about the cause or impact of the fire, despite the fact that it started in a bakehouse in Pudding Lane. Of Thomas Farriner, the baker in question, there are just a few details: he was apprenticed to London baker Thomas Dodson in 1629, became free of the Bakers' Company in 1637, and married

This plan, inscribed 'Mr Fariners grounde there the ffyer began', and drawn up seven years after Thomas Farriner's death, shows the extent of his pre-fire property: some 1,394 square foot, which seems to have included a yard where he kept stocks of fuel. The plot was still vacant in 1679 'upon a Supposition that it ought perpetually to ly wast', but the decision was overturned and the ground surrendered to make way for a new building. Mr Harrice (*sic*) the cooper is named as the occupant of the property on the north side (see p. 90).

Hanna Mathewes at St Helen's Bishopsgate in the same year. By 1649 he had settled in the parish of St Margaret, New Fish Street, and in the Hearth Tax returns for August 1666 he was living in a fairly substantial property with five hearths and one oven in Fish Yard on the east side of Pudding Lane.[20] Farriner took an active part in parish affairs, and supplied bread to the poor and needy in his local community, serving as an overseer of the poor 1660–61.[21] By 1666 he was one of the main contract suppliers of ships' biscuits to the navy, and in this capacity held the official title of 'Conduct of the King's Bakehouse'. Most of his deliveries were probably made directly to the Naval Victualling Yard in Tower Hill nearby. After the fire, the King ordered the navy victualler to send sea biscuits to the refugees in Moorfields, but 'the markets were so well supplied that the people declined them'.[22] It is not stretching credulity too much to suppose that some of Farriner's biscuits might have been included in this consignment – if they were, it would have been the most extraordinary irony.

It is significant that the fire broke out in the early hours of Sunday 2 September, because Saturday was one of the regulation baking days and contemporaries noted that the Sabbath was the one day in the week when citizens who 'were wearied out' by their work could 'lye longest in bed'.[23] According to Farriner's account, the oven was extinguished at about ten o'clock at night; when he inspected it again at midnight, the still glowing embers were raked over and the doors and windows of the bakehouse were closed to reduce draughts. A stack of kindling had been left beside (or inside) the oven to dry so the oven could be fired in the morning. This in itself is an interesting admission since the ovens were not supposed to be fired again until Tuesday. Did Farriner have some kind of dispensation to bake at irregular and unofficial times to fulfil his orders for the navy? In any event, the cause of the devastating fire that followed is unknown. Farriner insisted that neither he nor any of his household had been negligent. Perhaps he was right. There are many possible explanations for the fire in his bakehouse; a guttering flame from a candle, a spark from the cinders, even spontaneous combustion of the flour. In the end, the burden of proof rested on the claims of a deranged French watchmaker, Robert Hubert, who initially confessed to starting the blaze, and then pleaded not guilty when indicted. Hubert was a scarcely credible witness; even though the government investigators concluded that the fire was an accident, he was a convenient scapegoat and was hanged at Tyburn on 27 October.

Little more is known about Farriner in the years after the fire (*see* p. 90), but he was evidently able to resume his trade because a stock of flour valued at £13 7s 6d with other household effects was listed in his probate inventory, dated 23 December 1670.[24] There are no known descriptions of Farriner's bakehouse, but some sense of its appearance and equipment can be gleaned from other bakers' inventories in pre- and post-fire London.[25] Thomas Poole, self-styled 'Whitebaker', had 3,100 'ship's biskett' at 9 shillings per hundred, valued at £16; 720 lb of coarse wheatmeal at £6; two old troughs, a kneading board, an old iron weighing beam and weights; and 39 old canvas bags at 6d per bag.[26] Most bakehouses had two or three wooden kneading troughs (with or without lids) fashioned from strong planks, which were scoured clean with a right-angled dough scrape. The bakers were careful to leave some dough behind so that the yeast spores could multiply and act as a raising agent for future batches. There were shovels or 'peels' for baking cakes and bread: made either from wood with a protective plate of iron on the blade, or from iron with a socket into which a short or long wooden shaft was inserted, 'by which all sorts of Bread and Dishmeats are taken out of the Oven, without hurt or danger'.[27] There were long broad boards with a hole at one end, used to carry unbaked bread, pies and pasties to and from the bakehouse. There were baskets, tubs and sacks, dough knives, shovels, beams, scales and weights, candles and spice boxes, bags of flour and grain; as well as piles of faggots and dried gorse for the ovens. Thomas Mitchell's bakehouse at the sign of the Sacaren's Head in Aldgate had several biscuit boards, various iron pots and 'a remnant of molasses', which was presumably used for sticky cakes and buns.[28] Every bakehouse had one or more bolting mills to grind and separate the meal from bran or other coarse grains; by means of which 'more meal will be taken from its Bran in one hour, than a person can searce or sift in a whole day'.[29] The mills were operated with a crank handle and the horizontal splats were covered with linen cloths to keep the grains from spilling out of the mechanism. Several bakehouses had moulding boards for fashioning the dough into loaves and rolls, and a few possessed a

(*opposite*) This tax record, compiled in August 1666, records the names of the residents in Pudding Lane and adjoining courts and alleys. The occupants paid a tax of 1 shilling for each hearth, which was collected twice a year.

x Henry Toogood playstirer	4	
1 Stove	1	
~~Widd Adams Cooper~~	1	
x Sarah Easton Tallowchandlr	4	
1 stopt up	1	
x Thomas Brooks fishmongr	2	
x Robert Berry Cooper	3	
x James Langdale porter	1	
Abraham Robbits	1	
x Mary Merrifield	1	
x Henry Browne Taylor	3	
x Edward Ratcliffe victualer	7	
x Daniell Harris Cooper	5	
Nathaniell Doggett Skinnegion	5	
Empty	4	
x Thomas Dalton Esqr	5	
Lawrine Joker widd	1	

Pudding lane, The East syde

x Richard Poole hooke&eye mkr	4	
Mary Collier Cooper	7	

Fish yard.

Hugh Amies porter	3	
Sarah fish Sparke	2	
Henry More waterbearer	1	
Thomas Birt Sexton	1	
Widd Thomas	1	
Empty. 5.	5	
Empty. 4.		
40	4 / 76	

23

x Mary Whitacre widd	2	
George Porter plastrer	3	
Widd Gander	1	
Benjamin Burstow	1	
Thomas Knight Glasier	4	
Alice Spencer	4	
Empty	3	
x John Bibie Turnr	3	
x Thomas Harrimer Baker	5	
1 own	1	
William Ludford plastrer	3	
1 stop up	1	
Jones	2	
x Susanna Nosse	3	
Empty	3	

Lambe yard.

William Burgis hooke&eye mkr	3	
Joshua Sands platewirker	2	
Empty	3	
x Nicolas Garter hooke&eye mkr	5	
Widd Grimes	1	
John Wardley Clothworker	4	
x William Walter Smyth	3	
John Wolfe porter	2	
John Hasleby porter	2	
Widd Pawley	2	
x William Greene Turner	2	
	60	

semi-mechanized kneading instrument called a brake – essentially a table supported by four or more robust legs with a long wooden pole attached to one side. The pole was bolted to the table with a hinged pivot which allowed the operator to move it up and down, and over and across the dough in a series of short, sharp thwacks.

Though some bakers were wholesale suppliers, most seem to have had a shop next to the bakehouse so they could supply a wide range of fresh bread, cakes and biscuits to a loyal and local clientele. The shops had an open hearth with bellows, tongs and fire irons, but were otherwise sparsely equipped with a few baskets and oddments of furniture: a chest, a cabinet, a table, a settle bed, leather upholstered chairs, and in one case an old carpet and a wicker chair. The larger establishments had a 'pastry' as well as the bakehouse, though these were primarily used for housing the bolting mill, for the storage of sacks and, in one case, in the loft above, 444 cwt of biscuits.[30] Smaller rooms beside or directly above the bakehouse held stores of flour and grain, bolting cloths, extra sets of scales and weights, assorted baskets and old sacks. The cellars and yards were stacked with wood and coals, the odd dough tub, and various kitchen implements such as iron pots, brass kettles, ladles, dripping pans and skimmers.

Some bakers, like John Jarvis in the parish of St Katherine's by the Tower of London, kept part of their grain supplies in the City granaries. Many of the granaries were destroyed or severely damaged in the fire. On 19 August 1667 the Mercers' Company was told that the 'skreene, shovells, sives, Beame and weights' in the Bridewell Granary had perished, and that these items were also needed for the Bridgehouse Granary at the southern end of London Bridge. The wardens ordered replacements, and because they anticipated a sharp rise in the price of corn the clerk was instructed to find out how much grain the granaries would hold and to buy 'the best old wheate' at the most favourable rates 'for supply of the City when occasion shall require'.[31]

The Bread Seller and Water Carriers (*detail*), oil on canvas, by Jean Michelin (1623–1696).

Brick-maker & tile-maker

'[this] land nor any part thereof shalbee
molested or broken upp or in any wise medled
withall for or towards the making of Bricks.'
—*Clothworkers' Company*, 10 July 1668[32]

Building materials were in such great demand after the fire that
as soon as the embers had cooled enough for people to return
to the sites of their burnt homes and shops, they began to sift
through the rubble to salvage anything that they could find.
Bricks and tiles were cleaned and stockpiled for later use; roofs
on the point of collapse were carefully dismantled, and unstable
walls and chimneys were pulled down or shored up with bulks of
timber until they could be properly assessed by the surveyor and
repaired.[33] The Clothworkers' Company stacked their bricks with
other materials in a vault underneath the ruins of their hall, and
a week after the fire the Fishmongers erected a new wall using
recycled bricks without mortar in their haste to secure the site
and protect their boundaries from prying eyes and unwelcome
encroachment.[34] Bricklayers were encouraged to reuse old bricks
wherever possible. When Thomas Jones bricklayer was tasked to
clear and 'cleanse' the foundations of five tenements belonging
to St Bartholomew's Hospital in the Shambles, Newgate, he
was offered all the bricks that he could find as a reward for his
efforts.[35] Neighbours squabbled in their efforts to reclaim materials, and the Skinners' Company received a complaint that Ann
Evans, one of their tenants, had 'arrested' her neighbour William
Walker for 'intermixing' his bricks with hers.[36]

The homeless were desperate for materials to erect temporary
shelters; some were quick to spot an opportunity. When Arthur
Miles, a scrivener and a tenant of the Mercers' Company, saw a
'parcel of Old tiles' lying abandoned in the courtyard at Gresham

These burnt bricks and tiles were recovered from excavations in Pudding Lane. After the fire, wrote Samuel Rolls in *Londons Resurrection or the Rebuilding of London* (1668), people were penny wise and pound foolish. Bricks were plentiful but were 'never worse than they have bin of late, and yet never dearer'. Some were underfired and others bulked up with dross from the ashes and rubble. Many of the post-fire bricks recovered from excavations include ground-up clay pipes and other detritus.

College that had 'come off of the little shedd lately taken downe' he begged permission to buy them to set up a small shop in the 'Stone Walke'. The Committee overseeing the works at Gresham College (*see* p. 51) agreed that he could have them as long as the tiles were numbered and he paid the going rate.[37] The Wardens' Accounts for the year 1666–67 record Miles's payment of 10 shillings for 670 tiles.[38]

The need for bricks and tiles was so great that 'to encourage [their] more free and plentifull making … soe necessary to the rebuilding of the City', the leaseholders of all the lands in the suburbs and other open spaces surrounding the capital were urged to plough them up 'for gravel, Bricks, sand, loame or clay'.[39] By concentrating production around the City as much as possible the authorities hoped to keep transportation costs and prices to a minimum, which was set at £10 per rod. Only the garden plots were to be left untouched (*see* p. 113).[40] This order prompted a flurry of applications from enterprising individuals who hoped to profit from the venture. William White, who held 5 acres in the parish of St Giles-in-the-Fields from the City's tenant, Mr Reeve, was one of the first; his application to the Court of Aldermen on 6 November 1666 was swiftly granted on condition that there was no restrictive covenant or clause in his lease to prevent it.[41]

Not all of the brick- and tile-making projects proved a success. The Skinners' Company received a petition from Captain Jones to convert the Company's land in 'Sandhills' into a brickfield, but when the terms were set and the Company asked him to pay a £300 fine, Jones 'tooke his leave' and the whole enterprise collapsed.[42] Robert Markland, a leaseholder of Brewers' Company land near St Pancras Church in Middlesex, requested permission to break up 2½ acres for clay and on the remaining half-acre to erect a tile kiln with 'other conveniences'. New covenants were inserted into his lease, which was extended for a further term of 27 years and the Company asked Markland to supply them with 20,000 well-made tiles to 'be employed for their Hall and other building there', which were to be delivered free of charge. Within a few months, however, Marland had died. As his widow Elizabeth later explained, her husband had built three houses on the site but the land had proved unfit for tile-making. They had, she said, laid out a great deal of money on the whole venture. As she could not manage the 'business of the Tile-making [and] was very poore … [with] a great charge of children to maintaine', she asked to be discharged from the agreement. The Brewers decided that she should still pay the fine of £50 but in view of her 'condition' agreed to reduce her rent by £4 per annum.[43]

There were many other applications. The Clothworkers' Company received a petition from their tenant Samuel Horne to make bricks on 9 acres of Company land in Islington. His

'On the north side of London', 1665, after Wenceslaus Hollar (1607–1677). In the foreground three men are practising archery; St Paul's Cathedral can by seen on the skyline.

request was refused and he was told that no part of the land 'nor any part thereof shalbee molested or broken upp or in any wise medled withall for or towards the making of Bricks' without a special order from the Court. Horne tried again, and this time the Company decided that as long as he gave them 3 pence for every 1,000 bricks made and as many loads of dung as they asked for, he could go ahead, subject to an inspection of the land by a viewing committee. On 26 February 1668 the committee concluded that the ground 'held three spit deepe and was fit to make Bricks' and that it would be better to ask Horne to pay a fine for the land itself rather than for every 1,000 bricks produced. Horne said he would be prepared to pay £20 per acre, but as the season was 'soe farr spent' he could not begin to dig until the following year.[44] This comment is interesting because the weather conditions were of crucial importance for brick production: severe cold and frost made digging difficult or impossible and increased the fuel cost for firing; too much wind or rain could affect the drying process as well as the quality and number of bricks produced. Londoners were quick to complain when the smoke from the brick and tile kilns billowed across the City, and brick-makers were often fined for nuisances of this kind. So important were the weather conditions that in 1630 'A Proclamation Concerning New Buildings in and about the Cities of London' stipulated that 'the first digging [of the brick earth] be between the feasts of St Michael the Archangel and St Thomas the Apostle [29 September–21 December], and the second diggin, casting, or turning up of the sayd earth, to be at or before the last day of February then following.' In addition, the moulding of bricks should be done 'between the feast of the Annunciation of the Blessed Virgin Mary [25 March], and the last day of August yearly, and at no other time of season of the yeere'.[45]

After much deliberation, the Clothworkers' Committee decided that they needed independent, expert advice to establish the going rate for brick-making ground, and finally settled on £40 per acre or £360 for the whole plot with a lease term of seven years. It was agreed that after this time the ground should be brought up to its original level with 'dung and soyle' and manured. But when Horne heard of their decision he was much annoyed 'soe tooke his leave'. The whole matter became even more complicated when the lord of the manor decided that he should also receive some financial consideration, demanding £5 for every acre dug. Horne tried to claim back the money from the Clothworkers, who refused. After much toing and froing, the contract was finally signed. The last entry for this brick-making venture occurs in 1671/72, when it was drawn to the Company's notice that only part of the land had actually been used for making bricks, and Mr Horne's tenant owed them £80 in rental arrears.[46]

William Ridges Esq, citizen skinner and one of the governors at St Bartholomew's Hospital (*see* p. 44), also applied for permission to make bricks 'upon certain pasture ground' which he held from the hospital in the 'Common Fields' near the City's Pest House at Mount Mill to the north of the Barbican. Before his request was granted, a viewing committee inspected the ground so they could see at first-hand whether it would be detrimental to the local residents and 'what benefit may probably accrue thereby to the poore or otherwise to … Mr Ridges. A few weeks later the desired permission was granted; Ridges's lease was amended and the fee per acre of ground dug was set at £20. But a month later the governors wanted to know why William Ridges had made such little progress with the brickfield: did he wish to proceed, and if so what did he intend to do. They were reminded that Ridges had just spent £400–500 in building half a dozen houses on his rental land in White Lyon Court, Barbican, 'in such a convenient and substantial manner which wilbee to a future good improvement of the poore Revenues', in recognition of which he had been granted a 16-year extension to his lease with a small adjustment to his rent to reflect the improvements made. They noted, too, that Ridges had been minded to make a garden in 6 acres of pasture that he held near Mount Mill, and he was given permission on the understanding that it would not encroach on or in any way impede traffic on the King's highway. As for the brick venture, they decided to postpone the decision until Squire Ridges 'minde bee better understood'.[47]

When the Court met again on 28 November 1668, William Ridges's licence to make bricks was confirmed upon payment of a £100 fine and one proviso, that once the sand, gravel and brick-earths had been extracted and the bricks fired and made, he was to level the whole ground and lay it down to grass for grazing. A new convenant was inserted into his lease that he should not dig any part of the 4 acres beyond his lease term of four years, and that he should have free right of cartage near the Pest House on condition that any necessary repairs were made to the road and adjoining footpath. Further orders were made to confirm the contracts, and Ridges successfully arranged for an extension of his lease.[48] When he died in 1670, he left extensive property to his wife and five sons, including his house in Hornsey (*see* p. 204), 'two closes of land' near the Pest House, and 13 other houses in London and Middlesex.[49] The best evidence for his brick-making enterprise, however, comes from his probate inventory, appraised on 20 January 1670, under the heading 'In the Brick Field', which lists 500,400 bricks in the kiln valued at £239 8s; two clay carts, two hollow barrows, five 'crowding' barrows; two tables; two pairs of moulds; a pair of 'earth spades', other spades and two loads of sand, all valued at £243 8s.[50]

The governors of St Bartholomew's Hospital received other applications from their tenants to make bricks in the vicinity of the Pest House, but this soon caused problems because the only road leading into Old Street and from there to the City which was used for the cartage of bricks quickly turned into a quagmire.[51] There was a flurry of complaints from the local residents, who were annoyed by the noise, the constant trundle of carts under their windows, as well as the dirt and dust in their homes. The pathway running beside the road was churned up and the whole route to the Pest House became impassable. With some embarrassment, the governors read a report from the Lord Mayor and aldermen, to whom complaint had been made, that a certain Robert Botley, one of the tenants of the hospital, had destroyed the access roads with his cartage of bricks. Other hospital tenants who lived along the route were directly affected and voiced their own complaints, and so in an attempt to calm the situation the governors ordered Botley to repair the footpath and cart road from Old Street to the next bridge beyond the Pest House and Suckle House with immediate effect. To protect passers-by they also ordered that posts should be erected to protect the whole length of the footpath on the left-hand side, and that part of the route should be fenced in, leaving a 6–10 foot gap at various points for the wagons to squeeze through. In addition, Botley and his partners William Andrews and John Drury were to relay the entire length of the path and cartway with slabs and 'slight dirt', and the areas of compacted earth were to be covered with some 'good green Bavyns called Long Tayles' and upon these a good layer of fine gravel. Finally, they were to make good any defects and maintain the roadway for as long as required. Eight days' notice was given to allow them time to close off the road and obtain materials for repair.[52]

In July 1668, the Goldsmiths' Company paid William Andrews £3 18s for 3,000 bricks for the use of their new hall and tenement buildings.[53] Other orders followed. As the volumes increased, the road and path to the Pest House began to show increasing signs of neglect, prompting Widow Upton, a tenant of St Bartholomew's Hospital who lived near the Pest House, to complain to the governors that the footpath and cartway near her home were in a dreadful state of repair and the carts went too close to her house.[54] The governors agreed that she could install a bar across the road to stop all further passage until the necessary repairs were done.[55] But within months the constant flow of traffic and the ever present rumble of carts caused yet more problems. There were intermittent complaints from the tenants until in the spring of 1670 the governors announced that the cart road would be blocked up unless the brick-masters promised to put things to rights and pay their outstanding toll fees for cartage. Botley and Andrews agreed to the demands; however, a few months later Andrews was summoned before the governors and was told that all cartage rights would be withheld and the way stopped with a gate and turnpike unless he paid the monies due and made all the repairs to the path and road as they had asked. The matter was still unresolved in 1675, when Andrews was again reprimanded for defaulting, but by this date the City had been largely rebuilt and the peak demand for bricks and tiles had passed.[56]

Cooper

'after the late sadd fire in London (by meanes whereof most of his caskes were destroyed) hee was forced to supplye himself ... with forreigne Casks which he bought att Newbery in Berkshire.'
—*Alderman Jemmat*, 2 April 1667[57]

Hundreds of thousands of hogsheads, casks, barrels, kilderkins, runlets, firkins, tubs, buckets and other cooperage wares were lost or damaged in the fire. Filled with a huge array of commodities and everyday necessities – such as butter, alum, soap, oils, vinegars, strong waters, wax, sugar, glass, cheese, salted meats and pickled fish, dried fruits, nuts, dyestuffs, spices, drugs, figs, molasses, linseed, saltpetre, gunpowder, pitch, tar, wine, ale and beer – they were used for both short- and long-term storage, and played a key role in domestic life and commerce. The loss of so many cooperage wares was more than a mere inconvenience; it was a calamity of the highest order, and the coopers' trade was put under huge pressure to make new vessels or repair where they could. So great was the need that many coopers began to infringe the Company Ordinances. On 2 April 1667 the wardens found that Alderman Jemmat had 23 barrels and 3 kilderkins in his Houndsditch brewhouse that were neither marked nor sealed according to regulations. And there were two more unmarked casks in another brewhouse nearby. Jemmat could do nothing except agree, but by way of mitigation he explained that most of his casks had been destroyed in the fire so he had been forced to acquire new ones out-of-town. When these arrived he had asked Mr Norich, the Company's official 'sealer', to seal them, but Norich had refused because they were 'foreign' casks from a cooper in Newbury in Berkshire.[58]

There were other complaints. These included the 'great and notorious abuses of late time practiced' that beer had been put into ale kilderkins and other kinds of ale vessels contrary to the 'good laws of this kingdome and to the manifest deceit and detriment of his Majesties subjects'. In an effort to curb the practice, all vessels for ale and beer were to be distinguished by spoke-shaved markings on the heads and sides, and all ale vessels were to have three hoops around the booge (the widest part of the cask) and three more at the head. The sealers were to put 'in plaine figures' near the bung the true contents as prescribed by law, namely 32 gallons on an ale barrel and 36 gallons on a beer barrel; 'by them to bee gauged and sealed upon paine of being discharged from his or there sayed imployment'.[59] A special square-sectioned gauging rod was used to measure the casks; each face was marked with different graduated scales for ale, beer, wine and other liquids.

There are very few personal accounts for coopers in mid-seventeenth-century London, so it is impossible to gauge the impact of the fire on individual businesses. Some presumably profited from the increased work; others were badly affected. In 1667, for instance, Roger Morris, a cooper to the navy, asked for the prompt payment of two outstanding bills for £241 6s 3d and £26 5s because he had experienced 'a sad loss by the late dismal fire which [had] much impoverished his estate'.[60] But the most interesting evidence occurs in a case brought before the Mayor's Court in July 1667.[61] The key defence witness was none other than Thomas Farriner, citizen and baker of London, 'aged 54 or thereabouts', who appeared on behalf of Daniel Harris, citizen and cooper of London, in an action brought by his apprentice William Beck. It transpired that Farriner had lived more or less opposite Harris in Pudding Lane before the fire and had known him for the best part of twenty years (see p. 79). He knew the plaintiff, William, and believed that he had been well taught and instructed in the 'art of a wine cooper'. From his personal dealings with Harris, he believed him to be 'as carefull a man in looking after his servants as any of ye trade' and that he had given Beck everything he needed for his personal comfort and well-being. As a close neighbour and a frequent visitor to Harris's workshop, Farriner was aware that Harris had employed a journeyman to teach Beck to make dry casks and runlets 'for his further benefit and advantage of his trade' but he had also observed that Beck was a very careless fellow and spent rather too much time playing

Burnt barrel staves. One contemporary described the area around Pudding Lane as 'the lodge of all combustibles, oil, hemp, flax, pitch, tar and cordage'. Excavations at the south-eastern end of Pudding Lane in 1979–80 uncovered the remains of a brick-lined cellar filled with the carbonized remains of 20 barrels stacked in such a way as to suggest that they had been stored on five racks. Adhering to the wooden hoops and staves was a black viscous material, which was analysed and identified as 'Stockholm Tar', a kind of pitch used for waterproofing. It seems that the cellar was used as a store, so the proximity of this highly inflammable material to the bakehouse might have supplied the fuel that turned a small fire into a major conflagration.

around in the street instead of attending to business. As a result, Farriner felt that the money Harris had expended in trying to further Beck's career had been frittered away and wasted; and because, he said, Beck was 'addicted' to drink, it would have been far better if Harris had 'taken a boy that had bine industrious'.

Another neighbour, George Francis, citizen and grocer, aged 28 years, had a rather different opinion. He had known William well 'untill ye late dreadfull fire (that their houses were burnt)' and believed him to be very diligent in his master's business and had never seen him drunk, 'lying out' or keeping bad hours, but on the contrary had always found him to be very polite and hard-working. Other witnesses were produced in Beck's defence, but then on 12 August, 23-year-old Katherine Knight gave her deposition. She had known William Beck for about one and half years, having spent 12 months working with him as a servant in Harris's household before the fire. During the time she had been there, William had ample food and drink; his laundry had been taken care of; he had good accommodation and all other things 'fitting for an apprentice'. But she noticed that as soon as her master left the house William threw down his tools and would

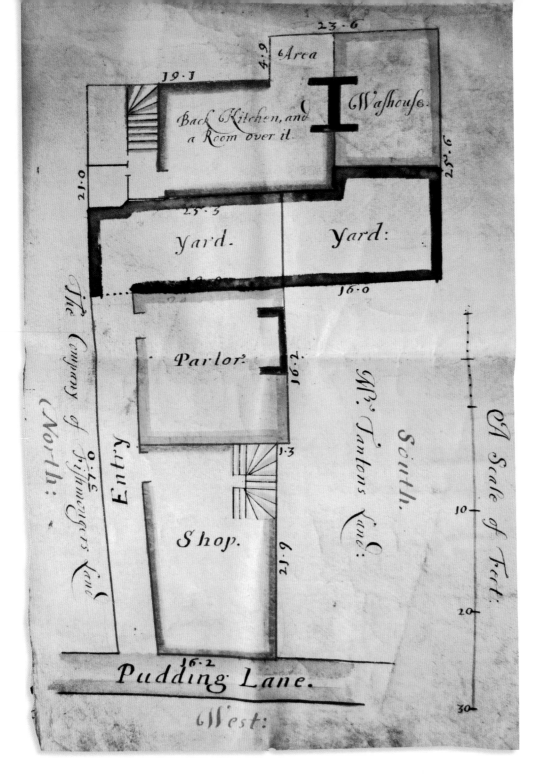

generally neglect his trade by 'playing and spending his time idly',
so that her master often had to employ a journeyman to finish
William's work and generally make up for the lost time. When
the fire came, her master was out of town on business, leaving
her mistress at home 'Bigg with child'. Beck carried a few goods
from the house, but then returned to collect his own things in his
'owne trunck', and, despite various entreaties from Katherine to

Daniel Harris evidently recovered quite quickly from his losses in the fire, because by 1674 he had moved next door to the vacant plot of Farriner's bakehouse (see p. 76). He later applied to the City Lands Committee for permission to erect a new building on the empty plot, and on 6 April 1682 the deed for the 'parcell of ground or soyle upon which the house stood where the late dismall fire first began' was drawn up. The lease term was for 40 years at a yearly rent of £12. A plan of the new property was made by the surveyor William Leybourn.

help them, had simply abandoned them to their fate. Katherine was certain that many goods of value had been lost which might well have been preserved if Beck had stayed and helped them, as 'he ought to have done'.

William Beck put his own safety before that of others, and if had stayed to help, as Daniel Harris later testified, more goods would have been saved from the fire. It is likely that the goods that were 'carried awaye' were household items and perhaps a few of the more portable tools, rather than stock-in-trade, since these items would have been impossible to move without the aid of several carts and a lot of extra manpower.

The stock lists of coopers' workshops provide a clear indication of the variety and scale of their holdings. Andrew Eagle in the parish of St Giles Cripplegate had 100 barrel boards, 220 tun staves, 200 white firkin hoops, 60 caps, 'three loads' of 3 inch planks and a further 26 foot of planks, 2 sections of trussing hoops (made from wood or iron), a new kilderkin stave, and 'ye shoop tooles & other things'.[62] Ralph Gunn, who lived in a one-up, one-down house in the same parish, had the following items in his shop and cellar: 4 barrels, 24 kilderkins, 3 four-gallon runlets, 2 firkins and a paire of old trussing hoops; 5 empty casks and 150 new kilderkin boards; 3,000 firkin hoops and a parcel of old boards with other lumber in the garret; as well as 'axes & adses & all other working Tooles whatever'.[63] John Wells of Bride Lane, who died in 1665, had an enormous stock. In the shop itself were 7 deal planks, 28 tun staves, a parcel of hoops, 4 screws, 6 jointing planes, 2 ploughs and a parcel of small tools, forms and lumber valued at £7 11s 6d. In the loft above were 52 tun staves, 105 short tun staves, 67 deal planks, 30 barrel heads, 56 kilderkin heads, 30 pipe staves, 2,200 kilderkin hoops and 600 firkin hoops, all valued at £27 3s 3d. His yard contained 673 foot lengths of 3 inch planks, 54 foot lengths of 2 inch planks, and 81 foot lengths of 1½ inch planks, with 1,850 barrel boards, 1 ton of pipes, 4 taps, 282 tun staves, a parcel of firewood and lumber, a wooden horse, and a parcel of pantiles. The cellar had more fuel, including a parcel of sea coal and smaller coals, a parcel of ordinary hoops, 12 beer barrels, 10 beer kilderkins, 11 ale kilderkins, 2 tubs and 131 labs, valued at £19. And this was not all. In storage elsewhere were 1,850 firkin hoops and 16,000 kilderkin hoops.[64]

Cordwainer

'she prayed them … consider that she had nothing else to live on.'—*Widow Theame*, shoemaker, 27 August 1667[65]

Sibbell Theame was employed by the governors of Christ's Hospital to make shoes for the orphans in their care. She had held an exclusive contract for many years, but in July 1654 the nurses responsible for the care of the youngest children complained that her shoes were not as 'serviceable as they should be', to the detriment of the infants' health. When Sibbell was summoned to a court meeting to account for her work, she explained that she could not make any improvements unless the Hospital gave her extra money to cover the cost. So the committee agreed to increase the purchase grants for shoes to 5s per annum, payable quarterly for one year, with the proviso that if any of the children who were 'put out to nurse in the Cittie with their mothers shall be found without shoes, or haveing bad shoes then the mother soe offending shall receive noe benefit from the hospital for a yeare after, either by money or clothes for keeping ye said child'.[66] A few months later the governors decided that Sibbell should only make shoes for the children resident in the Hospital itself and that these should be made 'very substantiall' with three soles rather than one. This ruling came as a severe blow to Sibbell, who argued that it would much 'prejudice her trade … the rest of her imployment being soe small'. She reminded the committee that she was a widow with three small children to provide for; struggled to pay her journeyman £20 a year to cut out the leather and manage her shop; and with the high price of leather, wax thread and other materials, she simply could not make the shoes to the required standard at the current rate of 3s 6d per dozen. The governors accepted her argument and raised her grant to 5s 6d per dozen.[67]

Sibbell settled down to her trade, but in the spring of 1655 she submitted a petition to the governors requesting that they

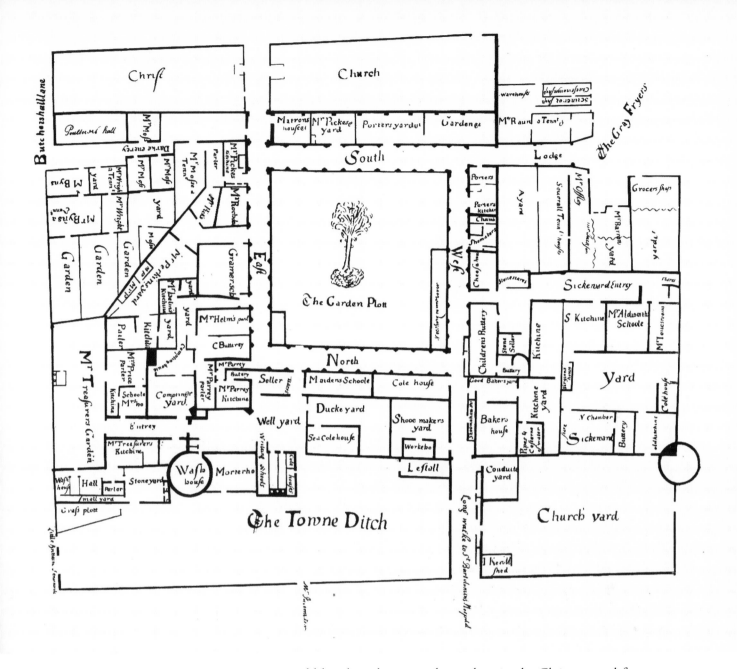

would be pleased to grant her a shop in the Cloisters, and for this privilege wished them to understand that her husband had made shoes for the Hospital for many years at very low rates and often at a considerable loss, and that her exclusive contract for supplying shoes had of late been 'disposed into other hands'. This last point was a particular concern since she found it difficult to maintain her business and provide for herself and her daughters. It was a persuasive argument and she was offered the shop for a yearly rent of 30s.[68] Other evidence suggests that Sibbell held the lease of several buildings in the precinct, probably in or near Shoemakers Yard to the immediate north of the Cole House, as shown on a *c.*1660 plan.[69] The shop in the Cloister is probably the one inscribed 'Shoemakers' on the west of the Cloister Garden between the Porter's house and the Cheesehouse, and it was perhaps from this new location that Sibbell issued the farthing trade token which bears her name, initials and occupation, 'SIBBIL THEAME CHRIST ASPITAL SHO MAKER', with the device of a shoe flanked by mullets.[70]

There are no records detailing the appearance and contents of Sibbell's dwelling house and workshop, but inventories of shoemakers' stock-in-trade from the neighbouring parish of St Giles Cripplegate offer some helpful clues. Robert Whittaker's shop contained 26 dozen shoes 'small and grate', as well as some trimmed leather, sole leather, two frying pans, two dripping pans, one jack with two spits, an iron grate, a pair of pot hangers, a fire shovel, tongs, fork and two irons. The garret contained various unspecified tools of the trade, alongside six sets of scales and a parcel of old lasts.[71] Richard Wright, one of the cordwainers who inspected Sibbell's work on company searches (see below), had 14 leather hides and two calf skins valued at £8 8s, 138 shoes in several sizes at £8 10s and several cut sections of leather for shoes.[72] John Heath had much less, just a pair of boot trees (used for stretching the leather to keep it in shape), leather offcuts, boot 'tops', welts and uppers, a hobbing iron, with lasts, soles and four dozen old shoes.[73] John Blow had a meagre amount of stock in his shop, with just 18 children's shoes at 39s, one hammer block and knives with a cutting board valued at 2s. He had 24 children's shoes in a 'Lodging Roome', a separate 'Cutting Room' containing 36 children's shoes and a parcel of leather. Three benches and a dozen lasts were kept in the garret, which suggests that it was used as an additional workspace.[74] The most detailed stock list is that

of Edward White, appraised in 1669, which includes 572 shoes for men, women, 'boys and girles', children's pumps and 'plaine sea shooes', as well as six pairs of boots, a dozen slippers, 7 calf skins and other hides, and 23 backs (a cut section for the heel of the shoe). There is no record of any tools. The rest of his household stock comprised some earthenware and glasses valued at 20s; an old table, with fire irons, jack and spit and lumber in the kitchen all at 12s; and a bed, bedstead and bedding at £2. The sum total is valued at £50 6s.[75]

Although nothing is known about Sibbell's working arrangements, she evidently had an uneasy relationship with the Hospital authorities and on more than one occasion narrowly avoided losing her place and livelihood. She continued to make very bad shoes 'not fitting for children to weare', whereby some had 'fallen sicke'. Then in 1655, following an altercation with the Hospital porter, Robert Guppy, she was reported to the governors for harbouring a young man for many years in her house as well as other 'men servants … att very ill houres'. Guppy also claimed that she received various goods from these men; he evidently hoped that Sibbell would lose her position, claiming that he could add a great deal more, 'only thought it his duety to acquaint them of the [current] businesse'. In response, Sibbell produced a written testimony that was read to the committee in which she acknowledged that 'shee was marryed' but had not harboured her husband in her lodgings even when he was employed as her servant, and she had

These children's shoes were filled with ash and fire debris when they were retrieved from a brick well in Queen Street in 1959.

certainly not welcomed other men into her rooms.[76] It was quite impossible for the committee to discern the truth since it was very much a matter of his word against hers, so Guppy was asked to make good his accusations with witnesses, and Sibbell encouraged to do likewise. Eventually the committee decided that for the 'peace of this house' both should be removed from their lodgings in the Hospital, but it would seem that this order was not carried out, because Guppy died in post and Sibbell Theame remained in her workshop until it was destroyed in the Great Fire.[77]

Sibbell was not the only shoemaker who struggled to meet the Hospital's standards, and other makers were chastised for making shoes 'not fitting for children to wear'. Most argued that the prices paid by the Hospital were too low and did not take account of the extraordinarily high price of leather, which meant that they could neither maintain standards nor fulfil their contracts. The governors eventually accepted that they needed to adjust their prices to reflect the current market value for leather, but did so on the understanding that if the wholesale rates for leather dropped, then so must the price per shoe. Sibbell Theame was further helped by the suggestion that the governors would buy the leather for her, but in 1662, as more shoemakers were needed to keep up with the ever-increasing numbers of children in the Hospital's care, she complained that although she enjoyed a house and two shops in the precinct she was entitled to receive preferential rates for her shoes because she had been making them for longer, and had lost 'a great deale of money' by so doing.[78] Athough her complaint fell on deaf ears, she remained one of the main suppliers for children's shoes, alongside Mr Brattle Preston of Duck Lane in the parish of St Bartholomew's the Great. From 1663 to 1666 Sibbell made 266 dozen shoes, and Brattle fewer at 174 dozen: a total of 5,280 shoes priced at 2s 2d per pair. The shoes were made in 12 sizes for children aged between four and fifteen years old and each shoe bore the mark of its maker.[79] Periodic inspections were made by officers of the Cordwainers' Company and the results of the 'Search' passed on to the governors, who recorded the details in the Court minutes. On several occasions Sibbell's shoes were found to be very sound, of 'good neates leather' and on the whole better than those of Brattle Preston, for which she received a little extra money for 'her encouragement'.

This gauge or foot-measure has scales for children's and adults' shoes. The shoes were probably marked on the sole to indicate their size.

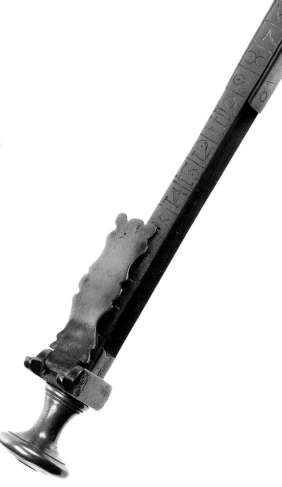

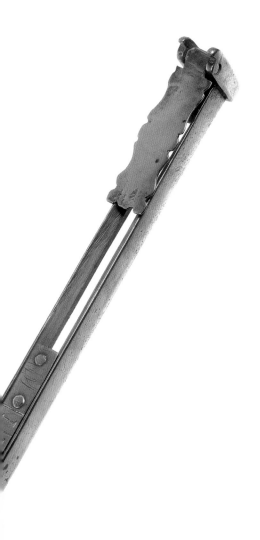

Then came the fire, and with it went Sibbell's workshop, the shop in the Cloisters, and seemingly also all of her leather and working tools. In a desperate attempt to find some kind of income, she approached the governors requesting leave to rebuild her shop in the Cloister that she might sell gingerbread for a quarterly rent of 30s. She asked specifically that the shop should be sited next to the Great Gate – a prime spot, approaching the Long Walk, the main thoroughfare leading to St Bartholomew's Hospital, and in addition asked for another shop within the 'ovall as formerly' for her men to make shoes in. Not content with this, she also asked that the whole charge should be borne by the Hospital and she should not pay any rent 'in regard she hath antiently made shooes for the house'. After some debate the committee felt that they could not help her, especially as it had been reported to them that she had kept very bad hours in the booth that she had erected in the Town Ditch, in which she was trying to make a living by selling drink. As a result, they decided that the door leading to the Ditch should be locked by the beadle punctually at 8 o'clock at night, and no one be permitted to pass through until morning. Sibbell promised to observe the time restrictions and said she would not permit any of the children to frequent her booth or to have any drink at unreasonable hours.[80] The promise was short-lived. On 27 August 1667 she was summoned to answer the charge of enticing one George Cox to her booth and plying him with drink. This offence was particularly serious, because Cox, a Cambridge scholar supported by the Hospital, had been sent down for drunkenness and keeping bad company. In desperation Sibbell asked them to reconsider as she had 'nothing else to live on', but the governors felt that they could not permit her to continue and she was ordered to sell what she had in her shed so that it could be pulled down. The Hospital steward was ordered to inspect the reserve stocks of beer and ale in her booth and to make sure that 'noe other drink be brought in'.[81] As for the supply of shoes, the shoe contract passed to Lawrence Johnson, who was asked to make 12 dozen shoes on 21 August 1667 'in behalf of Sibble Theame widdow'. Apart from a passing reference in the Hospital accounts for arrears of rent the following year, Sibbell's fate is unknown.

Draper & clothworker

'Upon Affidavit made by John Lee of Exeter fuller ye 11 pieces of purputanes brought in on ye proclamation are now in ye Dog house.'—*Lord Mayor's Waiting Book*, 13 October 1666[82]

The great 'Publick Cloth Markett of England called Blackwell Hall', lying on the west side of Basinghall Street near the Guild-hall, was a large building set around a courtyard.[83] The internal space was divided into different zones (each known as a hall) for specific kinds of 'broad and narrow' woollen cloth such as kerseys, baize, say and perpetuana, from Devon, Gloucestershire, Kent, Manchester, Reading, Somerset, Suffolk and Worcestershire. There were halls for blanket (undyed cloth), medley (mixed woollens) and Spanish (English cloths made from Spanish wool); with further areas for carpets, hangings and stockings of all kinds. Most of the halls were little more than a standing between one window and the next, generally divided by rails, pillars and intersecting walkways,[84] but in 1660 the Worcester clothiers were given an additional 'ten yards in length and the whole breadth of the said hall that is to say seven lights [windows]' on the understanding that if they ran out of space in the future, they could have more upon request for 'selling and stoweing of there [*sic*] cloths'.[85] All of the cloths from Essex, Suffolk, Hampshire, Surrey and Coventry and the so-called 'new draperies' were handled in warehouses in Leadenhall.

On 5 September 1666 Blackwell Hall burnt down. The Hall was administered by Christ's Hospital, and their records provide a graphic description of the disaster and its impact on Matthew White, a factor for Worcester cloths. White testified that he had sold several cloths in Blackwell Hall on 31 August 1666, and had made arrangements with the master porters for them to be

This painting by Egbert van Heemskerk (*detail*) shows the interior of a seventeenth-century London cloth merchant's or linen-draper's warehouse. The bolts of cloth have tabs at the ends which were used to record the names of the buyer and seller and the weight and quality of the material. By the 1660s drapers were retail and wholesale suppliers for woollen cloth and other textiles such as canvas and buckram, a loosely woven cloth made from hemp for lining curtains and upholstery. Drapers' stock in the pre- and post-fire period often included yards of plain and dyed linen, sewing silks, white, black and brown threads, bindings, tapes and printed and coloured calico.

delivered to the Star Inn in Fish Street Hill, a few minutes walk from Pudding Lane. A few days later, fire swept across the City. White was so preoccupied with other urgent matters that it was not until two days after the fire that he had a chance to enquire about his cloth. He made various enquiries and after a little while Mr Curtis, a porter, told him that some of his cloth was 'att a house neare the Artillary ground' in Moorfields, which indeed proved to be the case. But there was still a lot of cloth missing, which was worth £34 17s; despite repeated efforts to find it, and visits to various porters, White was at a loss to know where to turn and what to do. And, to add insult to injury, the master porters had 'bid him take his course, and will not make … restitution'. The master porters were present at the hearing, so the committee asked them to speak in their own defence, and 'they did acknowledge that one of them two clothes that hee speake of was miscaried and they supposed it was burnt'. They denied that Mr White had committed the cloth to any of them, and claimed that he had some 'remnants in his hands towards satisfaction for ye Cloth vallued to aboute £4 17s 6d'. It was a weak argument. The governors knew that it was standard practice for the master porters to keep a register of the cloth in their care, and to keep a record of its type and weight, as well as the names and habitation of the owners, buyers and sellers, so they wanted to know if the porters had properly entered the cloth in their ledgers and whether they had given 'security to make good such a loss'. They also wanted to know if the loss was due to negligence, to the unforeseen circumstances of the fire, or to a combination of the two.

Timothy Harper, the porter at the centre of the dispute, appeared with a written account, which was read to the assembled committee. It appeared that on the Saturday before 'the late dreadfull fire' Harper had received two cloths from Matthew White. But the same day, before he had had a chance to enter the details into his ledger, he had to go out on other business, and spent most of the day carrying cloth around the City. When he had finished the last delivery, he returned to Blackwell Hall, but found it shut. The next day, he 'was engaged upon the watch by means whereof hee could not come to the hall' (presumably in fire defence) and it was not until Tuesday morning that he was able to return to the Hall. His first task was to 'secure the two cloths', but as he could not find

A seventeenth-century linen and cotton twill fabric embroidered in wool with birds, insects, animals and flowing plants.

them he assumed that Mr White had already collected them, and with the 'fire comeing soe fast upon the hall [which] did soe amaze him as well as others that he forgot to aske Mr White whether hee had them or not'. A short time later, Mr White charged him with having the cloth. Harper made urgent enquiries and heard, quite by accident, from a fellow porter, that the some cloth had been removed from the Hall, but 'hee did believe the other was burnt, because hee was one of the last that came through the hall'. Matthew White was so angry that Harper undertook a search for the cloth at his own cost, procured a warrant, and 'used his utmost dilligence in searching' to the neglect of all other business 'to his great loss and damage ... hee being a poore labouring man, having noe other sustenance then his daily labours'. Harper eventually managed to track down 12 yards of cloth, which he delivered to Mr White, and soon afterwards heard that 19 yards more had been stashed in a warehouse in Horsleydown, Southwark. He told White about the latest find, and from that point on White took over the warrant and the whole business upon himself, so Harper naturally 'conceived himself thereby discharged'. After a certain amount of prevarication, the committee accepted Harper's claim that some of the cloth was lost in the Hall and burnt, but decided that he had been negligent – he should have carried away the cloth when it was sold or returned to the Hall to deal with it on Sunday, Monday or Tuesday. They concluded that Mr White should have some satisfaction for the loss, but reminded him that the porters were poor men and taking into account all that had happened the fine should be 'reasonable'. Mr White handed the affair over to the committee 'to make an end of itt', and they proposed that the porters should pay the sum of £20 between them.[86]

So much cloth was burnt that many drapers and clothiers outside London were quite 'undone by it, their whole estate lying there in cloth'.[87] While some tried to come to terms with the scale of the loss and its devastating impact on their livelihoods, others, more fortunate, were left to hunt around for their stock which had been hurried away for safety. John Lee, a fuller from Exeter, did not have long to wait, and on 13 October, following a royal proclamation about harbouring stolen goods lost from the fire, was told that his cloth – eleven pieces of perpetuana (a strong woollen cloth used for upholstery and coat linings) – had been dumped in

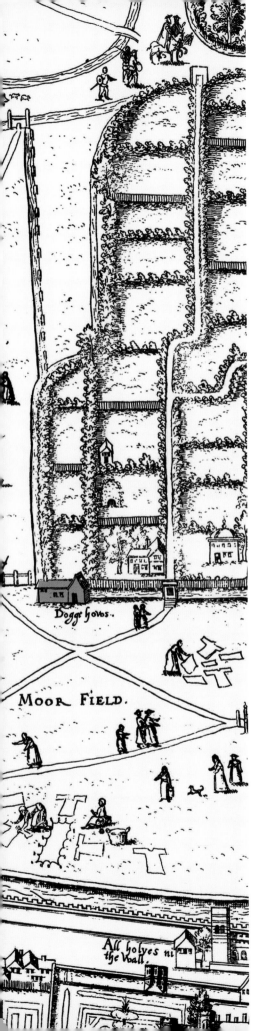

Dogge hows.

MOOR FIELD.

All holyes ni
the Voall.

the City Dog House in Moorfields. By happy chance, he was able to prove that it was his because the cloth still bore his mark: ten with the device ⊤ and three marked ☰.[88] The records provide no indication of its condition.

The most pressing problem for the clothiers, factors and porters was to find accommodation for their salvaged goods and space for new supplies, which began to arrive in ever-increasing quantities. Once the rubbish had been cleared and the ruined walls secured, sheds were built to house some of the cloth, and applications were made for space in the Leadenhall warehouses which had survived unscathed.[89] It was an immensely complex and challenging task for the warehouse keepers. Every little bit of space was needed. On 16 September the Gloucester clothiers asked if they could have the 'voyd place under the stayres' leading up to the East India Company's warehouse. The Colchester and Suffolk men had to move into the space formerly used for bayes (a lightweight cloth similar to flannel), while the clothiers from Bocking and Braintree in Essex were lodged in a room over the Spanish hall. There was so little space and so much demand that when Mr Denham, a Yorkshire factor, asked to set up on his own account he was told to 'have patience' and to wait until he could join in with others for a convenient place.[90] The overcrowding proved immensely trying. There were numerous complaints both from the clothiers and factors who had been displaced and from those who had been allocated a spot ill suited to their needs. Meanwhile, work on rebuilding Blackwell Hall continued. It was a slow process and by January 1668 the Essex clothiers had had enough, submitting a request that they might leave Leadenhall, as it was 'very inconvenient … and will not hold halfe their goods'. To alleviate their difficulties they were offered space in the 'late Spanish Hall and Gloucester Hall', and if these proved inadequate 'the Committee would take further care of them'. At the same time, the Wiltshire cloth was placed in the Spanish hall in a location that 'they enjoyed before the late fire', and the Gloucester factors dealing in red perpetuana came out of the Spanish hall and into the hall below, which forced other clothiers to relocate elsewhere.[91]

In January 1672, Christ's Hospital accounts record payments for the rebuilding of Blackwell Hall and the temporary accommodations of the clothiers, which amounted to £12,505 15s 10d.[92]

Engraver

'At this Court the Wardens making
knowne that the Companyes
Comon Seale and the small seale
hanging thereunto were in the late
fire burnt & consumed.'
—*Goldsmiths' Company*,
18 December 1666[93]

This seal matrix was made to replace the double-sided
Common Seal of the City of London, which was consumed
in the Great Fire of London. The obverse shows the walled
city with Baynard's Castle to the west, and the Tower of London
in the east. In the centre, soaring above the spire of St Paul's
Cathedral, is the figure of St Paul, the patron saint of the City,
with a sword in his right hand and a standard bearing the three
leopards of England in his left. The seal is inscribed SIGILLVM :
BARONVM : LONDONIARVM (Seal of the Barons of London). A
note in the City Cash Register for 1 December 1667 provides the
following details: 'Paid Master Robert Restrick Ingraver Twenty
pounds for makeinge a new Seale for the Cities use, finding silver
for the said Seale, the ould Seale beinge burnt in the said late sad
fier which hapned within the City of London.'[94]

There is little evidence for Robert Restrick's career as an
engraver. However, in 1661 he was sued in the Mayor's Court for
mistreating his apprentice William West. There were four main
charges: first, for failing to instruct West in the art of engraving,
chasing and embossing metal; second, for sending West around
the City with 'medicines to those who complained of sore eyes';
third, for beating him 'about Shrovetide last'; and finally, for
turning him out of his service. Two former apprentices, John
Brown and Samuel Cole, testified on West's behalf. Brown
claimed that during the whole term of his nine-year apprenticeship, Restrick 'did never (during the whole time aforesaid) teach

This seal matrix in silver, with a
modern steel mount, was made by
the engraver Robert Restrick in 1667 to
replace the Common Seal of the City
of London, which had been burnt in
the fire. The Haberdashers' Company
managed to preserve their ancient
seal in 'the late dreadfull fire' but lost
one of the keys to the box in which it
was kept. The wardens were forced to
break the lock to remove the seal. On
16 November 1666 a new lock and key
were ordered to be 'speedily made' in
replacement.

or instruct him … in the said art nor give him any manner of directions … but contrariwise' did as much as he could to prevent him from gaining any knowledge. Whenever Restrick had some engraving work to do, he always disappeared into a private shop which he 'kept locked … while he was at work', so that Brown was forced to creep up to the door and peek through a crack to see his 'manner of working'. And it was only, he claimed, by this subterfuge, the help he had received from others and his own diligence that he had acquired sufficient knowledge and skill to work as an engraver. Samuel Cole's term of apprenticeship had overlapped with West's for about a year, and during this time he claimed that Restrick had 'almost altogether employed him in going of errands to and fro to persons troubled with sore eyes (the Defendant driving a great trade that way)'. The final deposition for the complainant was from Ellen Dowse, Restrick's servant, who said that on 'Shrovetide last past' West had 'come into the Kitchen … with his arm all bloody'. Restrick's wife had heard a commotion; when she came into the shop to find out what was going on, Restrick had complained to her and had asked her to 'go and turn … William out of doors, calling him sundry very ill names'.

Robert Restrick's version of events was rather different. He said that West had in fact acquired a good deal of skill and knowledge in the art of engraving and might 'have been a great advantage to [him] and gained a good livelihood thereby' but for certain character traits that only become obvious over time. It transpired that West was lazy and spent far too much time in alehouses where he met with persons of 'idle and vain conversation'. The neighbours had often 'wondered' why West had been allowed to get away with his drunken behaviour for so long, and Restrick explained that during the Interregnum in 1659 he had entertained several of the King's friends and servants and so had not dared to 'cross the Complainant but was enforced to bear with him in sundry things for fear of being betrayed'.

The final deposition was taken from fellow apprentice William Parker, who explained that when West returned from his carousing he 'did stink of drink and would swear and curse'; he would spend too much time sleeping it off and then complain that he would never make a workman and 'that it were better for him to be a shopkeeper'. According to Parker's account on 'Shrovetide last past', while Restrick was out, West had taken the pattern of a seal sent by a town corporation to be engraved from his master's desk. Then, whether by accident or intent, West burnt it. When Restrick returned and found out what had occurred he was naturally 'somewhat moved'. There was a heated exchange. Restrick told West that he deserved to be beaten, but West lunged forward, grabbing and twisting Restrick's arm in a vice-like grip that caused him great pain and injury. West then tried to throw one of the stools at his master until Parker managed to restrain him; and then, when Restrick asked him to get back to work, he refused, which prompted Restrick to take up a stick and give West a blow or two. After this, he said, West immediately departed from his master's service and 'came no more'.[95]

Despite Restrick's sideline activities as a purveyor of eye medicines, he was evidently held in sufficient regard as an engraver to receive the City's commission for a new seal, and no doubt had other major commissions in the immediate post-fire period. But Restrick was not the only engraver who was employed to make new seals to replace those lost in the fire. On 18 December 1666 the Goldsmiths' Company gave directions 'for the speedy making' of their common seal and the smaller seal attached to it to Martin Johnson, seal engraver and landscape painter, who delivered the new seals to the wardens a few weeks later. For his workmanship and the cost of materials he was paid £7.[96] Johnson was also engaged by the Mercers' Company to replace their burnt seal, and he received £3 for 'Graving a new seale for the Company, namely for the silver Ivory & Workmanship'.[97]

Founder

'there shalbe one other Engen made [and] two of the Beadles ... shalbee trained upp for the safe lookeing unto and the management of the same; ... noe [other] person or persons whatsoever shall enter meddle or play with itt.'
—*St Bartholomew's Hospital*, 15 August 1670[98]

On 3 September 1666 an urgent warrant was despatched to Sir William Batten, Surveyor of the Navy, requesting all the 'water engines' currently remaining in the naval stores at Deptford and Woolwich to be brought up to London with 'all persons capable either by hand of judgment' to assist in the preservation of the Tower.[99] It is impossible to know how many fire engines and squirts were available and how many were destroyed or spoiled, but shortly after the fire the City founders were tasked with supplying new appliances and repairing and modifying worn-out and damaged equipment. Hundreds of new 'engines to quench fire' were purchased in case it should happen again,[100] and on 8 November 1666 Sir John Robinson, Lieutenant of the Tower, placed a massive order for 400.[101] More engines and hand squirts were ordered in response to an Act of Common Council on 15 November 1667, which split the City into four administrative divisions for the purposes of fire control. Each parish was to have two hand squirts, and the twelve main livery companies were to supply themselves with an engine, two hand squirts and other fire equipment. The aldermen were required to have one hand squirt each, and the lesser companies were to keep 'such a number of small engines ... as should be allotted them by the lordmayor and court of aldermen, according to their respective abilities'.[102]

The City institutions did not need official encouragement. The East India Company had their 'water engine' repaired at a cost of

The regulation of weights and measures was so crucial to commercial life that the Founders' Company were responsible for marking 'sizing' (assize) on all small brass weights made and used in the City and within 3 miles of its boundary. Some weights were salvaged from the fire. On 2 February 1667 the Plumbers' Company reported that the brass weights 'with ye Chequer [Exchequer] stamp on them ... now at Mr Thomas Aldworths shall there remain by his consent to ye use of ye Company when they shall require ye same'.

£7 9s;[103] four months after the fire the Leathersellers decided that 'the Engin remayninge in their Hall shall be … made serviceable again',[104] and there are several payments in the Wardens' Accounts to the founder Anthony Greene for its removal, cleaning and repair.[105] Anthony Greene was also engaged by the governors of St Bartholomew's Hospital, though it was not until 1670 that they finally got around to dealing with their old engine, the 'greatest part of it lost and broaken in the late fire'. Two of the hospital beadles were to be trained in its use, and there was a strict injunction that 'noe person or persons whatsoever shall enter meddle or play with itt … but onely those two Beadles soe appointed.' The following year, it was agreed that the founder and 'Ingen-maker' Anthony Greene should have £25 to cover the costs of manufacture and all the materials: 'ironworke Brasseworke and Timber worke' as well as, by way of part-exchange, the brass spout and 'what parte els remains'.[106]

A shed was built to house the engine in the little churchyard at the east end of the Long Walk close to the hospital gate, but when the engine was delivered the governors were unhappy with it, for 'it was not so good and well made as was expected'. As a result they decided that Greene should only receive £12 10s in part payment. Greene was rather annoyed and asked to have his engine inspected by someone with the skills to make a discerning judgement, promising to make good any defects found. None was found, and on 27 June 1672 the governors decided to settle their debt as soon as Greene added some pins and iron chains to the engine. Greene received his final payment in September and was given an annual maintenance contract of 16s to service the engine 'from time to time and from year to year' as need should arise. He was also given permission to use the engine 'upon every occasion that may happen by fire'.[107]

Although some founders were specialist makers of engines, pumps, squirts, and large items such as bells, capacity measures and cannon, the range of foundry products in seventeenth-century London was extensive. There was a particular concentration of

(*above*) This squirt held less than a gallon of water. On 7 June 1676 Daniel Man, Keeper of the Guildhall, acquired two brass squirts for £9 13s. Two more were purchased for the use of Newgate Prison; with a further sum of 3 shillings for 'ye ingraveinge with Citty arms & date'.[108]

(*right*) This engine was built in London in 1678 by John Keeling, a pumpmaker at Blackfriars. The wheels and most of the pumping mechanism are missing. It is the earliest surviving example known.

foundry workshops in Lothbury, close to the Company Hall, and by the late sixteenth century one Londoner noted that they made 'cast candlesticks, chafing dishes, spice mortars, and such like copper of Laton works, and do afterwards turn them with the foot and not with the wheel, to make them smooth and bright with turning and scrating (as some do term it), making a loathsome noise to the by passers'.[109] Most households had a wide selection of cast metal items, including pots, pans and kettles, candlesticks, snuffers, curfews and fire tongs, and irons, locks and measures; thousands of these items must have been lost or damaged in the fire. In the absence of detailed evidence, it is likely that the battered and slightly damaged goods were salvaged, patched and repaired, and the molten metals collected for their scrap value.

Gardener

'Sir William Batten … did dig a pit in the garden … and I took the opportunity of laying all the papers of my office that I could not otherwise dispose of. And in the evening Sir William Penn and I did dig another and put our wine in it, and I my pamazan cheese as well as my wine and some other things.'
—*Samuel Pepys*, 4 September 1666[110]

On 14 October 1659 the wardens of the Drapers' Company were embarrassed that the large garden next to their hall in Throgmorton Street was showing signs of neglect: the grass was unkempt, the hedges and gooseberry bushes overgrown, the paths uneven and rugged. A major overhaul was needed, but rather than invest in a 'new modell' they took the path of economy and opted for something far less radical, deciding 'with the least expence … to keep it as comely as it cann in the forme it now is'. Nothing was to be done until the spring; then, apart from a simple tidy and prune, the gardeners were told to dig up the old stone paths for new freestone paving to create better access and 'more decent passage'.[111]

The garden, the largest of its kind in London at this time, on a plot measuring 260 foot in length and 240 in breadth, was first and foremost a private space for members of the Company to enjoy. Occasional access was granted to neighbours and others, but this open-door policy caused problems: there were grumbles that the quiet walks and arbours had been used for cards and dice and had become the place of resort for 'idle young men'. There were even complaints that there were too many infants with their nursemaids, which created an intolerable racket. New restrictions were imposed, and the garden was only open to local residents at the weekends by appointment.[112] The garden is seldom mentioned in the Company records for the next few years, apart from incidental notes about a garden summer house and periodic payments for garden maintenance.

But everything changed when the fire reached Drapers' Hall on Monday 3 September. The beadle, porters and 'other pooremen of the Company' were pressed into service to carry goods from the Hall into the garden, and the silver plate and more valuable treasures were hurriedly bundled up and 'put into [the] mouth of a well of the Comon sewer in the garden for … presevation'.[113] The garden became a place of sanctuary. Personal possessions were piled up on the paths, and one local was so desperate to reach safety that he drove his cart straight through the garden wall.[114] Every piece of ground was covered with belongings, and for the next seven days and nights the Drapers appointed watchmen to guard their goods. Within a week the garden had become a complete wreck. The statues were blackened and chipped, and later accounts include payments for them to 'be clensed and painted'.[115] On 10 September the wardens met in the only space available to them, the garden house, but even this building was in a pitiful state, having been partly pulled down 'for prevention of taking fire'. Urgent repairs were made so that it could serve as a temporary lodging for the clerk, whose house had been 'consumed to ashes'; the wardens wanted him to remain at hand so that he could oversee the 'preservation of the writings and estate of the Company in and about the garden'.[116]

The preservation of the Carpenters' Company Hall, which stood on the north side of the Drapers' garden, was chiefly due to the large open space between them. On 2 October the Drapers, 'being now destitute of

(*previous spread*) A selection of seventeenth-century gardening tools and other implements, including a water engine (no. 43), drawn by John Evelyn for his unpublished gardening encyclopaedia *Elysium Brittannicum*.

a hall', asked for a meeting room in Carpenters' Hall, a small private closet to store their 'writings and papers' in, and the use of their kitchen, 'pastrie and butterie on such … daies of meeting'. They also wished to insert a door and passage into their garden, and this was agreed on the understanding that it was kept locked, with two keys made: one remaining with the clerk of the Carpenters and the other with the clerk of the Drapers. There were many other requests for rooms in Carpenters' Hall; even the Lord Mayor asked for 'house room' and for part of the adjoining garden as he was 'destitute of a fit and convenient house to keepe his Maioralty in'.[117]

The Grocers' Company had a garden next to their Hall, and from time to time this also served as a local amenity. It was used as a children's playground, for football and bowling, for storing timber, and even for drying clothes. The Company tried to restrict entry to designated keyholders, but with so much demand the garden began to look rather tired. The flower borders and box hedges were rather battered, and in 1664, 'upon report of the inconveniences arising by the continuance of the Bowling Alley, by the resort of general sorts of people admitted, and the danger to the garden, being made open and common therebye', the Company decided that the ornamental features were of little use, and that it would be cheaper to lay most of it to grass, with paths made 'in such a way as shall be most commodious and less chargeable to the Company'.[118]

Over the next couple of years the accounts record payments to the gardener Thomas Samney for mowing 'ye grasse plots', trimming the hedges, weeding, and pruning the vines. There were payments for paving and 'cleering the walkes', which suggests some damage to the hard landscaping, if not the plants themselves, and in the summer of 1667 the gardener was paid for 'raising & new laying ye garden & walke'. The renovations were evidently quite extensive, and the gardener acquired three new wheelbarrows for 24s 6d and a 'watering pott' for 5s 6d. Additional payments were made for the wages and breakfasts of a team of garden labourers for several weeks, with other expenses including 'mowing cutting & tryming ye hedges vynes & grasse plotts & other particulars', which came to £44 10s 6d.[119] The Hall was largely destroyed in the fire, but the garden 'tower' was

(left) 'The watering pot best to be liked', wrote Thomas Hill in *The Gardener's Labyrinth* in 1652, 'both for the finely sprinkling forth, and easie carriage of water in the same from place to place in the garden, is that much used in the chiefest Gardens about London.'

The red Gousberry
Ripe June 15

preserved and was put to use as a store for some of the Company's writings and treasures.

After the fire, many of the City gardens were put to alternative use. Sheds and booths were erected for shops and homes, garden houses were used for storage, and some were removed altogether to make way for new buildings, extensions and public thoroughfares. On 12 February 1668 it was decided that the two gardens adjoining the south-west angle of Leadenhall belonging to the 'late dwelling house of Mr Farringdon and the other of Mr Stock being 100′ square, vizt. each 100′ in length and 50′ in breadth' should be made into three convenient passages: one from Leadenhall, another from Lime Street, both 8′ wide; and the third, 14′ wide, from Gracechurch Street, as a 'very convenient place for an hearbe and fruite market'.[120]

Goldsmith

'Paid for redeeming the spoones belonging to Whittingtons Almeshouse which were pawned by the pooremen suddainely after the fyre for £3.10s and more paid 6s which the Tutor layd out for the Carriage of them and other things to save them from the fire in all two dozen of spoones.'—*Mercers' Company, 1666/7*[121]

Citizens did everything they could to remove prized possessions from the path of the fire, but such was its speed and destructive force that many were caught unawares. Samuel Pepys made prudent arrangements, placing his money and iron chests in his cellar and his bags of gold in his office 'as thinking that the safest place'. But these measures were not enough and within hours he was battling through the crowds with all his money, plate and 'best things' to Sir William Rider's home in Bethnal Green. A cart had been provided by a kind friend, which Pepys drove 'in my nightgown … and Lord, to see how the streets and the highways are crowded with people, running and riding and getting of carts at any rate'. He found his host exhausted, having been up all night receiving goods from friends, but Pepys was able to return home 'eased at my heart to have my treasure so well secured'.[122]

The City institutions strove to do likewise. But it proved an enormous challenge because so many of their members had battles of their own, were out of town, or simply too old and incapacitated to help. The Drapers' Company were able to save some of their plate by placing it in the well head of the common sewer in their garden (*see previous entry*), but were unable to rescue £446 worth of coins and some other silver locked in a till or cupboard in their counting house because Mr Burton, the former Renter Warden, had the key. As he explained to the Court on 26 October, he had been 'remote from the hall when the same tooke fire and ingaged in the preservacon of his owne goods and house'. The embers were still glowing when the Drapers employed a team of labourers to search through the rubble to see what they could find. A molten mass of silver and some coins, 'soe defaced as not to bee currant in payment', were recovered in the ashes, and the rest of the silver was 'supposed to bee melted in the Rubbish and … it is feared the greatest parte like to bee wholy lost'. The question then arose as to the true extent of the loss. The accounts for the previous term were scrutinized and a decision made that all of the molten and damaged coins were to be melted down and their value set against any monies 'due and resting upon the foote of [Mr Burton's] said accompt'. Later that day, the Company engaged the services of a silversmith to see whether he could 'refine the Rubbish and extract as much silver as hee can out of the same for this Companies use'. It was also agreed that the rescued plate should be taken out of the sewer, and lent to Sir Joseph Sheldon 'during his shrievalty giving caution for the return thereof'.[123]

Despite their losses, the Drapers were relatively fortunate. The master and wardens of the Merchant Taylors lost all of their plate in the fire, and the molten metal was gathered up and taken to Mr Taylor at the Tower mint, 'or any other person there', so that it could be refined and sold 'to the best advantage & benefit of the companie'.[124] The Grocers likewise agreed that their melted plate should be carefully taken up and grouped into parcels for sale as they were in urgent need of cash.[125] But in assessing their loss, they faced an additional problem because it transpired that most of their plate had been lent to the Sheriffs for a special function and it had just come back to the Hall a day or so before the fire. The plate, packed and transported in a set of locked hampers, had been left in a stack in the Hall for the attention of Mr Buckford, the warden responsible for its care. None of it had been checked or weighed, and Mr Buckford subsequently reported that he had been unable to deal with it as 'the fire was soe neere his owne house he could not spare tyme to come hither to dispose of it'.[126]

The wardens met on 4 December and Mr Buckford explained that he had four ingots and about 180 lb weight of silver from the molten plate in his custody; there was a good deal more besides, but as this was 'more drossey' he assumed that it would not yield

These spoons, the gift of Richard Whittington (1350–1423) to the Mercers' Company, were saved from the fire by the poor residents of Whittington's Almshouse in Paternoster Lane.

so much when it was refined. The melted plate was broken down into batches: the first was converted into three ingots, valued at £404 19s 9d; there were six ingots of 'fine' silver, fourteen pigs – seven marked with the number 'one', and seven with the number 'two'; and finally four 'cakes' of fine silver at 5s 7d per ounce. The total value was assessed at £678 17 6d, which included the assayers' fee of £2.[127] After some discussion, the wardens were concerned that the melted plate had produced a disappointing yield, representing less than half the weight expected, so a small committee was set up to discover where 'the loss and miscarriage arises' and report on their findings. Three months later the report arrived. Mr Walburge and Mr Holland, both employed as butlers to the Sheriffs, testified that they had placed all of borrowed silver belonging to the Grocers in the hampers and had done so in the 'presence of several witnesses'. They had delivered the hampers to the Hall, and had sent back everything that they had received apart from two spoons, 'which Mr Walburge acknowledged to be wanting and to be answered by him'. The committee were satisfied that they were telling the truth, so Mr Buckford was asked to hand over the £7,000 worth of ingots extracted from the melted plate so they could be sold for the Company's best advantage.[128] Despite various entreaties, they were kept waiting, and on 2 May 1667 the wardens demanded that the full number of silver ingots in the house of Mr Buckford, late warden, should be delivered immediately to 'bee by them converted into money by the most beneficiall & improvable way'. And it was made quite clear to him that if he refused they would be forced to refer the matter to the Lord Mayor and justices. The wardens also agreed that a proportion of the melted plate should be reserved so that when the Company's financial position had improved they could commission new pieces in replacement. These were to be engraved with arms and inscriptions both 'for the donors memorial & future encouragement of succession of moneys' in the Company's support.[129]

Even though most corporation plate was rescued from the fire, many companies were forced to convert it into cash to discharge their debts and offset as many of their liabilities as possible. It was a time for pragmatism, not sentimentality.[130] The Cordwainers' Company were obliged to sell all of their plate to raise funds:

On 5 July 1667 the Goldsmiths' Company decided to sell some of their plate. A detailed inventory was compiled so that 'ye benefactors guifts … [with the] coate of Armes & other inscriptions thereupn might bee carefully taken and ye same recorded in ye Companyes Court Bookes to the end such plate might be restored & made again when ye Company shalbee thereunto enabled.'

(right) The Wagon and Tun was made by Jeronimus Orth in Breslau, Germany, in 1548. The clockwork mechanism enabled it to run along the table; the tun or cask held rosewater, which was sprinkled over the hands of the diners. Given to the Mercers' Company by Master William Burde in 1573, it was one of the few Company treasures to survive the fire.

70 items in total, including 12 bowls, 13 wine cups, 5 beer bowls, 4 sugar dishes, 3 salt cellars, 3 tankards, a ewer and basin, and 7 gilt cups. A very detailed plate inventory was compiled recording the arms, makers' marks and donors' names and inscriptions, so that when they 'were in a flourishing condition again' new plate could be made and engraved by way of remembrance.[131] The Coopers' Company did likewise and concluded that their plate should 'bee speedily weighed & sold and the money's to bee raysed thereby are to bee disposed for & towards the discharge of the Companyes debts upon severall bonds under the Common seale'.[132] They also wished to retain some of the gifts of distinguished and honoured members as a 'rembrance of them'; so a reviewing committee was held to inspect the plate and the special gifts were laid aside and placed in a chest. Then on 18 October 1666, at the home of one of the wardens, a sale inventory was drawn up comprising 490 ounces of white plate, silver spoons weighing 250 ounces and gilt spoons at 20 ounces. Some items were sold immediately to Company members: Mr Norman bought half a dozen silver spoons weighing 12 ounces; and Captain Cooper went home with a bowl, flagon, dish and spoon. The rest was sent to a broker acting on behalf of the goldsmith Sir Robert Vyner; there is a later entry in his hand recording the amounts raised. The silver plate was valued at the rate of 4s 11d per ounce; the silver spoons and plate 'not silver' at 5s per ounce; the gilt spoons were rated at 5s 4d per ounce; and the whole lot was valued at £195 10s.[133] The Cloth-workers took 736 ounces of burnt plate to the goldsmith John Gray for a cash payment of £184 5s,[134] and the Mercers' Company kept ten of their most treasured items (which are still in their possession today) but sold the rest to pay off the accrued interest on their bond debts.[135] The plate sales were handled by Rowland Worsopp (Worship), a member of the Company and a practising goldsmith, who had also lost his property to the fire, and was occupying a makeshift workshop 'betweene the columns in the walk in the Great Yard' at Gresham College.[136]

The impact of the fire on the lives of individual goldsmiths is far more difficult to assess. But in these troubled times one man's loss was very much another's gain, and some goldsmiths unaffected by the loss of their home and business premises must have benefited by the sudden demand for their services. Molten

Silver rattles with bells and a stick of coral for teething known as curralls, were produced by Evodius Inman and Gilbert Shepperd. The coral tip on this rattle has been replaced with a whistle.

metal needed to be weighed and refined; fire-damaged items were recycled or refashioned; and, as more and more of the City corporations sold their plate collections, there must have been a limited and short-term boost in business.[137] Sadly, the evidence for this activity is slight and, for the most part, circumstantial. There are a few tantalizing references in the Clothworkers' Company records, which include payments for the installation of an iron staple to 'hang the Goldsmiths scale on when the Plate was weighed att ye Mr & Mrs Chetwinds house', payments for portage of plate to 'Mr Grayes the goldsmith in Bishopsgate Street',[138] and further sums to him for new cup at £25 1s 6d and £6 'for burnishing the remainder of the Companies plate rescued from ye fire'. Later payments include payments of 12 shillings for 'amending the Companies staffe' and 7 shillings for carrying the 'Companies seales to the late Masters house and weighing the Companies plate there'.[139] For other goldsmith–jewellers it was a very different story, and some were reduced to penury. A few weeks after the fire, for instance, the jeweller John le Roy asked the Countess of Castlemaine for the 'speedy payment' of £357, which she owed for a diamond ring valued at £850 and other work undertaken on her behalf, as he had sustained great losses 'by the burning of his house by fire'.[140]

The Goldsmiths' Company records provide a little more detail, though information about the fate of particular goldsmiths and the impact of the fire on trade is largely lacking. The Company were able to preserve most of their plate thanks to the efforts of alderman goldsmith Sir Charles Doe, who rushed from his house in Cheapside to the Company Hall in Foster Lane. He was just in time to see John Brattle, the deputy assayer, and Mr Rawson, the beadle, loading up a hired cart with their personal possessions and goods. The cart was requisitioned and rapidly filled with the Company's writings and plate, which were transported to safety in Edmonton, Jasper Hodson the carter receiving £5 for his trouble.[141] Brattle, Rawson and their colleague Richard Morley, who was employed in the assay office, complained that they had 'severally lost in the late fire by preserving [the goods] of the Companyes', and they demanded compensation for the loss of their personal effects as well as 'several goods of trade'. A committee was appointed to investigate the affair and Brattle and Rawson were asked to provide an itemized list of their lost property. Brattle's assessment amounted to £38 10s, besides a number of unspecified items worth £7 or £8; Rawson claimed that his losses were in the order of £84 13s; and Morley claimed for various 'household goods'. Six months later, the committee decided that Brattle should be compensated as the cart he had provided for his own use was used for the Company's service. He received £40. The committee were less inclined to accept the beadle's evaluation, though they did acknowledge that he had in 'some measure' tried to preserve their plate and other things, and in doing so had lost some of his household goods; for this and his efforts in retrieving some molten silver from the rubbish in the Hall,[142] and other 'extraordinary services in the Companyies affaires to November last', he was given £30. Morley was granted 30 shillings for his strenuous efforts in 'loading of the cart with the Companyes concernes'.[143]

It is clear that some plate was lost from the assay office at the time of the fire because in July 1667 the goldsmith–jeweller Daniel Maddox complained that he had not received any compensation for a caudle cup and cover, which Sir Charles Doe during his term of office had removed 'to make a trial of the goodness thereof but lost in ye last fire.'[144] Prior to the fire, Daniel Maddox had a house and workshop at the sign of the Golden Unicorn in Cheapside; when this was burnt down he was forced, like so many others, to find alternative accommodation elsewhere.[145] It seems that he relocated to Cripplegate Ward for a few years, because in 1668 he was discovered to have made some poor-quality curralls (probably some kind of teething rattle with bells and coral), 'unduly charged with copper or brasse wyer'.[146] The inventory compiled after his death in 1670 shows he had a small shop in Aldersgate Street, as well as two new shops on the site of his former property in Cheapside. The Aldersgate shop seemed to comprise little more than a stall with a shop board, a cupboard, a chest of drawers, a glass showcase, a flock bed and assorted bedding, two stools upholstered in turkey-work, a bell, a pair of candlesticks, a scale beam, two locks and a sword – all valued at £2 15d. But Cheapside was evidently his main centre of operation. The inventory for these shops included a great quantity of silver plate of 'several sorts' worth £692 14s 9d, a silver tankard pawned for £5, some small plate and other 'small wares' at £81 2s 6d, burnt and broken

silver at £16 15s, and 276 ounces of broken and 'uncertaine silver' at £64 8s. The stock list also includes some old lace, 20 guinea coins, 4 ounces of gold crowns and other broken gold, 'old plate', 'old silver', plain and enamelled gold rings, 15 rings with diamonds and other small stones, some 'slight stone' rings, a locket with 33 diamonds, 83 small loose diamonds, 25 'fowle' emeralds, 5 garnets and amethysts, 22 rubies, and 7 other lockets and parcels of odd stones. The whole lot was valued at £1,119 19s 9d.[147] Whether any of the burnt, broken, old plate and coins were fire-damaged goods, or simply part of the goldsmith–jeweller's stock-in-trade is impossible to know, but it is tempting to conclude that he had a higher proportion of these kinds of items than he might otherwise have done in the years before the fire.

James Shaller, Samuel Boulton and Samuel Hawks were forced to carry on their trade in sheds in 'New Cheapside', Moorfields; Rowland Worship and others moved into Gresham College; and a few goldsmiths erected booths and sheds in Smithfield or moved further afield to Holborn, Fleet Street, Westminster and Southwark.[148] Having lost his Foster Lane property to the fire, Evodias Inman was one of the residents in Smithfield 'Rounds', and it was from here, presumably in an effort to retain and reinforce his links with his customers, that he issued a trade token by way of advertisement in 1669.[149] His move to a shed does not seem to have affected his business to any great extent, but he was evidently an awkward character, and he is mentioned quite frequently in the Company records for various misdemeanours, abusing the Company officers on search days, and refusing them access to his shop. After repeated attempts to retrieve samples of his work, the wardens resorted to subterfuge, employing Ann Terrett to purchase items on their behalf.[150] A parcel of small gold and silver wares – tobacco stoppers, curralls set with brass wire, rings with small stones and doublets (a colourless gem glued to a piece of coloured glass) and other items – was acquired, sealed in paper and carried to the Assay Office for trial, and on Tuesday 23 March 1668 Inman was summoned to appear before the wardens to account for a gilt locket set with brass wire, two rings set with white stones and a blue doublet, a plain hoop ring, all found to be worse than standard, for which he was fined 30s 11d. The items were all defaced and returned to him.[151]

Another resident of Smithfield was Gilbert Shepperd, who lost his home in Cary Lane, near Goldsmiths' Hall, to the fire. Gilbert successfully applied to the governors of St Bartholomew's Hospital for a tiny shop in the Hospital Cloister (*see* p. 48), but he died the following year, leaving the business in the hands of his widow Jane and son-in-law John Smith, to whom he left 'all such working tooles belonging to my trade in his custody and possession', a brass clock and the sum of £200.[152] The Company records include several references to Jane Shepperd and John Smith, whose 'goldsmiths wares were exposed to sale' at Bartholomew Fair and were removed for the purposes of assay.[153]

Sir Robert Vyner (1631–1688) made the regalia for the coronation of Charles II, and was appointed King's goldsmith in 1661. His property at the sign of the Vine in Lombard Street was destroyed in the fire. Sir Robert lent extensively to the government and incurred financial loss because the loans were not repaid. He was Lord Mayor of London in 1674–75, but was declared bankrupt in 1683.

Grocer

'And that by the said fire there were goods burnt and consumed … (not accounting the Raisins soe burnt as aforesaid) by Computacon about the vallue of fifty thousand pounds stock which by reason of the violence of the fire could no wyse possibly bee saved.'
—*Mayor's Court*, 1667

When the grocer John Benbow's household goods and stock were assessed for the purposes of probate in 1671, a memorandum was inserted at the beginning of the document to say that he had died during the plague in 1665. Shortly afterwards his property, goods and wares had been appraised according to the customs of the city, but in the following year 'the said goods & wares … or the greater parte of them were burnt & consumed in the late dreadfull fire & the apprizement in writing under the apprizer hands was then also burnt or is otherwise lost of miscarried soe that the executors cannot possibly give a particular account.' Only those few things which the executors were able to remember or knew from their personal dealings could be assessed, and these comprised debts owing of £26,457; desperate debts amounting to £6,076 19s 2d; part shares in four merchant ships (*Newcastle*, *Increase*, *London Merchant* and *The Golden Fortune*) with a combined value of £446; apparel, household and shop goods at £438; and in 'ready money' the sum of £446 17s 6d. From the scant details that have survived, it seems that Benbow's commercial arm stretched far and wide with trading interests in Lisbon and Seville and in the American colonies of Virginia and Maryland. He was not alone. Grocers needed

During the refining process sugar syrup was poured into conical earthenware moulds to set. Most of the sugar imported into London in the 1660s came from Barbados and Jamaica.

a network of contacts at home and abroad to maintain a viable and thriving trade; one has only to look at the kinds of stock they supplied to see how important these links were to the success of their business. Grocers had to procure a wide range of commodities for their customers, and in the immediate pre- and post-fire period there was a particularly active trade in ginger, turmeric, aniseed, cloves, coriander, nutmeg, fennel, rice, raisins, pepper, tobacco, currants, raisins, French barley, starch, honey, almonds, liquorice, figs and various sugar products – brown, white, fine, coarse, sugar candy and molasses.

Francis Smarfoote in the parish of St Giles Cripplegate had a fairly typical array of stock, though he seems to have been mostly employed as a confectioner rather than a retail grocer, because his shop included an oven and a small grate, a stack of charcoal, a wooden bowl, 3 pecks of flour, a baker's peel, rake, tray, scale, weights and a stone mortar. There was a table and counter and a few nests of small, large, flat and long boxes. The commodities included all sorts of conserves and preserves, including 3 lb of marmalet (a fruit paste of quince and other

Caudle cup and posset pot. Caudle and posset were hot, spiced drinks of curdled ale or wine whisked into an emulsion with cream, milk and eggs. The 'grace' or aerated foam on top of the posset pot was scooped out with a spoon and the remaining liquid sucked through the spout.

fruits, often embellished with a stamped design and housed in a round wooden box), 25 lb of cakes and biscuits, 40 biscuit frames (for moulding and shaping), 2 lb of macaroons valued at 1s 10d, ginger roots, stacks of oranges and lemons, 4 lb of 'lemon chipps', 34 ounces of 'posset-meats' of all sorts, almonds, brown sugar and comfits.

Grocers often specialized in particular commodities such as spices, tobacco, sugar or dried fruit. Raisins were the mainstay of 32-year-old grocer William Clapham's business. On 25 February 1667 he was summoned to the Mayor's Court with his trading partner Abraham Wessel.[154] According to their testimony, a month before the fire they had received 160 barrels of raisins from the merchant vessel *Partnership.* The cargo was unloaded into a warehouse at Fresh Wharf in London and the barrels were branded with the merchants' mark. On 2 September the fire swept through the warehouse and all but six were burnt; and Clapham estimated that a further £50,000 of goods were lost from the same wharf, 'which by reason of the violence of the fire could no wyse possibly bee saved'. Abraham Wessell confirmed that the raisins had been landed and consigned to him by a bill of lading from Don Manuel Fero, a merchant in the port of Malaga, and that he had insured them for £150, or 20 per cent of their value, before 'hee had any newes of the arrivall of the said shipp the Partnership att Plymouth or any other part of England'.[155]

Haberdasher

'Gloves, pins, combs, glasses unspotted,
Pomades, hooks, and laces knotted;
Brooches, rings, and all manner of beads;
Laces round and flat for women's heads;
Needles, thread, thimbles, shears,
   and all such knacks,
Where lovers be, no such things lacks;
Sipers, swathbands, ribbons, and sleeve laces,
Girdles, knives, purses, and pincases.'
—*John Heywood*, 1544[156]

These hooks and eye have been fused into a molten mass by the blistering heat of the fire. They were found during the archaeological excavation of a fire-damaged cellar at the south-eastern end of Pudding Lane with the charred remains of tar-filled barrels, earthenware storage jars and other carbonized items (*see* p. 91).[157] The discovery of hooks and eyes is significant because there were three hook-and-eye makers working in this location in 1666: Christopher Peele had a house on the east side of Pudding Lane, and William Burgis and Nicholas Carter lived in Lambe Yard (*see* p. 79).[158] The cellar might have been backfilled with fire debris from one or more properties in the neighbourhood, but the evidence seems to indicate that there was a shop or workshop directly above, which had collapsed into the void. It is impossible to know if the congealed lump of hooks and eyes represents part of the burnt stock of Christopher Peele. What is certain, however, is that Burgis, Carter and Peele were members of the Haberdashers' Company, and that the area around Pudding Lane, at the north end of London Bridge, was a historically important centre of the trade.

The vast array of consumer goods retailed by London haberdashers was staggering. Hooks and eyes feature quite prominently and were made in various materials and grades for clothing and

upholstery. John Loyd, in the parish of St Giles Cripplegate, seems to have been a wholesale supplier to the upholstery trade; his shop contained ribbons, calico, canvas and buckram (a coarse woven cloth used for linings), some silk, thread, busks (strips used as a stiffener), and assorted, but unspecified, hooks and eyes.[159] John Bagnall had 2,736 hooks and eyes at 12 shillings per gross valued at £11 8s, and other knick-knacks such as tapes and bindings, 11,520 playing cards, tin tobacco boxes, primers and school books, buttons, pins and packthread. The haberdasher John Meadow's stock included a number of hooks and eyes (not quantified), various clasps, gloves, ribbons, wash balls, hair powder, shuttle-cocks, battledores, 1,200 pens, 14 red cloth purses, points, buttons, spectacle cases, 'pins of all sorts', scarves, hoods, laces, thimbles, dice, hawking bags, paper 'of all sorts', ink-horns, 'hankerchers', stomachers and knitting needles.[160]

Some haberdashers were specialist suppliers of stationary; some of clothing and accessories; and others of small metalwares. James Maythew, for instance, had a particular business in buttons; when his shop stock was appraised in 1661, he had 45,792 silver and textile-covered coat buttons 'of several fashions' ranging in price from 18d to 3s 6d per gross.[161] Thomas Strong sold a huge number of gloves; and Richard Eardley, Roland Fleming and Jeremiah Greene specialized in laces, ribbons and children's clothes.[162] But perhaps the most detailed information relates to Herbert Allen, who had a tiny shop at the 'signe of the Parrett' in the Royal Exchange just before the fire. The shop was sited on the outer west side of the quadrangle, either on the ground floor or, more likely, on the upper floor known as the Pawn (a derivation of the Dutch word *pandt*, a passageway) – there was a central corridor which ran around the entire quadrangle. There were 109 tiny shops crammed into the Exchange on the eve of the fire; when the building was consumed, most of the shopkeepers and traders were able to find lodgings in Gresham College (*see* p. 54).

Allen's name is not included in the lists at Gresham College, but when his goods were appraised for the purposes of probate in 1668 he was living in St Martin-in-the-Fields. His stock, listed under the heading 'In the shop on the Exchange', must therefore refer to the New Exchange on the south side of the Strand in Westminster, as the shops in Royal Exchange, Cornhill were not open for business until 1671.[163] Allen simply exchanged one shopping emporium for another. Whether he managed to remove most of his goods to safety or was forced to restock after the fire is unknown, but in either case he had an impressive array of goods, including English, French and Venetian point lace, 'yellow' French lace, lace bands, lace cravats, and other pieces of 'small' lace for trimming hoods, whisks and scarves, totalling £359. There were various articles of dress such as waistcoats, trousers, caps, mourning clothes, women's petticoats, sleeves and cuffs, hoods, children's gloves and infants' clothes, boot hose, French bands, screen fans, masks, and parcels of necklaces and bodkins. There were several pieces of lace, ruffs, cravats, hose, boot hose and linen items for women which were described as 'old fashioned', as well as '*alamode*' scarves and French-laced whisks. There were even several pieces of Holland and Cambrick cloth in the 'hands of work women to make up', valued at £5 12s. It was evidently a thriving business. His shop stock amounted to £1,077 16½s, and his whole estate was assessed at £2,301 8s 7d, with doubtful and desperate debts of £2,976 4s. And there is one significant entry at the end: the lease of 'the testators shop at the Exhange known by the signe of the parrett' at £40.[164] Perhaps Allen had taken his old shop sign to his new address so that he could maintain his links with his customers, or was he keeping his options open: did he intend to return to the Royal Exchange once the rebuilding work was complete?

Haberdashers sold all kinds of goods, including stationery. The brass travelling penner with receptacles for a pen and inkpot is engraved with the owner's initials 'WY' and the inscription 'Virgo fecit, 1654'. Virgo seems to have been a member of the Madin family of Sheffield.

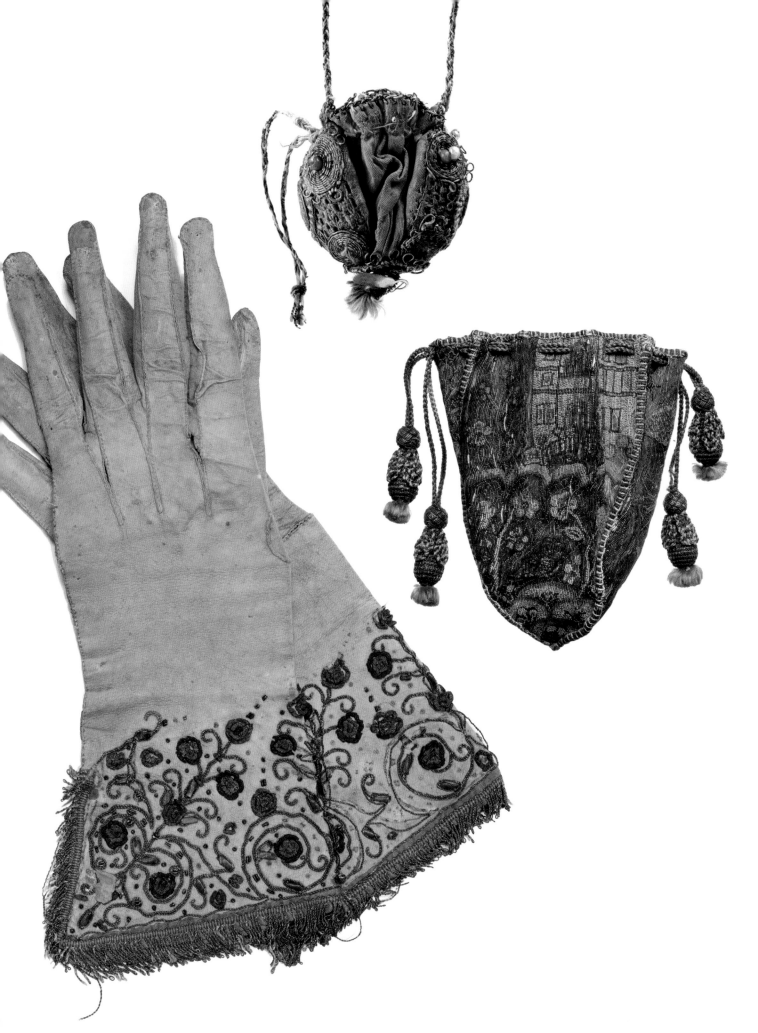

Ironmonger

'The bottom of the tar kettle is burnt out, but there is no one to mend it; a new bottom provided in London was, in the common calamity, burnt and melted.'—*Commander Thomas Middleton*, 23 September 1666[165]

A month after the fire, the governors of Bridewell Hospital requested that a 'great Iron keetle' should be provided 'to boyle the meate of the lunnatikes'.[166] The original kettle had melted in the fire. Detailed evidence for the loss of ironmongery wares of this kind is hard to come by, but there are several entries in the City livery company accounts which refer to burnt and damaged locks and keys and the replacement of iron grilles, bars, hinges and bolts.[167] Some companies were in such financial straits that every scrap of metal that could be retrieved from the ruins was gathered up for recycling and damaged ironmongery was sent away to be patched or wrought anew. Iron, like other metals, was so precious that the Fishmongers insisted that all the 'old iron … taken upp belonging to this Company [should] be kept in the great vault safe locked upp till this Court shall otherwise dispose of'.[168] The Plumbers decided that all the iron spits, racks and andirons which had been rescued and removed to a house in Morton should be collected together, and the clerk was instructed to sell them 'in ye Country for as much as he can'.[169] The temptation to 'remove' metal items from the ruins was great. A year afterwards the wardens of the Skinners' Company were astonished to find that the very heavy cast-iron fireback from their Hall, which had gone missing during the fire, had suddenly turned up 'in the custody of one in Shoreditch'. They ordered its immediate return and the Renter Warden was despatched to collect it.[170]

Apart from the ubiquitous fixtures and fittings – window grilles, catches, door furniture and the like (which are not counted

Two iron padlocks and one key melted by the intense heat of the fire. From excavations in Pudding Lane.

in inventories) – almost every house, and especially those with one or more hearths, had an extensive array of ironmongery. There were dozens of locks and keys for securing valuables, and there were sets of fire irons, fire shovels, fire tongs and andirons in most rooms. The kitchens were well equipped with iron spits, racks, jacks, grates, pots, firebacks, gridirons, frying pans and kettles, and there were hundreds of different kinds of specialist iron tools in shops and workshops. When a fire-damaged 'great tenement' in Botolph Lane at the north-east end of London Bridge was excavated in 1998, some interesting items of ironwork in various states and stages of corrosion came to light, including a small round grate, a broken waffle iron, some kind of goffering iron and 32 scorched and fused locks, two of which were burnt with the keys in place.[171] Archaeologists have suggested that the quantity and variety of ironwork represent the stock of an ironmonger or hardware retailer, but the number and range of items are far too small. Even a modest-sized house would have had a comparable number of locks and keys, and stock-in-trade inventories for ironmongers and blacksmiths provide a very different picture. Thomas Darker, a blacksmith in the parish of St Andrew Undershaft, for instance, had 47 lb of ordinary hinges, 54 pairs of small hinges and 29 pairs of hinges 'of all sorts'. There were 102 locks of various kinds

(unspecified), parcels of padlocks, 33 ward locks, 15,000 latches, parcels of tenterhooks (used for stretching cloth), sets of hobnails and 42,000 other kinds of nails, 3,000 bradawls, sets of screws, curtain hooks and rings, pack-needles, gimlets, chafing dishes, 120 sorts of pulleys and wheels, ladles, curry combs, chains for fire jacks and chains for dogs, fire forks, tongs and pot-hooks, frying pans, 55 lb of spikes, 39 lb of fire-shovel pans and 11 complete fire shovels, coffin handles and rat traps. And in the cellar there was 11 cwt of new iron, 10 cwt of old iron, 7 cwt of 'bushell iron', a 'pull-up Jacke foreged out with some other odd things', forks, files, hammers, and many other tools of the trade.[172]

The ironmonger Thomas Fowler, who had a shop in Bishopsgate Street, had an even more impressive stock of 740,315 individual items, including 550 different kinds of locks arranged and priced according to type: specific locks for trunks, chests,

By the early seventeenth century even the smallest London houses had a chimney and several heated rooms. Each grate or hearth had an accompanying suite of iron backs (used to radiate the heat back into the room), tongs, andirons, fire shovels, pokers and bellows.

cupboards, cabinets, pews and closets; English locks and Flemish locks; and locks graded according to their shape, size and mechanism. Even the spring-loaded variety were available in different sizes and qualities, and some were sprung for self-closure. Fowler sold tap borers for casks, tobacco tongs, 'steele' hammers, staples, looking-glass screws and screws of other kinds, all sorts of hooks and latches, hasps, curry combs, spit wheels, key rings, dog chains, hatchets, chaffing dishes, smoothing irons, trowels, fire irons, andirons, fire dogs, armour plate, garden hoes, shovels and spades – an exhaustive list.[173] The scale of Fowler's and Darker's stocks underlines just how important ironmongery was to everyday life, but also serves as a reminder of just how much ironwork was consumed in the fire and how many new articles of like kind citizens would have needed to furnish their homes and replenish their stocks.

Joiner

'Comes Simpson the joyner and he and I with great pains contriving presses to put my books upon, they now growing numerous.'—*Samuel Pepys*, 23 July 1666[174]

A couple of years before the fire a huge quantity of 'Brazilwood, pharnambuck and old Bahia wood' arrived in London and was immediately offloaded into a warehouse on Fresh Wharf by London Bridge. William Bird, the merchant owner, engaged the services of Abraham Russell at the Royal Exchange to broker a deal for sale, and in October 1664 the first consignment of 577 cwt of Brazil or pharnambuck (Pernambuco) wood at £4 per hundred-weight, with 77 cwt of 'old Bahia' wood (a type of rosewood) at £3 5s per hundredweight, was sold to George Perin in London. The following year Russell sold 286 cwt of young pharnambuck wood at £3 5s per hundredweight to Henry Makott and John Smith & Company. A further contract for sale for the remaining timber was made with Mr Leachmore and others; however, when Russell visited the warehouse shortly before the fire, over 30 tons of timber was still awaiting collection. The fire reached Fresh Wharf on 2 September and despite the efforts of the wharfinger, four porters and William Bird, the timber was 'utterly consumed as was the warehouse and all the buildings' on the wharf.[175] It was a devastating loss and Leachmore entered a suit in the Mayor's Court for compensation.

The fire destroyed thousands of tons of timber from wood-mongers' and carpenters' yards and from joinery, turners' and cabinetmakers' workshops. It consumed stockpiles of faggots and kindling, structural woodwork and untold quantities of furniture, so there was an urgent need to replenish stocks as soon as pos-sible. The City institutions with landholdings outside the capital made hurried arrangements to have their woodlands felled for rebuilding and repairs. The timber merchants supplied oak, cedar,

Mercers' Hall in Ironmonger Lane was destroyed in the fire. It was rebuilt between 1672 and 1682. A chapel was incorporated in the plan; the joiner John Baker was responsible for the carvings, including this ornamental gilded frond, 30 capitals costing 14 shillings each, and a magnificent altarpiece costing £30.

beech, poplar, chestnut, holly, box, sycamore, deal, walnut and all sorts of exotic woods for furniture-making inlays and veneers, for musical instruments (*see* p. 208), and for panelling, screens, canopies, chimney pieces and other interior fixtures and fittings. Joiners needed large stocks for their work. Henry Browne in Silver Street had two yards holding 6,575 boards stacked in 4′, 5′, 6′, 9′ and 12′ lengths, including 108 pieces of 'wainscotte' (panelling) valued at £134 8s, 200 planks of deal, and 90 12′ × 1½″ boards in a neighbouring churchyard. The whole stock was valued at £566 1s.[176]

The destruction of furniture must have been a major loss for many householders. The more readily portable pieces were perhaps carried or loaded onto carts; some of the larger items might have been dismantled (*see overleaf*); but many were simply too heavy or bulky to be moved and would have had to have been left behind. Pepys refers to beds which had been stripped down to the bare wood, both in his own home and in those of his friends, and a few days after the fire he employed a carpenter to help him set up 'bedsteads and hangings', which suggests that they had been taken apart.[177] Apart from chairs and stools, beds were the most common item of furniture in London households. There were grand beds with elaborate headboards, frames and canopies; 'half-headed' beds; 'folding' beds; and trundle or truckle beds on castors, which were commonly kept in the garret or shop for servants and apprentices. Joiners or cabinetmakers usually made the bed frames; most were drilled so that they could be strung with a criss-cross arrangement of cords to support the mattress (*see* p. 206).

Although some houses were sparsely furnished, many were stuffed full. Some rooms had so much furniture that it is hard to imagine how the occupants managed to squeeze around the bed or manoeuvre around the space without constantly knocking into a bench or stool. Some of this clutter can be attributed to natural hoarding tendencies, personal taste, sentiment and even fashion. But it is also conceivable that some of the rooms in the immediate post-fire period were overstuffed with furniture because those made homeless and in temporary lodgings might have been forced to squash everything they had into a smaller compass, or were perhaps also looking after other people's belongings.

Leonard Fryer, for instance, in 1667 had 51 items of furniture. There were three beds, a trundle bed, six leather chairs, two low

stools, three 'joyne stooles', one 'drawing table', one settle, one court cupboard, one trunk and a 'deale Box' in one chamber, and two beds, a chest, six low chairs and six low stools, a dressing table, trunk and hanging shelf in another. The main garret room held two beds, a court cupboard, a chest, a box, one 'joyned chayre' and a wicker chair, and in the adjoining closet were three more boxes and an old desk. The other garret had a bed and square table. All this in a house with four principal rooms.[178] Fryer is by no means exceptional; there are many examples of fully furnished rooms with half a dozen chairs of various kinds: chairs covered in Russia leather, plain chairs, joined chairs, high chairs, low chairs and 'elbow' chairs. Stools and forms were plentiful and many rooms had sets of drawers and chests of drawers. Desks occur with some frequency; these were generally kept in a small closet next to the main chamber or adjoining a shop. Bible boxes are also mentioned, and among the kitchen paraphernalia are occasional references to spice boxes and candle boxes with other small items of joinery in a shop or workshop. Book presses, essentially cupboards with hinged doors and adjustable shelving, were rare before the fire. Pepys's new cupboard was probably dismantled and removed to safety in the emergency. He later acquired twelve presses for his ever-growing book collection.

Boxes of this type were used for many purposes: for storing candles and other household stuff; for gloves, linen and fine textiles; for books, Bibles and sewing materials. Most are of flimsy construction since they were designed to stand on a table. The box makers were closely affiliated with the Joiners' Company, which accounts for the quality of the carving.

This oak gateleg or 'falling table' is a rare survival of London-made seventeenth-century furniture. The principal joints are secured with iron coach bolts with square washers, which would have enabled the frame to be dismantled so that an otherwise bulky item of furniture could be carried to upper floors where staircase access was restricted. A brass plaque bears the inscription: 'Sir Matthew Hale & the other Judges sat at this Table in Cliffords Inn, to determine the disputes respecting Property, which arose after the Great Fire of London AD 1666. Presented by R.M. Kerr Esq. L.D. 1893.' The table was probably supplied to Clifford's Inn shortly after the fire.

Although there was a huge amount of work for joiners after the fire, some struggled to make a living, and those who had lost their homes and stocks of wood and tools suffered keenly. The Bridewell Hospital accounts include a rather pitiful petition from Edward Searle, citizen and joiner, on behalf of his mother-in-law, Anne Marshall, 'an aged woeman [who had] fallen distracted by the late lamentable fire in London and losse of her house and goods'. As Edward explained, he was a poor man and a journeyman joiner with a wife and child to support; he did not have the money to maintain his family and was quite unable to support Anne, who needed to be taken into the care of the hospital for 'her cure'. The governors accepted that he was suffering great hardship and recommended that he should pay 2 shillings a week for Anne's stay in the hospital, which he was happy to accept.[179]

Leatherseller

'This day itt is thought fitt and ordered that 18 lether Buckets bee bought for this hopsitall in the Roome of those lately lost by the late dreadful fire.'
—*St Bartholomew's Hospital,*
4 August 1667[180]

Guy Cordier had 100 black cat skins, 20 white cat skins, 1 bear skin, 400 dog skins, 750 kid skins, 12 buck skins and several 'druggs to dye skinnes' in the garret of his house in Hogden in the parish of St Leonard Shoreditch. The workhouse contained a couple of pots to burn 'gauls' (presumably oak galls for tanning the leather), a pestle and mortar, three wooden bowls, a wooden bench and three tables. And 'abroad' were 104 yards of mohair (the woven hair of an Angora goat) in two-piece lengths.[181] Another skinner, in Tooley Street, had 9,400 coney skins, 1,000 black ferret skins, a parcel of beaver and racoon pelts, and various parcels of goat hides.[182] But these kinds of stock represented the luxury end of the leather trade and most of the ordinary everyday leather goods, bags, purses, belts, straps, saddlery, storage vessels and containers were made from neat's leather (the hide of an ox, cow or calf), which, if correctly prepared and tanned, had great tensile strength. The makers of costrels, bombards (jugs), blackjacks (tankards) and the like also made fire buckets.

Orders for leather articles of all kinds must have increased after the fire, but fire buckets were in particular demand. Not surprisingly the Leathersellers' Company were among the first to place an order: on 13 December 1666 they purchased 72 new leather buckets for their hall or 'some other convenient place for use if need be'. The following year the Company requested that three dozen of these new buckets 'shall have the Armes of this Society painted thereon',[183] and a few years later, Anthony Smith received

This leather bucket has been waterproofed with a layer of pitch inside. Each parish had a stock of fire-fighting equipment, which was usually stored in the local church.

£5 4s for '3 dozen of Bucketts against fire and new painting and repaireing them'.

Sets of buckets were acquired for the use of the Tower of London, and in 1667, when the Court of Common Council introduced a series of regulations 'for the better suppressing of fires', 3,200 'learthern buckets' were supplied for distribution across the City. At the same time, each of the twelve main livery companies were to 'provide themselves with thirty buckets'; the Aldermen and Sheriffs with 24, and the 'inferior companies, such a number … as should be allotted them by the Lord Mayor and Court of Aldermen, according to their respective abilities'.[184]

More buckets were gradually added to this number. Samuell Peirson was engaged to make 'three dozen of the best leather Bucketts according to the sample hereof which hee left here without painting to be hanged upp in the Court Roome of [Bridewell] hospitall against danger of fire'. For this work Peirson received £6.[185] A further three dozen leather buckets were procured for Newgate Prison at the same rate of 40 shillings per dozen.[186]

This leather fire bucket was found on the site of New Fresh Wharf at the southern end of Pudding Lane in 1974. Preserved under collapsed buildings and other fire debris, it was probably used to fight the fire and was dropped by accident in the chaos. There are traces of painted decoration – the year 1660 or 1666 and the initials SBB, indicating that it belonged to the nearby parish church of St Botolph Billingsgate. Records from the church show that the parish kept 36 leather buckets 'for danger of fyer'.

Looking-glass maker

'these sorts of glasses are mostly used by
lady's to look their faces in, and to see
how to dress their heads, and sett their
top knots on their fore heads upright.'
—*Randle Holme, 1688* [187]

The first serious attempt to manufacture looking glasses in
England occurred in the 1620s, when Sir Robert Mansell petitioned Parliament to make them of 'such perfection … that [they]
are now here made which was never wont to be in England before-
tyme'.[188] He persuaded Parliament that the enterprise would bring
employment to hundreds of native craftsmen, so he was granted a
patent to produce looking glasses at his glasshouse in Broad Street
near Bishopsgate. But his confidence was misplaced because the
Venetian and French glass houses continued to monopolize the
manufacture of glass mirror plate in Europe. Although there were
various attempts to bolster domestic manufacture by restricting
imports of 'Plates wrought into Looking-glasses', the demand for
mirrors was so high that the glass dealers in the capital found all
sorts of ploys to circumvent customs dues. In 1668 John Greene
and Michael Measey supplied two invoices with each consignment: one with the correct figures and the other set at a lower
amount to save duty. They even tried to conceal parcels of looking
glasses by asking their Venetian supplier, Allesio Morelli, to put
them into boxes so that they 'may not bee soe soone felt by our
searchers here'; and on another occasion Morelli was asked to
place them at the bottom of a chest with layers of papers on top so
that they could not be seen when the chest was opened.[189] When
the cases filled with 237 mirrors arrived, Greene was disappointed
with their quality and size, and so wrote to complain. He asked
whether Morelli had actually witnessed the packing and suggested
that, if not, they had both been 'abused to the vallew of above 100
livres'. If, Greene wrote, the quality did not improve, he would

stop sending orders to Venice for mirrors, as 'wee have so good made heer in England and cheaper'. Two years later, however, Greene placed another order for 314 Venetian mirrors of different grades: some diamond cut, others 'very good' or 'fine'; and in sizes ranging from 11½ to 24½ inches. He stipulated that they should be made of 'very Cleer whit mettle and Cleer and free from Bladders or great Sands or any other Blemishes or faults whatsover'.[190]

Almost nothing is known about the looking-glass makers of London before the fire, but from the mid-1660s onwards looking glasses start to appear in ever-increasing numbers in household inventories, so there must have been a number of independent makers and specialist suppliers like Greene and Measey to cater for this demand. Thomas Lee was evidently one of them. Nothing is known of his business dealings, but he evidently lost his property in the fire, because on 27 September 1666 he was given temporary lodging in a 9½ by 5 foot shed adjoining one of the Mercers' Company almshouses in Broad Street, next to Gresham College. Whether this was used for his trade or living accommodation, perhaps both, is unclear.[191] It is also uncertain whether Lee was a retailer, wholesaler or retail-manufacturer. He may perhaps have worked with and for someone else.

The probate inventory of Samuel Soane(s), looking-glass maker in the parish of St Andrew's Holborn, provides little more in the way of detail.[192] There is no evidence of on-site manufacture, no working tools or other items associated with his trade, and the shop was simply equipped with four old stools, a small table and 63 looking glasses 'great and small', the whole lot valued together at £27. The four rooms of his home were modestly furnished, and there were many 'old' items: old rugs; old curtains; old chests; old jack and weights, and 17 old chairs, all valued at just £47 5s 6d. Soane had debts of £61 5s, a clock and a piece of gold on pledge with pawnbrokers, but he had £236 of 'ready money' in the house at the time of his death, and his whole estate was assessed to be worth £485 16s 3d.

As the manufacture of plate-glass technology improved, looking glasses became larger and larger. These mirrors were probably imported, cut to size and mounted in decorative frames by specialists in London.

Mercer & silkman

'in regard they are antient and their sight dim that the penthouse over their doore might be taken downe, and such of their windows as are now little may be enlarged … [so that] all or most of them would be enabled to get something by winding of silke … towards their better livelihood.'—*Petition from Almsmen, 20 October 1663*[193]

When Bridewell Prison was destroyed in the fire, the artisan craftsmen who were engaged to teach the children a trade lost their homes and businesses (p. 25). Among them were the silk weavers Edmond Silvester, Nicholas Hayes, John Lea, Jeremy Caslyn and Randall Jackson, who were asked to keep their apprentices at work, and to find temporary accommodation 'in places neere unto the Citty where they can abide att the smallest rents till convenient houses maybe provided for them'. They were given several payments over the following days to cover their rents.[194] A few months later, Randall Jackson applied to the governors to have a little shed 'to lodge in att Bridwell' in the space formerly used by the beadle as a coal-hole, since he was 'forced every day to goe to Westminster for a lodging'. The governors agreed to his request so long as he built the shed at his own cost.[195]

The dispersal and relocation of tradesmen during and after the fire had a number of unforeseen effects. On 4 December 1666 Nicholas Horne, citizen and Merchant Taylor but by trade a silkman, complained to the Lord Mayor that up until the 'tyme of the dismall fire' he had dwelt in a house in Cheapside which had been known 'time out of mind by the signe of the *Anchor*'. When the fire destroyed his dwelling house and shop he moved into a new house in Jewen Street, resumed his trade and set up his old sign 'for a cognizance thereof and direcon' to his customers.

A *c.*1660–70 bodice of silk satin fabric with polychrome floss silk embroidery.

After a few days, Horne discovered that his former journeyman John Sharpe, with his partner William Heward, had taken a house in the same street and, contrary to the laws and customs of the city, had also put up the sign of the Anchor on their shop, in a deliberate attempt, Horne believed, to deprive him of his trade and steal his customers. And, to make matters worse, they had even added the words to the signpost: 'This from Cheapside att the end of Foster Lane.' When John Sharpe was asked to account for his behaviour he explained that he had actually traded under the sign of the White Hart with only 'an *Anchor* added' and suspended from his signpost as a 'marke & memorial of the place and person where and from whence hee received instruction'. He claimed that he had done nothing unlawful and had seen other people do the same thing without any dispute or controversy.

After some discussion, the Court of Aldermen felt that Sharpe and Heward had wilfully deceived and misled Horne's customers; that the use of the anchor was calculated to cause offence and if it remained would undoubtedly provoke further discord, jealousy and confusion. So Heward and Sharpe were ordered to take down the sign before the end of the week if they wished to trade as silkmen in the same street, and to make sure that they complied the Master Chamberlain would oversee the work. The Aldermen also felt that it was reasonable to assume that from the wording on the sign, customers would naturally infer that Sharpe and Heward had occupied Horne's corner plot in Cheapside before the fire, whereas in fact Sharpe's shop had been on the other side of the street. So Sharpe was told to obliterate or strike out the words

(*left*) Kidskin gloves with gauntlet cuffs of pink silk, tabbed and trimmed with gold and silver lace and embroidery.

(*above*) A man's linen cap embroidered with gold and silver thread, trimmed with sequins and gold lace.

'at the end of Foster Lane'; if he refused, the Chamberlain would take the matter in hand himself. A year later John Sharpe received a taste of his own medicine when his neighbour Christopher Portman used the sign of the White Hart for *his* new shop in Jewen Lane. Portman was ordered to take down the sign and to trade under another.[196]

The area around St Lawrence Jewry and the west end of Cheapside had long been the hub of the mercers' trade, but there were mercers (merchants in silk, velvets, brocades and other kinds of luxury textiles) and silkmen (primarily specialists in dyeing and spinning silk) in various locations around the City, with notable concentrations of silkmen and silk throwsters (weavers) in Holborn, St Giles Cripplegate and Spitalfields. Evidence for the silk throwsters' trade in the 1660s is relatively slight, but inventories show that they had in their shops as many as five to ten 'throwing' mills; a rich variety of machine- and hand-woven silk yarn; bundles of raw, damaged, fine and 'middling' quality silks from the Levant, Persia and Messina (Sicily); parcels of galloon (a braid of interwoven silver, gold and silk thread); and all kinds of black and coloured ribbon.[197]

Needlemaker

'by Imploying unskilful and unfit
persons as Women & young girls
in the Art or Mistery of making
of needles … a great number of
bad insufficient needles [have been]
made and put to sale.'
—*Needlemakers' Company*, 1668/9[198]

John Weaver was a needlemaker by trade. His house in the
parish of St Giles Cripplegate comprised six rooms spread over
three floors with a garret and a cellar. There was a room facing
the alley with an old chair and some hearth furniture; another
small room held an old table, four stools, a form, two old
cupboards and two iron dripping pans; and the cellar, which
doubled up as a store and workshop, held his tools and a massive
stock of just over half a million needles. Of these, 56,000 were
part-finished and 450,000 were ready for sale, which suggests
that Weaver was still making needles shortly before his death in
March 1663.[199] The needles are not itemized but they must have
been packed in numbered batches, probably in standard units
according to type, quality, weight and price.

As many crafts had their 'sole dependence upon the use of
needles' the range for sale in London was huge and the quality
diverse. There were coarse needles for leatherwork and upholstery; fine needles for embroidery; knitting needles; short, long,
narrow and broad needles; pointed and square needles; ordinary
needles and surgeons' needles.[200] When the needles were bright
and new it was evidently hard for customers to distinguish the
best from the worst, and it was only when the needles were put
to use and they snapped, were too blunt or turned to rust that
their true quality was exposed. So, in an attempt to impose some
kind of quality control, the Needlemakers' Company decreed

After the fire, London was supplied
with increasing numbers of foreign
needles made from iron wire rather
than steel. As many trades had their
'sole dependence upon the use of
Needles' and artificers travelled miles
to buy needles in the capital, the
London needlemakers' reputation was
brought into disrepute.

that only needles of the finest quality should bear a stamp and maker's mark.

Although the impact of the fire on the needlemakers' craft is unknown, the trade seems to have been put under increasing pressure from foreign competition, and in 1668 the needlemakers submitted a petition to the King about the great quanities of needles 'dayly imported … from parts beyond the Seas', which were for the most part 'falsely and deceiptfully wrought'. The main problem was that the needles were made of iron wire rather than tempered steel. As soon as they arrived in the capital they were marked, covered in new paper and packed in English style to disguise their origin; then sold, bartered and exchanged in London and elsewhere 'to ye great abuse and deceipt of his Majesties subjects'. In one month the Company officers seized and destroyed 238,750 needles that were taken from a Dutchman in Crutched Friars, from a Dutchwoman in Wheeler Street, and from retailers in Broad Street, Houndsditch, Bartholomew Close, Bishospgate, the Minories, Southwark, Wapping, Moorgate, 'over against' St Clement's Church, East Smithfield, St Katherine's and Aldgate. Whether these needles were substandard wares of English make or foreign counterfeits – perhaps both – is unknown. What is certain is that many of the London needlemakers had been reduced to penury and were 'likely to be undone with their wives and families' by the flood of poor-quality goods on the market. And, to add to their woes, the London makers complained that they made all of their needles from steel, which cost them more in materials than the imported needles were sold for, so unless some 'speedy & effectual remedy [was] applied to prevent the Importacon of forregin & ill wrought needles' the needlemakers of London would lose their trade.[201]

But there were other deceits in manufacture; and as the demand for needles increased in the years after the fire, there were complaints that needlemakers had started to stamp ordinary needles to 'delude and deceive the buyers'. To make matters worse, the market was flooded with poor-quality needles which had been made by 'unskilled and unfit women and young girls'. The Company were particularly concerned that the women were not able to perform such ardous work through the 'weakness of their sex', so it was 'ordered and ordained' that no needlemaker

in London (man or woman) should engage a female apprentice. Provision was made for the widows of 'those men who in their life times had used the said Art' for at least seven years, and they were asked to present themselves to the Company so that 'care may be taken … [of their] several necessities'.[202]

Overseas merchant

'[We] have endeavoured to serve His Majesty to the utmost by advancing more money than they expect the … goods to fetch and the rather because there has been a loss on them by fire, and many buyers have not paid up and have become insolvent.'—*East India Company Committees*, 19 September 1666[203]

The East India Company kept large stores of goods in various warehouses across London. The fire spared the Company's headquarters in Leadenhall Street, but as the flames swept towards them so that a 'totall ruine was feared' the Committees responsible for particular commodities (such as cloth, nutmeg, green ginger, rhubarb and opium) tried to remove their stocks to safety.[204] Platoons of musketeers stood guard so that the evacuation could be conducted as smoothly as possible; none of the merchants was allowed to take away their own goods lest it cause widespread panic, confusion and further loss. Cartloads were conveyed from the City to the house and garden of Dr William Clark, the Vicar of Stepney, and to the homes of Mr Crowther and Captain John in Mile End. Removal costs and other expenses in preserving goods from the fire amounted to £534.[205] Despite their best efforts,

On 13 December 1666 Samuel Barnard swore an affidavit stating that several contracts relating to the customs and excise were burnt in the fire, as well as 80 tally sticks to the value of £136,424 2s, dated from 24 April 1663 to 16 May 1666. Tally sticks were issued as a form of receipt; the notches, cut with different profiles, record the amounts. The sticks were split lengthwise, with the stock held by the borrower and the foil by the lender.

most of the saltpetre in the Custom House was lost, as was almost all of the pepper stored in the cellars underneath the Royal Exchange.

The first task was to assess the loss. The Committees realized that some of the goods which had been rescued from the fire – including 43 casks of cloves, 10 bales of cotton yarn and 227 bags of pepper – had been removed from the warehouses before they had been weighed and properly entered into the Company's ledgers. The greater problem was to recover as much as possible of the spoiled pepper from the ruins of the Exchange. Labourers were employed to sift the rubble, and some 110 bags of pepper were recovered and sent down to William Ryder's sugar house in Woolwich to 'be cured and lodged there'. The pepper was transported downriver under the care of a turkey merchant who was charged with supervising the work of 'curing'. He was also asked to collect

up the empty bags and send them back to London as they were in such short supply and were greatly needed for other purposes. [206]

In the meantime, warehouse space was urgently needed for the Company's stock. Some of the City warehouses were full to bursting, while others, taken over as a temporary store in the emergency – including the walks and gardens at Gresham College – had to be vacated in a hurry so that the space could be used to accommodate the shopkeepers from the Exchange. [207] The Great Warehouse at Leadenhall was inspected and surveyed to make sure that the floors could withstand the 'further burthen of goods into it'; but the Cinnamon Warehouse nearby was judged so full that the Company could not admit anybody into any part of it, 'without great inconveniency and hazard to the goodes'. The Committees were asked to draw up a list of suitable stores and

by 19 September a shortlist was produced which included a large warehouse at Haydon House 90 foot long and 24 broad; three warehouses adjoining Mr Partridge's Brewhouse, the largest at 100 foot long and 40 wide; and Nicholas Panning's warehouse in St Mary Axe. But this was not enough and the Court agreed that the merchants needed to look for extra space elsewhere and should enquire about the use of the City granaries. Space was in such short supply that the buyers were called to clear their goods and remove them as quickly as possible. A special order was also made for the pepper, and it was agreed that every effort should be made to trace the owners by the numbers and marks on the bags.[208]

On 28 November, the Committees produced a report on the burnt pepper, and it was agreed that the East India Company would buy off the interest on the pepper that had been properly weighed and cleared through the accounts, and for the remainder burnt at the Exchange; so the merchants could have their money returned with interest. The following month the Committees for buying goods ordered some new bags for the burnt pepper; all of the remaining 1,755 bags of pepper, ranging in price from 4d to 1s 4d per pound, were brought together from the various warehouses for 'sale by candle'. The best pepper, from Malabar and Quilon in India, was valued at 1s 8d per pound.[209]

The fire must have had a lasting effect on merchants trading overseas. While its real impact is impossible to measure, some information can be gleaned from a few documented cases in the Mayor's Court. On 20 November 1667, for instance, John Ewing, a 30-year-old London merchant, appeared on behalf of John Gordon, an English merchant resident in the 'Cittie of Cadiz', with whom he had been in regular correspondence for the past seven years and whom he knew to be 'just and honest' in all his dealings. Spanish and English documents suggest that before the fire Gordon had been engaged as an agent in London on behalf of Andrew De Coniq, a Dutch merchant in Cadiz. According to Ewing's testimony, in early July 1666 the merchant ship *Charles V* from Cadiz arrived in the Thames laden with wines, pine nuts, dates and other commodities. The goods were consigned to Gordon's care, and removed to various locations in the City: most of the dry goods to a warehouse in Tower Street and the wines to cellars in Cross Lane near the church of St Dunstans-in-the-East.

Martabani jars were made in South China, Indochina, Siam and Indonesia and were first traded from Martaban (in Burma) by the Arabs, Portuguese and, in the seventeenth century, by the Dutch East India Company. They were used as containers for water, oil and ginger in syrup. The East India Company imported 86,802 lb of green ginger worth £2,531 14s into London in 1662–63. This jar, dating to *c*. 1650, was found on the site of St Bartholomew's Hospital.

Ewing testified that Gordon had done his utmost to 'sell & dispose' of the goods as quickly as possible, but that they had all been burnt in the 'lamentable fire in London'.

Further details were supplied by Robert Dodd of London, cooper, aged 38 years, who said that he had inspected the consignment in the hold and had seen '91 Butts of sherry wines marked ADC', which had been consigned to John Gordon. Upon closer examination, however, he had noticed that eleven were 'for the most part leaked out and empty', so a further nine butts' worth of wine was used to fill up the partially empty casks for sale. Seven butts were sold immediately: one at £23 10s and the remainder at £24 each. Dodd knew this because he had been present at the sale and had subsequently delivered the casks to the purchasers. John Gorden and his servant William Bellamy had tried to sell the remaining 64 butts of wine but had been unable to do so. Then on 2 September the fire reached the cellars in Cross Lane, and all of the wine was destroyed, together with the pine nuts, dates and other items in Tower Street. The deponents all testified that the loss was not due to Gordon's actions or negligence and confirmed that he had done his utmost to preserve the goods from the fire. De Coniq's claim of negligence was overturned, and he was ordered to pay the outstanding customs dues, which were set at £387 18s 8d: the standard duty for wines in the port of London at that time. A final document in Spanish demanded that De Coniq should also pay £196 6s 1d, being the residue of £397 9s which Gordon had 'disbursed on his behalf in the Citty of London', besides other petty charges.[210]

Painter

'the little flower-pott [painting] … the
finest thing that ever I think I saw in
my life – the drops of Dew hanging
on the leaves, so as I was forced again
and again to put my finger to it to feel
whether my eyes were deceived or no.'—
Samuel Pepys, 11 April 1669[211]

London had a thriving international art market. One contemporary writing in 1665 suggested that the capital was 'a collection
and digest of all men and things … [and home to] the best
Artsmen in the Nation'.[212] The public appetite for art is impossible
to measure, but from the 1660s onwards there was a marked
increase in the ownership of paintings in London households. A
single picture was the norm, though some houses had three or
four, and a very few upwards of ten. The glazier John Brace was
exceptional in having 17 pictures 'great and small' in his dining
room, with three more in the 'widow's chamber'.[213] Most are listed
with other household items so individual valuations are lacking,
and apart from occasional references to 'landskips', 'mythologies'
and, more infrequently, a 'fruitage', 'flower piece' or portrait, the
subject matter is seldom given.[214] Still-life paintings were probably
much more popular than the evidence from inventories suggests;
Samuel Pepys was particularly struck by the virtuosity and verisi-
militude of a 'little flower-pott' painting in the London studio of
the Dutch artist Simon Verelst.[215]

Although it is impossible to know how many paintings in
private ownership were lost or damaged in the fire, records suggest
that most of the art collections held by civic institutions and the
City livery companies were removed to safety with other valuables
and preserved. But there were a few close calls. As the fire swept
towards Barber-Surgeons' Hall, the officers were faced with the
challenging task of evacuating one of their greatest treasures:

Within the painting, the following labels appear:

HENRICO OCTAVO OP E MAX REGI ANGLIAE
FRANCIAE ET HIBERNIAE FIDEI DEFENSO
RI AC ANGLICANAE HIBERNICEQ
ECCLESIAE PROXIME A CHRISTO SVPREMO
CAPITI, SOCIETAS CHIRVRGORVM
COMMVNIBVS VOTIS HAEC CONSECRAT

TRISTIOR ANGLORVM PESTIS VIOLAVERAT ORBEM
INFESTANS ANIMOS CORPORIBVSQVE SEDENS
HANC DEVS INSIGNEM CLADEM MISERATVS AB ALTO
TE MEDICI MVNVS IVSSIT OBIRE BONI
LVMEN EVANGELII TVLVIS CIRCVMVOLAT ALIIS
PHARMACON ADFECTIS MENTIBVS ILLVD ERIT
CONSILIO, QVO CELEBRANT MONVMENTA GALENI
ET SELERI MORBVS PELLITVR OMNIS OPE
NOS IGITVR SIMPLEX MEDICORVM TVRBA TVORVM
HANC TIBI SACRAMVS RELIGIONE DOMVM
MVNERIS ET MEMORES QVO NOS HENRICE BEASTI
IMPERIO OPTAMVS MAXIMA QVEQVE TVO

BVTTS
I·CHAMBER·
T·VICARY
·I·AYLEF
·N·SYMSON·
·E·HARMAN·
X·SAMON·
·I·MON FORDE
·I·PEN
·N·ALCOKE
W·TYLLY

Henry VIII and the Barber-Surgeons, oil on panel. Hans Holbein the Younger began a cartoon for this picture, which was completed and painted by others. The picture was commissioned to celebrate the union of the Barbers' Company and the Guild of Surgeons in 1540. Large sections have been overpainted to disguise the damage caused by the fire.

the large panel painting of *Henry VIII and the Barber-Surgeons*. Described simply as 'H ye 8th picture' in the company accounts, this monumental work was carried to safety by six porters under the supervision of Mayor Brookes and Captain Carroll, who later received £1 each for their trouble. The porters were given 8s 9d to share between them. A further sum of 14 shillings was given to the beadle Peter Smith, for 'getting home severall flags & pictures'. Although the Court minute books have been lost and details are lacking, it seems that the painting had been hung on the wall of the Anatomy Theatre, which had direct access into Saint Giles Churchyard. From there it was but a short journey into Moorfields, where the Company treasures were first removed, and thence to Holborn Bridge to the home of one of the Company tenants: John Phillips, John Harris or Robert Westbroooke.[216]

But this relatively short journey was evidently not without incident, because the painting seems to have been quite badly damaged: in 1667 the accounts record a payment of £1 6s 8d to Mr Farre for 'mending King H ye 8th Cup & picture'.[217] It is unclear what the 'mending' actually entailed, since a goldsmith was later commissioned to repair the cup, and payments were subsequently made to Thomas and Mary Green, painters, according to a later set of annual accounts.[218] Further information is supplied by Samuel Pepys, who went to the 'Chyrurgeon's-hall, where they are building it new', on 29 August 1668. After examining the Anatomy Theatre, which had survived the fire, Pepys applied himself to the main purpose of his visit: to see 'their great picture of Holben's' and secure it for a bargain price. He offered £200, 'it being said to be worth £1000'. But it was not to be. Pepys was disappointed by its condition: 'it is so spoiled that I have no mind to it, and is not a pleasant, though a good picture.'[219] Perhaps the Barbers had a greater regard for their painting than they were given credit for.

The Plumbers' Company removed their pictures to a house in Morton, where they remained for some years until the Hall was rebuilt.[220] The Coopers' records for 4 March 1672 include the following entry: 'voted that severall pictures formerly hanging up in the old hall & being preserved from the great fire in London bee cleansed and putt in frames and soe hung up in convenient places'.[221] The Royal College of Physicians managed to remove their pictures to safety, but a note in Dr Merrett's hand regarding items preserved from the fire (*see* p. 14) mentions 'Dr Harveys & Fox's pictures without frames', which suggests that the paintings were unframed to facilitate removal.[222]

Nothing much is known about the stocks of London painters, painter–stainers and art suppliers in this period. Inventories are few and, for the most part, unspecific, but some meagre details emerge for the painter–stainer John Robinson, who lived in a tiny house of two storeys in St Giles Cripplegate. The garret held a couple of flock beds, two rugs, four blankets and two pairs of flaxen sheets, and two items of stock, 'two coloured stones to grind two colours withall', which were separately itemized and valued at 10 shillings. The room below had another bed with curtains and bedstead, a truckle bed, a table and a chest of drawers; and the kitchen was furnished with a cupboard, a table, six chairs, a fire iron and eight pewter dishes 'great and small'.[223] Far more fulsome is the inventory of the painter–stainer Leonard Fryer, also of the parish of St Giles Cripplegate, who had a reasonably large and well-furnished home. He had a workhouse containing 'all that belongeth to ye painting trade' valued at 6 shillings, but the

Gulielmus · Harvey · M·D·

William Harvey (1578–1657), unknown artist, oil on canvas. This portrait is one of two paintings rescued from the Royal College of Physicians during the Great Fire. It has sustained a great deal of damage. The sitter's right hand is distorted, possibly the work of an eighteenth-century restorer.

list of debts includes entries for 'painting a signe of ye nagshead & Rainbow in Jewen Street' for £1 13s; various payments for work done for the Earl of Bridgewater; and for other unspecified work in London Wall, at the Rose in Bartholomew Close, in Lothbury and in Islington. Fryer had a sign in the garret with other lumber and £322 9s 10d in money in the house at the time of his death in February 1666.[224]

There was much work for painter–stainers after the fire. There were large and small-scale contracts for buildings, as well as individual commissions to refurbish shop signs and other odd items. The Plumbers' Company engaged Thomas Evans to paint 'two dozen of buckets for the use of the hall with the Companyes wares & the date of the yeare of our lord at the rate of twelve pence for every bucket'.[225] Similar orders were placed by the City Corporation to Edmond Pickering painter to decorate four dozen buckets for Newgate Prison, and eight dozen more for the Guildhall and for the use of the Lord Mayor and Sheriffs.[226]

Pewterer

'This day the Court tooke into Consideracon that they had bought some pewter before the fire, And by reason of the destruction & unsettledness of the tymes, they had not yett fully satisfied the pewterer, And therefore have this day ordered yt what shalbe due to him, shall forthwith be paid him.'—*Brewers' Company,* 2 *May* 1667[227]

By the 1660s many Londoners had in excess of 200 lb weight of 'fine' and 'coarse' pewter in their homes. There was more pewter on the market than ever before, and enterprising and skilful craftsmen could make a name for themselves and 'a considerable business'.[228] There were technological advances in production too, and pewterers were constantly challenged to come up with new designs to satisfy the capricious tastes of their customers, for, as one Londoner wryly observed, 'we change the fashion of our pewter as often as we change the fashion of our hats'.[229]

Hiring pewter for dinners and special events was big business. The livery companies hired in plate for feasts even though members sometimes grumbled about the cost. The Drapers' Company tried to minimize 'expence and discontentments' by ordering new pewter, which was stacked in the kitchen for daily use. To cover all future contingencies, a pewter contract was issued to Mr Jackson to provide sets of fine pewter 'at his owne charge', as well as 'rough pewter as the Cooks shall desire'. The pewter was to be scoured clean and returned to his house, for which he would receive the yearly sum of £3 10s.[230] The wardens were quite satisfied with the arrangement, but in due course Mr Jackson complained that his services had been abused; the Company had had more dinners than usual and his yearly

allowance barely covered his costs. He asked for an increment of 40 shillings.[231]

Pewter was even hired out to private homes, so pewterers and victuallers tried to safeguard their property by ensuring that their wares were clearly identified with ownership marks, initials and other devices, as Samuel Pepys found to his cost when he made the mistake of inviting friends home for a meal on 'washing day'. Finding the house in disarray, the cupboards bare and the kitchen out of bounds, he sent out for a ready meal but was much vexed to find that 'my people had so little wit to send in our meat from abroad in the cook's dishes, which were marked with the name of the cook upon them; by which, if they observed anything, they might know it was not my own dinner.'[232]

One of the most significant boosts to the pewterers' trade in the seventeenth century was the expansion of catering provision across the capital. This development was prompted by the need to feed a massively increasing population, but was also a reaction to changes in the dietary and drinking habits of Londoners as 'dining out'

became an increasingly important part of social, cultural and business life.[233] There was a need for pewter as never before. When the tavern and alehouse proprietors started to compete with ordinaries and cookshops in the 'trade of victualling', they needed to extend the range, quality and variety of their pewter stocks to serve the needs of their customers. New vessels were needed for the revolutionary hot non-alcoholic beverages of coffee, chocolate and tea which took London by storm; by the 1660s coffee houses had large stocks of 'fine' and 'coarse' pewter in their kitchens, and parcels of pewter coffee pots, dishes and porringers in the public rooms.

Surviving examples of mid-seventeenth-century pewter show signs of heavy use and abuse, but the fact that they have survived at all is remarkable as pewter was too valuable to be discarded lightly and always had the spectre of the melting pot hanging over it. Where possible pewterers was asked to replace missing lids and handles, and battered vessels were given a new lease of life with a judicious repair and patch, but even so pewter was regularly replaced – it has been estimated that tavern pots and kitchenware had a life cycle of perhaps 20 or 30 years before they were sold for scrap.[234] When raw materials were scarce, pewterers were almost entirely dependent upon supplies of 'old' vessels to maintain levels of production, and some craftsmen with entrepreneurial flair tried to ensure a ready supply by offering their regular customers a part-exchange deal of old pots for new. Little wonder, then, that Londoners did what they could to reclaim molten pewter from the rubble of the fire. The Clothworkers' Company employed two men to dig up the molten pewter from their charcoal cellar.[235] The Grocers' Company accounts include payments of 25 shillings for 'casting ye melted pewter'. In the following year their pewter stocks were gradually replenished with orders to Nicholas Kelse, Richard Collyer, Daniell Ingoll and Robert Moulins for '36 dishes of the sorts following: 6 at £10; 12 at £7; 12 at £5, and 6 more at £4' – all at the somewhat inflated rate of 14d per pound. The usual price for fine pewter was 9d per pound, and for coarse pewter 7d per pound. They also acquired 6 dozen trencher plates, 3 pasty plates, 3 dozen saucers, and 3 large and 3 lesser dishes, all of which were stamped with the Company's coat of arms at a cost of £27 15s 9d.[236] Some Companies had to wait quite a while to renew their pewter; for example, the Clothworkers held on to their

Illustrations from The *Academy of Armory* (1688) of a pewterer's metal-forming 'studdy' or horse-head anvil (*left*) and a polishing wheel.

molten metal 'remaining in and about the hall & yards' until 1668 when they were finally able to commission some new pewter for 'feastivall daies to bee held at ye hall as occasion shall require'.[237]

The fire consumed Pewterers' Hall in Lime Street and one of the pewterers' greatest treasures, a 'Table of Pewter with every mans Marke therein' (since 1522 pewterers had had to register their mark on a set of pewter plates at the Hall), as well as their property holdings across the City. But, on the plus side, there was a massive, if short-term increase in work, and it was a boom time for pewterers who had not suffered personal loss. There was so much scrap metal on the market that the projected scheme to bring in extra supplies of tin from the stannaries in Cornwall was completely undermined, and when Nicholas Kolk tried to offload some tin ingots in his custody he could neither set the price nor return them to their owners as they had been melted and 'altered by ye late fire'.[238]

The impact of the fire on individual pewterers is very difficult to measure. John French, who lived in the parish of St Katherine's by the Tower, managed to escape its worst effects; when he died, in 1669, he had several casting blocks in the cellar, and his shop contained a mixture of 'new' and 'old' alloys, 'fine' metal, some old and new lead, some alchemy spoons, and various tools of the trade. His son Alexander already had some moulds and the 'majority of his beams and scales' in his house in Beech Lane, Ludgate, which suggests that some part of the business had already been transferred to him. There were more moulds with the pewterer Mr Priest, as well as various outstanding sums both owed and owing for metal.[239] The shop in St Katherine's was run by French's widow Abigail; it was evidently a thriving business because she took on two apprentices a few years later.[240]

Some pewterers were far less fortunate. William Archer was criticized for selling pewter from a booth in June 1667.[241] Thomas Dickenson and Miles Haviland also had to move into makeshift booths and sheds in Smithfield. Although Dickenson eventually managed to find a permanent shop in the area, Haviland was forced to move away from the capital, because in 1670 he was noted 'to be long absent from London and address not known'.[242] All sorts of schemes and strategems were found to keep businesses afloat. Some pewterers, like John Higdon, tried to earn some

money and maintain their client base by placing items in 'divers places'.[243] And he was not alone, because a few months after the fire several pewterers, including five in Southwark, were selling other makers' work in their shops, both as a commercial venture and to help their brethren in time of need. John Higdon probably benefited from this arrangement, for in due course he was able to re-establish his business in the parish of St Giles Cripplefield. When he died in 1673 he was living in a modestly furnished one-up, one-down house; the lower room and cellar serving as a shop, filled with a stack of fine pewter, 200 cwt of coarse pewter, 1 cwt of solder, 6 lb of lead, as well as 150 cwt of iron, which suggests that he was making other sorts of items as well as pewter to supplement his income.[244]

Plumber & pipe-borer

'a great part of the leade that covered Lambes Chappell belonging to this Companie neare Cripplegate was lately taken off the said chappell by some persons whoe had attempted to carry the same away. But being discovered made theire escape and left the said leade behind them.'—*Clothworkers' Company, 18 April 1667*[245]

The fire destroyed most of the City's piped water supply. The tidal pump and water wheels in the first two arches of London Bridge, installed by the Dutch hydraulic engineer Peter Morris (Morice) in 1575, had burned down leaving large tracts of the southern part of the City without water. Most of the lead cisterns and quills (small pipes) had vaporized or melted into fused lumps; many of the well heads and conduits were damaged or destroyed; the drains and sewers were blocked; and most of the above- and below-ground network of wooden water pipes used for mains supply were fractured. There were complaints across the City. The most urgent task was to restore the London Bridge Waterworks; enough money was raised to cover the cost against a promised future return to the investors of £2,000. But there were many local difficulties. A couple of months after the fire, the Goldsmiths' Company found that the 'sinck which should convey the water out of the Hall yard is stopped to the prejudice of the vault or cellar lyeing under the same'. Workmen were ordered to investigate and mend the defect as soon as possible.[246] There were urgent complaints about the lack of water serving Newgate Prison, and the Lord Mayor directed

Molten mass of lead containing the stem of a clay pipe and some sherds of pottery, from Queenhithe Dock.

that a kettle and other 'accomodacons for the Prisoners there' should be installed forthwith. At the same time, the City plumber John George was asked to prepare a clear and 'perfect' plan of the pipe networks across the City and investigate 'ye Aqueducts of this Citty [and] how the same may bee repaired maintained or imployed to the Cittyes best advantage'.[247] Dozens of orders were placed with the Chamberlain's Office for new conduits in Cripplegate, Holborn, Gracechurch Street and Cheapside; for mending pipes at Fleet Bridge; for laying pipes to the conduit heads; and for conveying water through Ludgate Hill.[248]

The New River Waterworks in Islington lay well beyond the burnt area, so the governors of the New River Company were able to supply new pipes to the northern parts of the City without too much difficulty. But they also saw an opportunity to extend their network south into those areas previously served by the London Bridge Waterworks. This encroachment prompted an immediate outcry from the widow and sisters of Mr Morris (the grandson of the founder), who complained that the 'citizens may bee in a short time compelled to [be] served from [the New River Company] at unreasonable rates, when they shall have beaten down all other waterworks & specially this, which is more ancient & furnished much better water than the new River'.[249]

Water companies, civic institutions and private individuals needed urgent help from teams of plumbers and specialist pipe-borers. The old and damaged pipes had to be removed and new sections laid as quickly as possible, but all this work took time. So much time that many plumbing faults were left unresolved. A year later, the Skinners' Company were told by one of their tenants that 'by reason of the constant running of the watercock in St Hellens and the defects in the Gutter the Companies house in his occupacon … the Timber that lieth on the side of the Gutter is much rotted & impaired';[250] and it was not until 9 June 1669 that the Drapers' Company were able to place an order for a new set of pipes to 'be laid and brought downe for the conveyning of the water for … the hall (with cisterns at the topp guilt with the Company's armes).[251]

Elm wood with its twisted interlocked grain was the preferred timber for water pipes, as it had great tensile strength and was re-sistant to splitting. Short lengths of trunk with a drilled bore, each

about 8 foot long, were laid end to end. One end of the trunk had a socket and the other was tapered so that the trunks slotted into one another to form a continuous pipe. The pipe junctions were reinforced with bands of iron and lead to minimize splitting and leaks, and at intervals spigots and lead pipes were inserted in a series of small holes, which directed the water into the buildings. To ensure a good supply of water for fire engines and squirts, an Act of Common Council in 1668 ordered that pumps were to be placed in all wells, and fireplugs inserted into the main pipes belonging to the New River and London Bridge waterworks.[252]

Daniel Fillops in the parish of St Giles Cripplegate was an elm pipe-borer; his shop contained 'toules' and two shancks, 18 buckets and spouts; a grindstone, a small parcel of 1½″ boards, a parcel of 'square Elme' at £17 10s (bulks of timber that had not been drilled), a horse, cart and harness, and a 'parcell of pipes bored and a few rafters' at £3.[253] Plumbers inventories in the immediate post-fire period are rather more detailed. Robert Tuckwell's shop stock, appraised on 25 July 1667, comprised eight brass moulds to 'cast pipes and one iron mold with knots staves & cords to them', all at £40 10s; six brass moulds to cast leaden bars, valued at 30s; another set of brass moulds to cast small weights; 25 tons 3 cwt 96 lb of 'sother'

(solder) at 6d per hundredweight; two melting pots, two pairs of beams and scales, ropes, and 'severall things aboute ye shop'.[254] Samuel Eames had properties in Spitalfields and Bunhill Fields. His shop and warehouse contained 16 cwt of lead bottoms for stills (distillation equipment); 1 ton 8 cwt of new sheet lead and 6 cwt 32 lb of pipes; 2 tons 1 cwt 46 lb of old lead; five small pipe moulds, moulds for weights and flower pots; 200 cwt of coarse old brass, and two pots with 'all tooles and utensils belonging to his trade'. The whole was valued at £142 6s 5½d.[255] The most comprehensive stock belonged to Samuel Peach of the parish of St Andrew's Holborn, who had other properties in Kingstreet, Bloomsbury and Spread Eagle Court off Grays Inn Lane. His shop included 1 ton 13 cwt of new sheet lead, 19 cwt of 'ring weights', 1 gross of small weights, 10 cwt of new leaden pipes, 5 cwt 63 lb of sodder (solder), 1 ton 7 cwt of hard metal, and 2 tons 2 cwt of old lead; as well as various parcels of weights, a melting pot with 'iron work belonging to it', scimmers and ladles, one sheet-lead mould and pan, one pipe and pipe mould frame with strikes, shafts and dresser, and 'all other wooden tooles thereunto belonging', as well as a cart for the pipe mould, ten sodder stones, some brass pulleys and tackle ropes, a brass force pump, four brass pipe moulds, some

'The Waterhouse', 1665, after Wenceslaus Hollar (1607–1677). The New River and reservoir were created in 1609–13. Water was brought to London via a network of pipes from springs near Ware, Hertfordshire, 40 miles distant.

soldering irons, hammers, a knife and 'other tooles belonging to a Plumer's trade'.[256]

It is clear from inventories and plumbers' accounts that lead prices were relatively stable immediately after the fire; though new lead cost on average 4 shillings more per hundredweight than old lead, which would have made a great deal of difference to the overall cost of a replacement roof, gutter or drain.[257] So one of the greatest labours in the days, weeks and months after the fire was to recover as much of the molten lead from the ruins as possible. The scrap lead was needed for new pipes, cisterns and gutters, but also for solder, window cames and roofs. Much of the salvaged lead was cast into pigs; for instance on 5 October 1666 Mr Read, plumber, took some of the old lead from Bridewell Hospital to melt into pigs of lead at a rate of just 6d a hundredweight. A kettle was set up in the courtyard for the purpose, and the hospital steward supplied the necessary fuel.[258]

The demand for lead was so high that all of the City institutions asked plumbers to sift through the rubbish to reclaim as much lead as they could find. A week after the fire the Mercers' Company wardens attempted to dispose of the 'heape of lead Rubbish' in their Chapel to those who would offer the most for it.[259] Payments in the accounts were later made to George Widmerpoole for the 'scummings and Ashes' of melted lead; for cartage to Gresham College for weighing and housing; and finally to Thomas Ballard, plumber, for casting about 16½ tons of lead at 9d per hundredweight; the whole amounting to £13 7s.[260] The City institutions hoped to recoup some of their losses from the sale of the scrap metal, and the plumbers were keen to obtain it at the lowest possible price, even if this meant that they had to sift through the rubble to find it.[261] Months after the fire, there were applications from plumbers seeking permission to sift for lead. In November 1667 William Hayes asked that he might buy all the lead in the rubbish at Skinners' Hall, which he would sift for their use. The Company agreed that he could have it as long as he gave them an advance payment of £9 with the promise of 20 shillings more should it prove 'soe much worth'.[262] These exclusive contracts were of great benefit to the City institutions and to the contracted plumber, since there was so much competition for work and soaring demand for the raw materials.

The plumbers had so much work that some were tempted to take short cuts. In October 1666 it came to the attention of the Court of Common Council that one plumber (unnamed) in Aldersgate Street had had the misfortune to set his house on fire during the night because he had started to melt lead in his cellar. The plumber was told to stop work immediately and a viewing committee was appointed to inspect the property to see whether it could be used for plumbing work in the future.[263] The following year Peter Smart was questioned by the Plumbers' Company for using unmarked sother (solder), which he agreed was true, but argued that it had been 'formerly marked but being burnt in ye late fier in London it was unfit for use', so he had been forced to 'new mill it'. Some 9,000 lb had been used already, but he promised to mark the rest in the next few days. He was fined 'ye several sums' of 30s, 20s and 10s, but the Company eventually agreed to reduce the fine of 10 shillings to 5 shillings.[264] Smart's comment about milling is interesting because most lead at this time was cast into pigs or sand-cast into large sheets. Milled lead was a relatively new innovation, and as the sheets were much finer it was generally deemed unsuitable for building.

In September 1668 the Plumbers' Company were concerned that 'divers persons of this Company' had taken in 'plumbers that are forreingers' to help them in their work. Some of these 'forreingers' had probably come from the suburbs or home counties, but as non-freemen they were prohibited from working in the City, it was unanimously agreed that henceforward if at any time any freeman member of the Company employed or set to work any 'forreign' plumber either as a plumber or plumber's labourer that he should receive a fine of 40 shillings for the first offence. These measures, however, did not prevent non-freeman from setting up on their own account. For instance on 21 September 1668 John Channell was proceeded against for opening and keeping a plumber's shop, 'he not being a freeman of the Citty of London'. An action against him was brought in the Mayor's Court at the suit of the Chamberlain of London, where it was eventually agreed that he should pack up his goods and leave town. Channell asked if he could have grace to remain in town for a few more days to collect outstanding debts 'for worke that he hath done in & about London', but promised to shut up his shop immediately and to

pay the clerk of the Plumbers' Company so much money 'as the charges which had bene disbursed in presenting the suite against him and also to satisfy the informer'.[265]

In early June 1667 the governors of St Bartholomew's Hospital were slightly surprised to hear that the two men appointed to relay the flagstones in Christ Church, nearby, were far more interested in sifting through the rubble for lead; so it was agreed that they could have all the pieces they found 'under the bigness of six shillings worth' and that anything bigger was to be left to the Hospital's use.[266] The larger lumps were handed over to the Hospital's plumber, Mr Talbott, to be melted down into roofing sheets, and so precious was this material that the Steward of the Hospital was directed to oversee the casting process.[267] It was a prudent decision because by weighing the lead the governors knew exactly how much they needed to buy for the new roof; they could offset some of the costs of replacement by selling the old lead in part-exchange for new, and at the same time could make sure that they were not short-changed. It was perhaps as well that the governors took such a keen interest in their property because there were increasing reports across the City of scrap metal pilfering. Just a few months earlier the Clothworkers were horrified to hear that the lead on Lamb's Chapel in Monkwell Street near Cripplegate, which belonged to them, had been stripped 'by some persons whoe had attempted to carry it away but being discovered made their escape and left the … leade behind them'. The sheets of lead were secured by the local constable and the sexton of Cripplegate parish, but a few days later the Company decided that it would be safer to remove the lead from the chapel to Mr Coles the plumber in Fleet Street, and that an account should be taken of its weight so that the chapel roof could be replaced 'with all expedicion'.[268] The sexton received two payments of 2s 6d for his part in securing the lead.[269]

Lead ingot found beneath the piles of old London Bridge.

Spectacle-maker

'From the Exchange I took a coach, and went to Turlington, the great spectacle-maker, for advice, who dissuades me from using old spectacles, but rather young ones. And doth tell me that nothing can wrong them more then for me to use reading-glasses, which do magnify much.'—*Samuel Pepys*, 4 November 1667[270]

Ordinary spectacles and their cases were retailed by haberdashers, but it was also possible to have a private consultation with a specialist spectacle-maker and order bespoke lenses and frames. Pepys bought rolled-up paper tubes (about 3 inches in length with a small orifice at the end), which helped to minimize glare and reduce binocular vision, and several types of spectacles from John Turlington's shop in the Royal Exchange in Cornhill, but unfortunately he suffered from long sight complicated by astigmatism, which could not be corrected with contemporary lenses. Candle-light caused his eyes 'to be sore and run', and in 1666 he decided to acquire tinted 'green spectacles [to] get them right'.[271]

The spectacle-makers had shops across the City but there were particular clusters in and around the Royal Exchange and the immediate vicinity of Cannon Street. This changed after the fire.

Spectacles found on the site of Tabbard's Inn, Southwark, from a seventeenth-century context. They may in fact date to the eighteenth century.

When the Spectacle Makers' Company met on 3 October to assess their losses they were unable to hold a full meeting because so many of their members were 'dispersed into several remote parts as yet unknown'.[272] Evidence for this displacement is hard to find. Some moved to the Minories; some found accommodation in Southwark and Westminster; a few ended up in improvised booths in Smithfield; and John Turlington occupied a shed just 7½ foot by 5½ foot against the wall of Gresham College and Broad Street.[273]

Shortly before the fire the demand for spectacles was so high that thousands of frames and lenses were imported for domestic assembly. The port books for the year 1662–3, for instance, include references to 17,652 pairs of spectacles at 15 shillings per dozen and 3,468 lenses at £12 per dozen. By 1669, however, the volume of spectacle imports had dropped significantly to just 587 dozen (7,044); though the price pre- and post-fire remained the same. The imported spectacles and lenses came from Italy, and the high cost of the lenses suggests that they were made from finely ground and polished rock crystal.[274] It was perhaps the high cost of lenses that tempted some London makers to practise all kinds of deceit. John Sheppey, with his wife and servants, was caught 'grynding

A public spectacle. The first recorded evidence for the London Stone, a block of oolitic limestone, occurs in a twelfth-century document. It was originally sited at the southern end of Candlewick Street (now Cannon Street) opposite St Swithin's Church. In 1598 the antiquarian John Stow wrote of 'a great stone called London Stone, fixed in the ground very deep, fastened with bars of iron'. The stone was badly damaged in the Great Fire, which destroyed the church and surrounding buildings; afterwards just a small part stood proud above the level of the street. In 1671, 'bad and deceiptful' spectacles were smashed against it – a ritual form of public humiliation because of the severity of the offence.

of watch glasses' and setting them in frames in the parish of St Botolph's Bishopsgate; and Elizabeth Bagnall, a widow and whole-sale haberdasher in Cannon Street, had 264 English spectacles, 'being all very bad both in the glasse and frame not fit to be put to sale'. Although Elizabeth explained that her husband and 'her man' were both lately dead and she did not know where they had bought them, the wardens decided that her entire stock of spectacles should be confiscated. A warrant was obtained from the

The Spectacle Seller, c. 1646, by Adriaen van Ostade (1610–1685)

Lord Mayor and the spectacles were brought to the Mayor's Court at the Guildhall, where they were found to be 'bad and deceiptful' and condemned to be 'broken defaced and spoiled both glass and frame' by smashing them against the London Stone in Cannon Street with a hammer.[275]

Some of the best evidence for the spectacle-makers' trade relates to John Clarke, who had a house in London Wall. It is unclear whether his shop was burnt, but in January 1667 Clarke was in arrears with his quarteridge (a quarterly payment or subscription to the livery company), and in the following year was fined 20 shillings for selling 16 pairs of spectacles fashioned from 'looking glasse ground only on one side'.[276] Yet more 'deciptful work' was discovered, and following a visit from the wardens Clarke offered to break the spectacles himself and promised to 'deale noe more in them'. The wardens were not so easily dissuaded: they smashed the glass, leaving him with the 'whited copper' (probably tinned copper) frames. Clarke was furious and complained 'of the greate losse he had susteyned by the late dreadful fire and the losse in the defacing of these 31 dozen of spectacles'; that they were all foreign spectacles made by John Hill, and he would stop dealing in them. The wardens were somewhat mollified and he was fined 10 shillings. But a few days later when John Hill was asked to give his own account of the spectacles, he 'utterly denied the making of them'.[277]

Clarke continued in his trade as a spectacle-maker and retailer. When he died in 1674, having moved to new premises in Leaden-hall Street, the wares in his shop and dining room comprised 22 glasses 'great and small' and some frames at £84; 264 spectacles and some old frames, as well as some 'burning glases and pros-pects'; 24 dozen combs of several sorts; 34 dozen knives and forks; and 12 dozen canes and sticks. His debts included payments of £5 2s to Mr King for spectacle frames; 2s 10d to Mr Robinson, a glass-seller, for 'filing and other things'; and to Mr Read, a 'looking glass frame maker', the sum of £4 4s.[278]

Stationer

'Then we fell to talk of the burning of
the City; and my Lady Carteret herself
did tell us how abundance of pieces of
burnt papers were cast by the wind as
far as Cranborne; and among others,
she took up one, or had one brought
her to see, which was a little bit of
paper that had been printed, wherein
there remained no more nor less then
these words: Time is; it is done.'
—*Samuel Pepys*, 3 February 1667[279]

There is something particularly poignant about this entry in
Pepys's *Diary*. While other eyewitnesses describe the billowing
clouds of black and sulphurous yellow smoke hanging like a pall
over the City, and the strength of the easterly winds that fanned
the flames into ever-greater fury, Pepys's words help to capture the
true scale of destruction and the swirling mass of papers that were
consumed and reduced to ashes.

The speed and ferocity of the fire took many by surprise.
Bundles of papers were swept up under arm, rolled up into cloth
or thrown into an ill-fitting container, and amid the panic things
were lost. Papers came loose, books were dropped and damaged;
leases and bonds were burnt.[280] Documents and books ended up
in all sorts of odd places. A few days after the fire, a parcel of
books was retrieved from the City dog-house in Moorfields;[281]
the Weavers' Company lost their 'large book wherein was a copie
of the Companies Ordinances and other concerns',[282] and some
papers belonging to the Skinners' Company were found in the
street by the sexton of the local parish. Thankfully these precious
documents were returned and small sums of money handed over
as a reward. The Sexton received for 'paynes, care and honesty'
2s 6d.[283]

*Bishop King's sermon before the King
from St Paul's Preaching Cross*. This
detail, from a diptych by John Gipkin
in 1616, shows the shops of stationers
and booksellers tucked within the
buttresses of the Cathedral. The smoke
from the chimneys blackened the
walls.

The City institutions faced many trials and tribulations in their efforts to save and reclaim their 'bookes and writings', but their misfortunes were as nothing compared to the losses sustained by members of the book trade. The stationers and booksellers were hardest hit because they made the fateful decision to remove some of their stock to St Faith's Church within the crypt of St Paul's Cathedral. The precincts of St Paul's and its immediate environs had long been the hub of the book trade; stationers, printers, booksellers and bookbinders occupied many of the sheds, stalls and shops in the churchyard and neighbouring lanes. This location offered distinct commercial advantages. Many of the city's scholastic and educational institutions were located nearby, including St Paul's School and the grammar schools in St Martin-le-Grand and St Mary-le-Bow. Doctors' Commons, the 'common house' of the civil lawyers, stood in St Paul's Churchyard, and a little further afield were the legal scriveners in Holborn and Chancery Lane and the Inns of Court. By the 1660s, there was a large community of booksellers and stationers in Holborn and the Strand, and in the streets around the Royal Exchange in the heart of the City, where specialist books, prints and pamphlets were sold to the mercantile community and those engaged in international trade. Almanacks, travel books, guides, charts, maps, information and news items found a ready market among the traders and businessmen frequenting the taverns and coffee houses nearby.

St Faith's was the parish church of the Stationers' Company; its location deep within the stone-walled Cathedral was certainly convenient. Thousands of books started to arrive during the next two days (the Cathedral remained untouched by the fire until Tuesday, 4 September), and each stationer was probably allotted a special spot for his stock. There are no detailed lists, but some sense of the variety can be gleaned from the inventories of stationers and booksellers just before the fire. Thomas Driver, a bookbinder near the Bishop's Head in St Paul's Churchyard, had 24 Bibles of 'several sorts' valued at £7 4s, his tools, a cutting press and two ploughs (used for trimming the pages), three beating hammers, and a 'sett of letters', all valued at £2.[284] William Kendall had 12 small books, one Bible and one [New] Testament valued at 10s; and 5 lb of metal clasps for Almanacks.[285]

On Tuesday 4 September, Londoners were horrified to see St Paul's Cathedral alight. The fire blazed around the Cathedral precinct and ignited the scaffolding which had been installed for repairs to the tower; and as the wooden structure began to burn, the flames soared ever higher, reaching up to the roof itself. Rivulets of lead began to rain down on the walls, and, as the heat intensified, the leaded windows began to sag, bow and finally crack. The wind-driven sparks set other parts of the structure alight; and the roof lead, 'no lesse than six akers by measure', turned into a molten mass.[286] One onlooker saw 'the great beams and massy stones, with a great noise, fall on the pavement and break through into Faith's Church underneath'.[287]

It is difficult to imagine how the stationers and booksellers coped with the enormity of their losses, but the few personal accounts that do survive present a disturbing picture. Before the fire, Mrs Andrews had been responsible for distributing issues of the *London Gazette*. She had a long-term contract with Mr Newcome, a book supplier and printer, and was usually able to buy a fourth, if not a third, of the stock from his press. But on 12 November 1666 she was constrained to write to James Hicks, the postmaster, to explain that the next issue of the *Gazette* was 'now far off' because the fire had burned her goods and she had 'no clothes but those on her back'.[288] Mr Newcome had left town or was otherwise 'removed' and Hicks found himself with a large pile of Newcome's books in his care. As he explained to a friend on 12 November, this had 'put the book women into straits, and unless some

provision is made for them, they must leave him to dispose of the books as he can'. He added that the women 'run much hazard' by attending him in his temporary accommodation in the church-yard, 'where the stench of earth is offensive and unwholesome'; and he had great sympathy for Mrs Andrews, who for weeks had diligently observed the directions given about the *Gazette*, but had been unable to proceed because of Mr Newcome's curious be-haviour. Whether the shock of the fire had resulted in some kind of nervous collapse is unclear, but Hicks felt that he had to find some way round the problem, and planned to send Mrs Andrews to someone else as she was a 'discreet woman and deserved en-couragement'. He added that Mr Newcome 'behaves so strangely that others say they will sell his books no more, at hazard of their health, through all ways, and at such a distance.'[289]

Richard Royston lost his house and shop in Ivy Lane near St Paul's to the fire. He managed to find shop space within the precinct of St Bartholomew's Hospital, though these rooms were ill suited to his trade (*see* p. 47). As he explained in a letter to the King and Council, though he abhorred all thoughts of disloyalty he had been constrained to buy some unlicensed books because he was reduced to great extremity. 'In compassion to the losses sustained by his stationer', Charles ordered that Royston should receive £300 from the Treasury.[290] Many booksellers and stationers from the Royal Exchange moved into temporary accommodation at Gresham College. Ralph Smith a bookseller, took a space between the columns in the 'walk in the Greate Yard'; another bookseller, John Clark, had a small spot next to the gate at Broad Street; the stationer John Cade leased the site of the former Civil Law room and adjoining stable for £12 per annum on the under-standing that 'hee to leave itt in the same condition as he finds it', which is a little hard to comprehend! He later applied for extra room in the hayloft to accommodate his stock and permission to install a sink and reroute the pipework through the stable to the common sewer. Another stationer, William Lightfoote, erected a wooden shed in the cellar passage leading from the Quadrangle yard into Bishopsgate Street, and Edward Greene took a space in the Long Gallery (p. 50).[291]

A little more is known about Edward Greene in the years after the fire. By the time of his death in 1668, he had a dwelling

Still Life of Books by Charles Emmanuel Bizet d'Annonay (1633–1713).

house and shop in Fore Street, Cripplegate; a shop in the newly built Royal Exchange; and seven leasehold tenements in Grub Street. He must have salvaged some if not all of his stock at the time of the fire in order to trade at Gresham College, but when the probate inventory was compiled he had two separate trading interests: stationery at Fore Street; haberdashery at the Royal Exchange. It is quite likely that he had been active in both trades for many years, but it is also possible that he sustained particular losses to the stationery side of his business, which prompted a shift towards haberdashery. It is noticeable that the value of the haberdashery (£237 1s 6d) was five times more than his stationary stocks (£48 1s 10s), though it would be unwise to read too much into this since he might have invested in the haberdashery side of his business to restock his shop in the Exchange, or sold a lot of stationery in the months before his death. The Fore Street shop had a counter, with various boxes, book presses, shelves, 156 reams of paper of many kinds: demy, Dutch, 'pott', royal, gilt, 'horne' (presumably the paper backing for a horn book), 'fooles capp', 'Morless', 'flowre de luce', Venice and coloured. There were 18 bundles of brown paper, 8 dozen cards, 2,592 pieces of paste board,

Horn book, horn ink-pot and scriveners' knives, used to erase errors from parchment or vellum. The pounce pot contained powdered cuttle-fish bone or finely ground pumice, which was sprinkled over parchment to provide a smooth, grease-free surface for writing. The abrasive also helped to break up some of the surface fibres, making it more receptive to the ink. The pot has a dished top to receive any surplus powder.

a parcel of quills and pens, some pewter and 'leaden' standishes, some hard wax, pieces of vellum and parchment, and 20 shillings worth of printed books.[292] The list of papers is particularly interesting because paper was in such short supply after the fire that the stationers and printers were given royal dispensation to import as much as they could from the Continent. When Greene died the value of his estate was assessed at £638 1s 9d; his debts amounted to £1,338 18s 7d; and he had just 20 shillings of 'ready money' in his house.

The printer John Ogilby, who had lost £3,000 worth of reserved stock in the fire, obtained a licence to import 10,000 reams of printing paper from France, 'duty free, in such vessels as he can procure'. And Christopher Barker, the King's printer, gained permission to import 1,000 bales of paper, 'for carrying on His Majesty's business, having lost large quantities by the late fire, and the present scarcity rendering paper so dear'.[293] The scarcity of books and paper affected prices. On 2 October 1666 the Stationers decided to increase the price of psalters by an extra 16 shillings a quarter, psalms by an extra 6d each and primers by 20 shillings a gross. The prices for ABC books and horn books were unchanged.[294]

The Stationers' Company made provisions for the stocks of their members, and soon after the fire they managed to secure the use of St Bartholomew's Hall for a year, and hired several warehouses in and around Smithfield and St Bartholomew's Court.[295] There are various estimates of the losses sustained by the stationers, with some contemporaries (who were not members of the trade) suggesting a figure of £150,000, and John Evelyn upwards of £200,000, noting in his diary that the 'magazines of books, belonging to the Stationer[s] … were all consumed burning for a weeke following'.[296] The only reliable evidence comes from the Stationers and printers themselves. Cornelius Bee and partners, booksellers, assessed their losses in the fire at £13,000 for 1,300 copies of the *Critici Sacri*, which represented just a proportion of their stock.[297] The evidence from probate inventories suggests that many printers and stationers were able to resume their business quite quickly after the fire even though they had sustained heavy losses. George Hurlocke's shop and warehouse in Rood Lane in the parish of St Magnus the Martyr, at the north end of London

Bridge, was burnt. But after the fire he had moved to Bethnal Green (he had in addition seven leasehold properties in Thieving Lane in Westminster). When he died in 1668 he had 687 books in his shop, including 13 Bibles, 19 reams of paper, a parcel of books in 'quires & sticht', a 'sea Waggener' and five sea charts, as well as a cutting press, plough and cutting board, all valued at £39 7d. The warehouse had 14 books in folio valued at £9 3s, 10 folio bound sea books and 26 sea charts valued at £8 15s, two reams of waste paper, and books in quires of several sorts, the whole valued at £221 14s.4d.[298] James Crumpe. in the parish of St Bartholomew the Less, probably survived the worst events of the fire, though he must have sustained significant losses as a shareholder in the Stationers' Company. When he died in 1668 he had a vast stock in the warehouse and in a room over the kitchen, including 459 Bibles in different versions and languages, including Latin, English, Dutch and Welsh. There were dozens of primers; common prayer books; 389 Welsh 'service books in quires, 87 more sowed and gludd and 18 more bound and 12 large ones att – 20 shillings' and other theological texts; Greek and Latin grammars; 'children's books'; plain and gilt horn books; and parcels of cat-skin, calf-skin and turkey leather for bindings. Crumpe also had a large number of books 'abroad att Binding'.[299]

Some of the most important evidence, however, comes from the Stationers' Company Stock Book for the year August 1666 to September 1667, which provides a fairly detailed inventory of the 'English Stock' in the Treasurer's Warehouse printed 'for beginning a stock again'. It begins with the words: 'After the sad and never to bee forgotten Judgement by the fire which upon the 2d 3d 4th and 5th days of September 1666 destroyed the greatest part of this City, and in the Common calamity our Hall, Warehouses and stock of Bookes and other goods therein.' A long list running to several pages follows, arranged for the most part under subject headings such as 'psalters', 'almanacks' and so on. There were 1,608 reams of paper and 823,112 books, which included 48,000 English primers and 11,608 Scottish primers. The value of the books added since the fire came to £4,386 15s 6½d and the inventory as a whole was assessed at £11,900 2s 8½d.[300]

Tallow chandler

'Some have been burnt by ... setting candles under shelves; some by leaving candles near their beds; some by snuffs of candles... If you will use candle all night, let your candlestick be a pot of water brim-full, and set it where it shall stand; then light a candle, and stick a great pin in the bottom ... and let it slowly into the water, and it will burn all night without danger.'
—*Broadside*, 1645 [301]

During the 1650s and early 1660s Anthony Joyce, a tallow chandler in Green Dragon Court, Cow Lane, near Newgate Market, held the main contract for the supply of candles to St Bartholomew's Hospital. Joyce was married to Kate, a cousin of Samuel Pepys; so in 1662 they decided to collaborate in a small business venture. Pepys agreed to buy 'tallow of him at a low rate for the King'; the profits were to go to Pepys's brother Tom and 'his kinswomen' for a dowry.[302] But the enterprise quickly faltered. Almost at once Joyce asked Pepys for extra funds; then on 16 June 1662 when Pepys inspected Joyce's tallow and compared it with the softer, whiter, Irish tallow which he had just procured for the Navy Board he was troubled by the difference and was unsure whether 'it be or no a fault'.[303] The relationship became rather strained. When Joyce made a decision to 'leave off his trade' and turn to innkeeping in January 1666, Pepys 'did advise against [it], for he is a man will know how to live idle, and employment he is fit for none.'[304] Then came the fire. On 5 September as Pepys wandered through the City, he made his way to Newgate Market, 'all burned – and seen Anthony Joyces house in fire'.[305] On 14 September Kate Joyce informed Pepys that her husband had lost £104 per annum but had seven houses left in Newgate.[306] The tallow-chandlery business was evidently affected, however, because eight days later the governors of St Bartholomew's Hospital were informed that Joyce had lost everything and could no longer fulfil the orders for candles.[307] His contract was discharged, but his losses had a lasting effect. Two of Joyce's properties were leased from the Hospital and Joyce was unable to pay the rents after the fire.[308] The tallow-chandlery side of the business passed to his brother William, who as a result of the fire had moved to Covent Garden, 'the trade being come that end of the town'; and Pepys heard that Kate and her husband had tired of their new occupation as innkeepers, and were keen to leave it. Joyce asked for Pepys's help in securing some kind of office work, but Pepys noted in his *Diary* that 'I know none the fool is fit for.'[309] Things went from bad to worse, and two years later Anthony Joyce 'went sober and out of doors in the morning to Islington' and threw himself into a pond behind the White Lion inn. Fortunately he was seen by a 'poor woman', who raised the alarm, and he was pulled out by 'some people binding up Hay in the barn there, and set on his head and got to life'. Joyce was recognized by a passer-by and carried home. His wife and friends were notified. When Pepys heard the news he hurried over to their house at the end of the working day to find Joyce 'in his sick bed (I never was at their house, this Inne before), very sensible in discourse and thankful for my kindnesses to him; but his breath rattled in his throate and they did lay pigeons at his feet … and all despair of him, and with good reason'.[310] Joyce explained that he had attempted suicide because he had forgotten to 'serve God as he ought since he came into his new employment [and had lost his reason due to] his great losses in the fire'. He died the following day. Pepys made arrangements with his widow to secure some of his portable goods and valuables since the property of suicides was forfeit to the Crown.[311]

The governors of St Bartholomew's Hospital had to find new suppliers for their candles. The contract was taken up by Brian Ayliss in the Old Bailey and John Gale in Cursitor Lane, who were able to profit from Joyce's misfortune as they lived just outside the burnt area. The order was split between them: each was asked to make 40 dozen (480) candles at the going rate of 5 shillings per dozen.[312] It seems that there was a significant increase

in the volume of candles supplied to the hospital immediately after the fire, which perhaps accounts for the need to have two suppliers rather than one. The ledgers show an annual expenditure in 1665 of £37 3s, but in the three months after the fire the Hospital spent £28 8s on candles, and when the next set of accounts were produced in April 1667 they included another payment for candles of £9 12s.[313] This increase is not easily explained, though it is possible that more candles were needed to cater for the influx of tradesmen and shopkeepers who had taken up residence within the hospital precincts (*see* p. 48).[314] It is also possible that the Hospital harboured many of the injured, but sadly there are no surviving records of treatments, nor any evidence for medical practice in the Hospital accounts during this period.

Nothing more is known about Ayliss's work, but John Gale seems to have had a slight edge on his competitor since he was personally acquainted with one of the governors.[315] It was perhaps for this reason that Gale's contract was extended, though he seems to have been a rather tricky character. In October 1665 he was reprimanded for his abusive language and behaviour when the wardens of the Tallow-Chandlers' Company tried to search his workshop; for this offence and for refusing to pay his search money he was summoned before the Lord Mayor 'to answer for his contempt'.[316] This misdemeanour had little effect on Gale's career, and he continued to supply candles to the Hospital for several years.

Lighting in the home and street was a carefully regulated affair. In 1662, for the maintenance of the highways and sewers and for the 'preventing of the Mischiefe of Fire that may come by Negligence, Treason or otherwise', Parliament ordered that all houses with a street frontage must suspend a lanthorn in front of their property.[317] The large cresset lamps and lanthorns were lit at prescribed times and in particular months of the year (1 March to 1 October) 'from such time as it shall grow dark until nine of the clock in the evening upon pain to forfeit the sum of one shilling for every default'. The lighting levels were also controlled, and householders were ordered to buy candles of 'twelve in the pound' or greater. Candles posed a considerable fire risk. On 2 March 1665 Pepys was horrified to discover that two of his serving maids had slept fully clothed with their bedding next to the fire, and a 'candle burning all night'.[318]

(*above*) This trade token was issued by Anthony and Katherine Joyce. The obverse is inscribed ANTHONEY·IOYCE with three stags; and the reverse has the address AT·HOBORN·CONDED [conduit] and their combined initials – 'I' over 'A' and 'K'. Katherine, née Fenner, was a cousin of Samuel Pepys. Anthony Joyce abandoned his trade as a tallow chandler to become an innkeeper; this token might have been issued to advertise his new business venture.

(*left*) Cressets, ironwork baskets often mounted on a pole and filled with hemp soaked in rosin or pitch, were used for street lighting.

It is impossible to know how many candles the average household consumed, since much would depend on the location, size and configuration of the property, the number and positions of the windows, the proximity of other structures and the occupant's wealth, health and livelihood. The tiny houses in back alleys, facing onto long narrow passageways and overshadowed by the jettied upper storeys, would have been in semi-permanent darkness; and light levels were further reduced because windows were often obscured by latticework, shutters and awnings. There were frequent grumbles about the lack of light, and about the various nuisances caused by neighbours blocking light to the detriment of trade and well-being.

The candlemakers' trade was split into two distinct branches, the makers of tallow candles and the makers of wax candles; but, apart from the difference in the raw material, which was reflected in the quality of the candle and its price, both trades employed similar techniques and used very similar sets of tools. Although Londoners were well aware of the distinction, the generic term 'candlemaker' is generally used in contemporary documents, so in the absence of any other detailed evidence it is impossible to know what kinds of candles were produced or supplied. Candlemakers' inventories include a wide range of tools and equipment. There were parcels of cotton and cord for the wicks, and vats, tubs and casks for the tallow, which was supplied in different grades and qualities in hardened blocks and in semi-liquid form. Mary Lee's workhouse in Charing Cross, for instance, had 75 lb of hard tallow, 21 cwt of semi-liquid tallow, and 350 cwt of coarse black tallow.[319] Some inventories include supplies of pitch, red lead,

brimstone and rosin (a type of resin made from the distillation of crude turpentine oleoresin), which were used to make torches of the kind used for street lighting. Every inventory includes a chopping block, which was used to cut the wicks to the desired length. The block, which rested across the workman's knees, was pierced for a wooden peg or stock, against which the lengths of wick were measured. There were tools to break up the blocks of tallow for melting, and fire forks and scrapes for raking the furnace. There were baskets and tubs for straining and rendering the molten tallow and an instrument called a ladder, which rested over the rim of the tallow tub to support the strainer. The candle moulds were made from copper or lead and took the form of a tank with two lateral bars of iron which could be levered up and down with a crank to coat the wick with layers of tallow or wax. Wax chandlers used a chafing dish to melt the wax and a candle wheel to create an even coat on the wick as it was drawn through the molten wax.[320]

Although the scale of production varied from business to business, tallow and wax chandlers seem to have been retail manufacturers. Some had one room which doubled-up as a workhouse and shop, while others had the luxury of a separate shop with one or more working rooms nearby. The shop spaces were equipped with a counter, assorted boxes and baskets, scales with sets of iron and brass weights, mops, brooms and lanthorns, and it is likely that the candles were arranged in packages according to weight, shape, size and price. Mary Lee had 444 new candles and 46 'broken candles' in her shop; James Jeater had 24 dozen 'ready made'; and Henry Jordan had a vast stock of 7,200 candles in his cellar workhouse.

In 1664 Samuel Pepys started to burn 'wax candles in my closet at the office to try the change and to see whether the smoke offends like that of tallow candles'.

Tobacconist

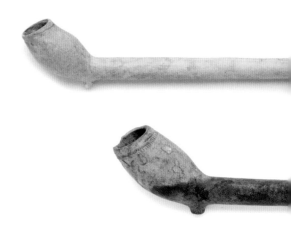

'from henceforth noe person whatsoever shall take a Pipe of Tobacco or absent himselfe from the Table dureing the sitting of this Court without licence under the Penalty of 12d to be paid to the use of the Fellowship.'—*Carmens' Company*, 3 February 1670[321]

Smoking was an obvious and ever-present fire hazard, but the habit was so well entrenched that several livery companies tried to curb the practice 'for the prevention of any danger and inconvenience … that may hereafter happen'. The anti-smoking policies were first restricted to the parlour, the large private members' room adjoining the common hall: in November 1657 the Drapers' Company forbade anyone to smoke in this room 'uppon paine of forfeture of twoe shillings six pence for every pipe so take or smoked'. The fines were to be set aside for the use of the poor.[322] The Cordwainers introduced even tighter rules: on 18 July 1665 members were told that 'noe tobacco shall for the tyme to come be bought at the charge of this Company att any tyme hereafter'; no one should smoke in the Great Parlour or Court Parlour and the few pipes provided at the Company's charge were reserved for the sole use of members.[323] Many other companies adopted similar rules and regulations but the habit evidently persisted because the Carmens' Company were compelled to stop members leaving the room for a smoke during committee meetings.

   If smoking was frowned upon in some circles, it was actively encouraged in others. The public rooms in taverns and coffee houses were stocked with pipes and smoking accoutrements, and some coffee house proprietors sold tobacco over the counter. Apothecaries suggested that powdered tobacco leaves killed lice and other vermin, and tobacco smoke 'injected in the manner of a clyster, is of efficacy in stoppages of the bowels, for destroying

James I, in his 1604 *Counterblaste to Tobacco*, wrote that men should be ashamed to sit at table 'tossing of *Tobacco* pipes, and puffing of the smoke of *Tobacco* one to another, making the filthy smoke and stinke thereof, to exhale athwart the dishes, and infect the aire … [it is a] custome lothsome to the eye, hatefull to the Nose, harmefull to the braine, dangerous to the Lungs, and in the blacke stinking fume thereof, neerest resembling the horrible Stigian smoke of the pit that is bottomelesse.'

snail worms' and even for the recovery of 'persons apparently drowned'.[324] Londoners were actively encouraged to smoke during times of plague, and in 1665 Samuel Pepys bought a roll of tobacco to 'smell and chaw', which helped to calm his nerves.[325]

The volume of tobacco imports into London was so great that one contemporary suggested that 'whole ship loads … are brought over to our nation, that the Custome thereof is sufficient to maintaine a Navy or an Army'.[326] The smoking habit spawned several subsidiary trades with their own specialisms: there were tobacco merchants, brokers and factors, tobacco sellers, tobacco pressers, tobacco cutters and tobacco pipe makers. Some had very little in the way of materials and stock, while others had a quite considerable business. Rowland Bill in Norton Folgate occupied just one room, with a bed, curtain and valence, a few household goods valued at £8, a parcel of tobacco pipes and tobacco clay at £5, his wearing apparel and working tools, all valued at just £20 10s.[327] In contrast, the pipe maker John Martin in St Giles Cripplegate had 29 moulds and 6 screws in his workshop, 20 tuns 'in Tobacco Clay' valued at £24, and 2,880 tobacco pipes at 18 pence the gross valued at £1 10s; with some chaldrons of coal, a wooden grater and other 'lumber for ye trade'.[328]

The wooden pipe moulds were made in a huge number of shapes and sizes for 'smooth' pipes; 'gleased' pipes; pipes with short, medium and long shanks; and pipes with or without a heel at the foot of the bowl. The tools included a 'shanking board' used for rolling long strips of clay to form the shank, moulding wires to pierce the shank, and a trimmer to produce a smooth, burnished surface.

One half of a two-part wooden tobacco pipe mould, with longitudinal grooves on the sides and a pair of peg holes for keying the two sections of the mould together. One corner, cut on the diagonal and aligned with the rim of the pipe bowl, probably served to hold a 'stopper' to shape the internal wall of the bowl. The shape suggests that it was made between c.1580 and 1610. It is the only mould of its type known to exist. It was found on the Thames foreshore.

(*left*) Tobacco rasp and box.
(*below*) Carved to imitate a roll of twisted tobacco and painted for ornamental effect, this late-seventeenth-century sign hung outside a tobacconist's shop in Gresham Street.

Tobacco pressers were used to smooth the tobacco leaf into sheets, and a special engine with a crank-driven mechanism controlling the rotation of the drum and cutting wheel produced tobacco in fine or coarser grades for smoking. William Stackhouse had two press rooms with 24 old cutting wheels and 11 presses, a separate cutting room with an engine and six standing presses, and some cut tobacco in the warehouse at the back of the yard.[329]

Robert Travis, tobacco seller, had a house by 'ye postern gate' in Watling Street and a 'power mill' in Crayford, Kent. The Watling Street property was destroyed in the fire, but within the year Travis was back in business. When his house was appraised for probate in September 1667 the shop stock included 2,737 lb of Virginia tobacco, one hogshead of 'neat' tobacco (a hogshead held between 500 and 1,300 lb), quantities of cut tobacco at 5d, 10d and 16d a pound, and 26 lb of Spanish tobacco, three reams of paper, 12 tubs, 7 boxes, 1,728 tobacco pipes, an engine, two presses and other trade items, the whole lot valued at £189 10d. His debts amounted to £463, but his overall estate was assessed at £689 17s 2d.[330]

Trunkmaker

'Paid for three Trunckes to put the
Companyes writeings which were taken
out of the Treasury in the late fire.'—
Goldsmiths' Company, 16 November 1666[331]

Trunks and chests are the most frequently listed item of furniture
in seventeenth-century household inventories, and they survive in
greater numbers because they were relatively cheap, portable, not
subject to the vicissitudes of fashion and had multifarious uses.
There was scarcely a house, great or small, without a trunk or
two. They appear in almost every room: in garrets and cellars, in
bedchambers, parlours and closets, in shops and warehouses; they
were used for short- and long-term storage, and made ideal receptacles for clothing, personal effects, papers, valuables, tools and
goods. They were made in a wide variety of materials and sizes,
though most were constructed from wood overlaid with leather,
strengthened with metal straps, studs and corners. Inventories
describe 'old trunks', 'empty trunks', leather trunks, and trunks
with coverings of canvas and red velvet. Paper-covered trunks
are also mentioned; these were a source of concern to the Society
of Trunkmakers, who submitted a petition to the Leathersellers'
Company on 4 April 1665 about the several 'Abuses ... daily
committed in their said trade contrary to the lawes and ordinances
of this society and to the great descredit of his Majesties subjects
by which if not timely prevented will utterly undoe their trade of
trunkmakeing by recovering trunks with paper in stead of leather
and putting on leather hinges in stead of iron with other false
doings not fitt to be practised.'[332]

   Thousands of trunks were used to convey goods to safety in
the fire. Many were lost or damaged, but even when the trunks
themselves survived, the padlocks or one or all of the sets of keys
were burnt or missing.[333] This problem was faced by the Cutlers in
their temporary lodgings at the 'Beare neere Bridge foote', so they

ordered a new chest with four keys for their writings and treasure; one key to be kept with the master and one each for the three assistant masters.[334] New trunks were also needed to house goods which had been grabbed in haste. On 18 September 1666 it was agreed that the master and wardens of the Pewterers' Company 'should provide a couple of sea chests to secure ye Books deeds Records or whatsoever writeings belong to ye Company, which through ye rate of ye late terrible fire are now in ye custodie of Mr William Rawlins loose as he conveyed them from ye hall'.[335] After a while the storage of Company goods in members' houses became something of a problem and there were several demands that items 'might be removed'. The long-suffering Benjamin Albin had to wait until 1671, when he finally complained to the Skinners about the 'temporary' storage of goods lodged in his house, asking that they might be removed 'and be disposed of' to some other convenient place, and a box or chest purchased 'as will hold them'.[336]

The trunkmakers who managed to salvage their own stocks in the fire, or who lived and worked beyond the fire-damaged parts of the City, would have had massive orders for repairs and replacements. The only known surviving inventory for a trunkmaker seems to be for Thomas Pope, a leatherseller, who lived in King Street, Westminster, in the parish of St Martin-in-the-Fields. This inventory, appraised on 6 January 1672, is quite detailed and provides some indication of the scale of his business and stock-in-trade, which amounted to 522 trunks, 33 portmanteaus and 31 close-stools. The stock was split across two sites. The King Street house had two garrets, one containing two trunks, three 'great' tubs, some canvas hangings, Russia leather and seal skins, a box of candles, some glue, 30 glasses with 'leaden screws', and a pair of andirons and fire irons. The warehouse 'up one paire of stairs' held 205 trunks 'great and small'; 15 close-stools, 21 portmanteaus and 24 buckets, all valued at £152 17s 9d. In the shop were a further 191 trunks of various sizes, 23 close-stools, some nails, locks and other lumber, valued at £48 1s 6d. The yard and shed contained 84 split deal planks, 400 inch boards, 4,000 half-inch boards and more lumber at £27. The second site was a shop in Whitehall which contained 126 trunks, 16 close-stools, 12 portmanteaus, and more nails and locks valued at £63 1s. Pope had two further properties in Southwark. His whole stock and assets were valued at £495 13s 3d.

This seventeenth-century coffer or till, covered with embossed and gilded leather, has a hinged lid and falling front to serve as a writing desk. The lid opens to reveal a shallow box compartment lined with linen and plain paper (a later repair). Behind the hinged front are six drawers, known as 'tills', with green ribbon tags for handles.

Turner

'and I to Tower-street, and there met the
fire Burning three or four doors beyond
Mr. Howells; whose goods, poor man
(his trayes and dishes, Shovells &c.,
were flung all along Tower-street in the
kennels, and people working therewith
from one end to the other), the fire
coming on in that narrow street, on
both sides, with infinite fury.'
—*Samuel Pepys*, 4 September 1666[337]

Richard Howell was well known to Samuel Pepys: they were
both employed by the Navy Board, for which Howell was
principal turner; they were close neighbours, attended the same
church, and on occasion met socially.[338] On 3 December 1661
Pepys received some of Mr Howell's 'turned work to file papers
on', which he thought 'very handsome'.[339] A few months later he
received an invitation to dine with Mr Howell and some friends
of his, 'officers of the tower', at the Mitre Tavern. But when Pepys
arrived in the room that had been hired for the occasion, he
found 'at least twelve or more persons and knew not the face of
any of them, and so I went down again; and though I met Mr.
Yong the upholster, yet I would not be persuaded to stay, but
went away. And walked to the Exchange and up and down, and
was very hungry; and from thence home – where I understand
Mr. Howell was come for me to go thither, but I am glad I was
not at home.'[340] Pepys subsequently dined with Mr Howell and
two officers of the East India Company.[341]

A few years later he borrowed Mr Howell's horse so that he
could travel to Erith, 'it being a horrible cold frost to go by
water'.[342] In June 1665, in his office garden, Pepys had such a long
and profitable discussion with Richard Howell about the corrupt
practices of the Navy paymaster that as soon as Howell and the

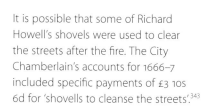

rest of the party had gone he rushed to write it all down so that 'it be for ever remembered'.[344]

From his diary entry for the 4 September 1666, it is clear that Pepys was extremely sorry to see Richard Howell's desperate situation. The more so, perhaps, because Howell was ill, living, as he himself put it in his will of 10 December 1660, in a 'vale of misery'. The trail of dishes, trays and shovels strewn along the kennel (an open drain or gutter at the edge or middle of the street) provides a graphic picture of the emergency and the desperate effort to save as much stock as possible. Although later evidence suggests that Howell did manage to remove most, if not all, of his goods to safety, it came at great personal cost, for nine days later he was dead. A memorandum inserted at the end of the will states that he was 'late of the parish of St Margaret Patens, London' and had died within the Tower where he had sought sanctuary.[345]

On 29 September 1667 Richard Howell's property was appraised for the Orphans' Court; listed among the debts owed by the testator are entries for 'carmen and porters'; 'more Carmen'; and finally 'other charges in the tyme of ye fire', which amounted to £16 5s 8d. The inventory also refers to the ground of his dwelling house 'burnt downe' in Tower Street, which was valued at £100; to a house in Savage Garden in Tower Hill occupied by his widow;[346] to another large property and garden in Greenwich; and to a part-share in the ship called the *Royal Katherine*. The Savage Garden property, which was probably acquired immediately after

It is possible that some of Richard Howell's shovels were used to clear the streets after the fire. The City Chamberlain's accounts for 1666–7 included specific payments of £3 10s 6d for 'shovells to cleanse the streets'.[343]

On 21 November 1660 Samuel Pepys wrote in his diary: 'This morning my Cosen Thomas Pepys the Turner sent me a cup of Lignum vitae for a token.'

the fire, comprised two garrets, a hall, a parlour, a widow's chamber, a dining chamber, a kitchen, cellar and vaults. The inventory suggests that a substantial part was given over to the store of goods: one of the garrets was stuffed full of 360 shovels and 'spade trees', with remnants of 'striped stuffe', old coverlets, six leather hides, a bed, a mattress, a trunk and other lumber; and the hall held 6 dozen water scoops valued at 42s, 20 old shovels and spades, with some bandileer collars, three leather bottles and eight small brass lamps. The cellar held 4,946 lb of boxwood; 17,935¼ lb of 'corn wood'; 716 lb of 'greenewood'; 728 lb of 'speckled' wood; 12,320 lb of *lignum vitae*; some 'lanthorne trees, heads and bottoms'; and a beam scale and weights. The whole cellar stock was valued at £80 9s 10d.

The entry for *lignum vitae* is particularly significant because Pepys kept a note in his private papers which suggested that Howell had overcharged for supplies of *lignum vitae* – a tropical hardwood used extensively for rigging tackle and blocks.[347]

Upholsterer

'Twoe of the patterns for chairs presented by the said Mr Veamer (one att 10s the other att 13s a chaire) were best liked. And he had order to make up three dozen.'—*Coopers' Company*, 29 September 1670[348]

One of the most striking features of London household interiors in the immediate pre- and post-fire period is the use of the colour green for upholstery and other soft furnishings. Almost every home had green rugs, green curtains, green cushions and green chairs. Just occasionally the monotony was broken with a little white, grey, sad (a dull or neutral colour), and increasingly red and blue. The stationer Edward Greene had four rugs, eight curtains and a valence of 'mouse coloured' perpetuana – possibly a reference to their faded and worn condition, rather than their true

A canvas cushion embroidered on the upper side in polychrome silks with a pastoral scene. Mid-seventeenth century.

colour.[349] William Lane, a clothworker in Bartholomew Close, had a 'Greene Chamber' with rooms named according to the colour of the hangings: 'Pintado', a printed or painted flecked fabric from India, and 'Purple'.[350] His wife's chamber was furnished with a tester of 'yellow sarsnet' (sarcenet silk).[351] It is noticeable that merchant taylors, clothworkers and drapers tended to have a wider variety of textile furnishings, and in these households the usual green carpets and curtains were more often than not embellished with 'Irish stich and silke fringe'.[352] Where detailed information is provided, households generally had a mixture of new, old and second-hand furnishings; the older items naturally relegated to the garret or workshop for the use of the servants and apprentices.

The fabrics varied enormously, from very cheap coarse canvas and buckram (hemp) to pricey figured or embroidered silks, satins, tapestry and velvets with hangings and curtains to match. Almost every house had soft furnishings in serge, a durable woollen cloth with a diagonal weave; and 'striped stuff', a worsted with parallel threads, sometimes in a printed version, was the fabric of choice for the less important rooms and for poorer households.

The choice of colour for household furnishings was largely a matter of personal taste and cost, but there were changes in fashion too, and by the early 1670s almost as many households had red furnishings as green. For some the *alamode* switch from green to red was relatively simple, as many chairs and stools had loose covers. So, when Samuel Pepys decided it was time for a change, he was able to alter the 'chairs in my chamber, and set them above in the red room, they being Turkey work: and so put their green covers upon those that were above, not so handsome'.[353] The process of switching the covers was made all the easier because the open edges were fastened with tapes or, more commonly, hooks and eyes (*see* p. 130). The reference to turkey work is particularly interesting because this distinctive tough, colourful cloth was one of the most popular upholstery fabrics in London – according to one petition 'there were yearly made and vended in the Kingdom' about 60,000 turkey-work chairs, a staggering number even allowing for exaggeration.[354]

The turkey work used for upholstery, curtains and cushions was very much a product of domestic manufacture, but London household inventories also include references to the genuine article.

Detail from a late-seventeenth-century wall or bed hanging of twilled cotton and linen embroidered in red wools or 'crewels'. The complexity of the design is unusual. Even rarer is the inclusion of four coats of arms: the City of London, the Merchant Taylors' Company (shown in reverse), and those of the Escott and Hastings families. It is possible that the hanging was made to commemorate a link by marriage or business partnership between two London Merchant Taylor families. Other features include various biblical scenes: Adam and Eve, Abraham and Isaac, David and Abigail, Esther and Ahasuerus, Daniel in the Lions' den, the Nativity and Susannah and the Elders.

Among the long list of imports in the London customs accounts for 1662–3 are 2,343 Turkish carpets, valued at £3,574 10s. Each carpet was priced at £1 10s. In the next set of customs records, for the year 1668–9, the overall volume of carpet imports had trebled, with 1,033 'turkey carpets' and – a new addition – 8,350 pieces of 'striped' carpet.[355] Whether this increase was due to the fire, or was just part of a general fashion trend and greater consumer wealth is impossible to know. What is clear is that London upholsterers had bulk orders from the City institutions that had lost all of their chairs and soft furnishings in the fire. The Grocers placed an order with Mr Steed for a 'dozen high Turkey worke chaires at 10 shillings apiece;[356] the Mercers bought eight turkey-work chairs for 7s 6d apiece, and another dozen at 12s apiece.[357] The turkey work used for upholstery was almost certainly of English make. In 1670, when the Coopers' Company needed to order some new upholstery they asked for two quotes from Samuell Veamer and 'one … Jackson'. Both men brought in some fabric samples for the chair cushions, and after some deliberation the contract went to Mr Veamer, who happened to be a freeman of the Company, for two different styles of cushion in turkey work, one priced at 10 shillings and the other at 13 shillings a chair. Veamer was asked to make up 3 dozen, 18 in one pattern and the rest in the other, for the use of the Great Parlour.[358] At the same time, the Goldsmiths placed an order for a dozen turkey-work chairs, 'which were bought after the late fier' at a bargain price of £5 8s;[359] and two years later the Pewterers acquired '16 new Turkey-Work chaires' at 13s apiece.[360] The variation in pricing was probably due to differences in chair size and the amount and quality of upholstery required, rather than the bargaining skills of the upholster and client.

London shops continued to sell all kinds of turkey-work fabrics for upholstery and soft furnishings. In 1670 the draper John Young had 43 turkey carpets and three Persian 'stript' carpets in his shop, valued at £109 10s, with 234 turkey-work 'backs and seates', five old seats and two backs at £66 13s.[361] In the same year, William Ridges's (*see* p. 86) stock included 398 Turkey carpets old and new; 3,091 ells of new and secondhand tapestry hangings with and without silk fringing; 260 'skinns of old and new lether Carpets'; 10 dozen turkey-work backs and seats for chairs; two upholstered

A cream satin coverlet lined with red silk, embroidered with silver-gilt thread, cord and silver purl (laid over padding), trimmed with vandyked silver-gilt bobbin lace. In the centre are the arms of Sir Robert Abdy who was created Baronet in 1660. Sir Robert married Catherine, the daughter of Alderman Sir John Gayer, in 1643.

cushions for couches; several odd pieces of turkey work; 18 fine turkey-work chairs; several more odd remnants and lumber, all valued at £1,023 6s 4d. There were more tapestry hangings and other furnishing items elsewhere.[362] The appraisers were careful to draw a clear distinction between 'turkey' and turkey work in order to distinguish the imported article from the home-made product.

One of the most important parts of the upholsters' trade was to supply soft furnishings for the bedroom, including cushions, bolsters and mattresses. London household inventories include many types of mattress, which varied from the more expensive feather fillings; to the middle-priced flock – either tufts of wool and cotton waste or pieces of unspun sheep's wool; to hemp or straw. The covering materials were usually canvas or a robust woven linen called tick, which was strong enough to keep the sharp feathers from poking through the fabric. Mattresses were probably used to protect vulnerable items from damage in the rush to escape the fire, either as a lining for a cart or rolled around a few personal possessions. When Peter Garretson's inventory was drawn up in 1667, all he had apart from his wearing apparel were 'several odd thinges' and a feather mattress and bolster.[363]

The upholster William Soule, in Cloth Fair, near St Bartholomew's Hospital, had a lot of bedding materials in stock. One of the three garrets contained a bedstead, a mattress, a white rug, a pair of old pillows, a pair of grey curtains, a bundle of window curtains, and – rather suprisingly – a still, possibly used for the distillation of dyestuffs. The other two were stacked with items directly associated with his trade, including: a beam scale and weights, 211¾ cwt of 'mill flocks' – presumably offcuts of waste from a woollen or cotton mill; 350 lb of feathers and a parcel of 'old tukes' (ticking) and 3 cwt of coarse tew (or tow – a blend of hemp and flax), used for coarse sheeting and upholstery linings. Next to the dining room was the 'Cleavers roome' containing seven pieces of old valance, a couple of pictures, one hanging shelf, a pair of grates, andirons and other hearth furniture. There were two warehouses, one seemingly set behind the other. The larger of the two held four feather beds, nine flock beds and bolsters, four pillows, 29 rugs in various sizes, six pairs of blankets, 14 sets of curtains and valences, and six turkey-work chairs. The smaller warehouse held six turkey-work chairs, 28 featherbeds, bolsters,

two parcels of blankets, five pillows, 29 rugs, nine pairs of striped curtains and valences, a parcel of ticks, other 'stript stuffe' and a parcel of skins. The shop stock, valued at £86 1s, held 'several' turkey carpets, valued at £14; a parcel of serge remnants, at £10; various kinds of ticking, at £22; some printed 'stuffe', at £14; strings of silk and worsted, at £2 1s; and a few more remants of cloth, at £22; together with some shelves, a table and other lumber, £2. Another room next to the shop contained more beds and mattresses, a rug, a blanket, four chairs and stools, an old table, carpet and 'old hangings about the roome'. The total sum of inventory was assessed at £860 10d.[364]

A small fragment of seventeenth-century carpet from Turkey and 'back-stool' chair covered in English turkey work with the date 1649 worked into the design.

Virginal-maker

'[The] River full of lighter[s] and boats
taking in goods, and good goods
swimming in the water; and only, I
observed that hardly one lighter or boat
in three that had the goods of a house,
but there was a pair of virginalls in it.'
—*Samuel Pepys*, 2 September 1666[365]

London was a renowned centre for virginal-making. This
instrument, signed 'JACOBUS WHITE FECIT 1656', was made by a
member of one of the most important virginal-making families in
seventeenth-century England. It was made at a time when domestic
music-making had reached new heights of popularity, spurring one
contemporary to suggest that 'such as have any naturall ability and
fitnesse to Musick be Encouraged and Instructed therein'.[366] More
and more Londoners acquired musical instruments to play in the
comfort of their homes, 'chos[ing] rather to fidle at home, then to
goe out and be knockt on the head abroad'.[367] But domestic music-
making could prove a trial, as Samuel Pepys discovered when Mrs
Temple 'after dinner fell to play on the harpsicon till she tired
everybody, [so] that I left the house without taking leave, and no
creature left standing by her to hear her'.[368]

James White was the third generation of his family to make
virginals. Like his father Thomas, he was admitted as a freeman
of the Joiners' Company. He was resident in Old Jewry in the
spring of 1666 and must have lost his property when the street
was consumed by fire.[369] Whether he returned to this location or
moved elsewhere is unclear, but he clearly had sufficient resources
to resume his trade; he perhaps had time to remove his stock and
household goods to safety. At some point White joined forces
with Ralph Dallam, an organ maker, a partnership that continued
until Dallam's death in 1672. It is difficult to determine the precise
nature of their collaboration, but the association must have been

This instrument is constructed from oak, pine, spruce, cedar, popular, beech and boxwood; the keys are inlaid with ivory, oak and walnut. Much of the original painted decoration has been lost. The compass is BB – c3, 50 notes, with an additional jackslot for the C key.[370]

mutually beneficial, not least in reducing some of the costs in running an independent business and setting up as a sole trader. White completed two organ commissions after Dallam's death: one for Greenwich parish church and the other for Christ's Hospital; yet in Dallam's will he is given the title 'virginal maker'.[371]

Pepys's comment about the numbers of virginals rescued from the fire is interesting because relatively few keyboard instruments are included in London household inventories at this time. Perhaps Pepys was inclined to exaggeration, but, even if he was correct, were they actually 'virginals'? Virginals and harpsichords have a broadly similar shape, and as all of the instruments carried away from the flames must have been closed and piled up with other goods, it would have been very difficult for Pepys to tell them apart. The differences are so subtle that John Playford, in his *Musick's hand-maide … for the Virginals or Harpsycon*, drew the reader's attention to the difference, remarking that a virginal is 'strung with one course of strings; the Harpsichord with two or more, and is fuller and louder'.[372]

Though little is known about James White's business, a probate inventory for a Thomas White of St Giles Cripplegate, dated 2 March 1664, has survived.[373] Could this be the father of James and Thomas White junior or another member of the family? Thomas White senior was made free of the Joiners' Company in 1621 and it is possible that he moved away from Old Jewry to allow his son James to take over the business. The appraisers do not give the occupation of the deceased, but the stock is suggestive of a virginal-maker's trade and includes links, cord and packthread, fuller's earth and sand, rosin, tags and nails, white and brown paper, size (both white and black), red, white and black lead, red ochre, linseed oil, turpentine and varnish, glue, green copperas, verdigris, Spanish brown and 'small quantities of other colours', as well as 'Engoy wood and deal boards'. Virginals were always painted, usually on the inside of the coffered lid, the soundboard and case front. The two surviving instruments by James White are both embellished with embossed papers, so it is possible that the white and brown paper in the inventory was intended for a similar purpose.

The second inventory, appraised on 26 April 1661, for John Hayward in the parish of St Helen's Bishopsgate, is unequivocally that of a virginal maker.[374] The garret contained a parcel of planes, chisels and 'edge tooles' small and great, with two old and empty chests, three brass moulds, three benches and other lumber. There was 'one Virginall frame' in the dining room, but the shop had three benches, a settle bed, five cedar planks, a rubbing stone, three glue pots, two iron ½ cwt weights, four handsaws and a bowsaw. Also in the shop was the lease of a mortgaged house in Bishopsgate Street, which had been paid off, as well as some working clothes in linen and wool. The entire household contents were valued at £37 2s 8d. John Hayward's son took over the family business. On 4 April 1668 Samuel Pepys visited Charles Hayward's workshop, noting in his diary:

> Up betimes, and by coach towards White Hall, and took Aldgate Street in my way, and there called upon one Hayward, that makes virginals, and did there like of a little espinette (spinet), and will have him finish it for me: for I had a mind to a small harpsicho, but his takes up less room.[375]

Watchmaker

'But Lord, to see how much of my folly and childishnesse hangs upon me still, that I cannot forbear carrying my watch in my hand in the coach all this afternoon, and seeing what-a-clock it is 100 times. And am apt to think with myself: how could I be so long without out one.'—*Samuel Pepys*, 13 May 1665[376]

By the end of the seventeenth century, some 4,000 people were employed in the capital's watchmaking industry and London was one of the leading horological centres in Europe. Clocks and watches were prized possessions and Pepys was clearly delighted to receive a watch as a present in 1665. The following year he purchased a 'minute' watch, and this was soon swapped for an up-graded astronomical timepiece 'with many motions'.[377] Inventories show that large clocks and the smaller portable 'larums' (alarm clocks) were generally installed in the dining room, passageway or kitchen; and watches are listed under the heading 'plate', though they are seldom described or individually valued.

Some of the large clocks in livery company halls were rescued from the fire; the only suggestion of damage comes from the Plumbers' accounts, which include a payment to the clockmaker Mr John George for repair.[378] How individual makers fared in the immediate post-fire period is difficult to assess, though it is certain that many of those living and working in Blackfriars, near St Paul's Cathedral, in Cheapside and in various locations around the Royal Exchange must have suffered greatly. Mr Knotford erected a temporary workshop in the inner yard up against the wall of the stable in Gresham College, and the Mercers' Company received a request from Benjamin Wolverton for a 6 by 4 foot

A gold filigree and blued-steel pair-case verge watch by Benjamin Hill, c.1660.

shed in Broad Street, for which he paid an annual fine of £7 7s (p. 50).[379] The lease term was seven years, but by the time of his death, in 1669, he had evidently found new accommodation nearby. His household goods included a bedstead with red petuana curtains and valence, three feather beds, one straw pallet bed, two bolsters, five pillows, five blankets, two rugs, six chairs, a cradle, some hearth furniture, a trunk and a set of drawers. He had a halberd and musket, and the kitchen was equipped with a small table and four old chairs, a parcel of tinware, a spice box and 99 lb of pewter. The trade items comprised a vice, two 'old Cristall cases and a parcel of old brass and steele for worke' valued at £5, a parcel of 'boxes unmade up', and nine 'fine cases' of silver valued at £3 13s 6d. The shop contents comprised just a 'small standing watch, two vices and other tooles' at £5. The value of the whole inventory was £89 6s 3d.[380]

Rather more is known about the clock- and watchmaker Benjamin Hill, who was sworn a free brother of the Clockmakers' Company in 1640.[381] By 1646 he was living with his wife Gunnett (the daughter of a clockmaker) in Boar's Head Court, Cock and Key Alley, just off Fleet Street, and from 1646 the parish records for St Dunstan's-in-the-West record the births of eight children, the last stillborn in 1655.[382] When Hill's property was listed in the 1666 Hearth Tax Assessment he had seven hearths; a large number by any standard, and certainly in comparison to his neighbours, most of whom had two or three.[383] A few months later, however, Boar's Head Alley and the Cock and Key Court were consumed in the fire, and Hill moved to a slightly smaller address in Fetter Lane, where he remained for the rest of his life.[384] He became senior churchwarden at St Dunstan's in 1669, and was buried there on 13 September 1670.[385] In his will, written three days earlier, he left his 'Clocks Alarums watches and other materealls Tending to my Trade being of Gould Silver Brasse or any other metalls … unto my wife and to my eldest sonne John Hill to trade therewith as God shall hereafter enable them.'[386]

When Hill's stock was assessed for the purposes of probate on 21 October 1670, the shop was filled with all kinds of clocks and

This silver verge watch by Benjamin Hill, in a piqué-leather case, had a running time of 16 hours. The back of the case has a rotating cover to protect the winding hole. *c.* 1660.

watches with 'diverse motions', watches with springs and some without, clocks with alarms and some with bells, rough movements for clocks and watches, several movements 'in their boxes plaine & others showing the day of the moneth', watches in silver cases, hanging watches and clocks without weights and springs, watches in gold boxes, assorted boxes and cases of silver and brass in 'divers fashions', two 'turkey-figured clocks with alarms', pendulum clocks, all sorts of frames and wheels, chains, 16 small bells and 6 dozen silver hooks, 34 bezels for the watch glasses, 20 pendants (for suspension), 1,656 watch keys, 240 watch glasses, and a dozen crystals cut in oval and round fashion, as well as a pumice stone (probably used for fine polishing of brass and steel components), some parcels of odd metal, files and other 'utensills belonging to the trade'. The whole lot was valued at £626 13s 6d.[387] There was a small market in exporting English watches and clocks to the East, so the reference to 'turkey-figured' clocks might indicate that these timepieces were designated for Eastern trade.

There are no references to timepieces in any of the other rooms in the property, so it is possible that they had been transferred to

the workshop after Hill's death to become part of the inventoried stock. The workshop space was large enough to accommodate a bed, with 'old curtens and vallens' as well as an old chair and table and a worn and frayed carpet; small comforts for a journeyman or apprentice while they kept some kind of guard on the stock overnight (*see* p. 40). The most valuable items must have been put away in a locked cupboard or trunk in another part of the house for added security. Such precautions were very necessary. Several years later an advertisement appeared in the *London Gazette* to advise anyone who had been robbed of a silver calendar watch in a filigree case with a black satin ribbon and an old winding key, signed Benjamin Hill *fecit*, to go to Newgate Prison to recover it. The watch had been stolen by Laurence Keck, 'who used to wear Whiskers, but lately cut off', a well-known felon who had been convicted 'and suspected to have committed many Robberies … near Royston in Hertfordshire and Counties adjacent'.[388]

Notes & references

ABBREVIATIONS

The following abbreviations have been used to reduce the volume of entries for the manuscript sources and other key works. Some of them indicate the location of the record, followed by the classification code. Most of the livery company records are held by the Guildhall Library (GL); but some are retained by individual companies. The terms used to describe similar sets of records vary from institution to institution, so only those most commonly used have been abbreviated here. The records in the London Metropolitan Archives (LMA) include all the material formerly held by the Corporation of London Record Office (CLRO). In some cases the old CLRO references and the newer LMA codes are combined.

Add.	Additional manuscript
BBH	Bridewell and Bethlem Hospitals
BL	British Library
CB	Court Book/s
CH	Christ's Hospital
CM/B	Court Minutes/Court Minute Books
CO	Court of Orphans, including Common Serjeant's Books, 1586–1773 (series CLA/002/01), Orphans' Inventories, [1600]–1773 (series CLA/002/02)
CSPD	Calendar of State Papers Domestic Series
EIC	East India Company
HAC	The Honourable Artillery Company
HMC	Royal Historical Manuscripts Commission
GL	Guildhall Library
GR	Gresham Repertories
JCC	Journals of the Court of Common Council
LMA	London Metropolitan Archives
LMWB	Lord Mayor's Waiting Book
MC	Mayor's Court
ML	Museum of London
PEC	Peculiar Court of the Dean and Chapter of St Paul's Cathedral
PROB11	Registers of Wills proved in the Prerogative Court of Canterbury
REP	Repertory of the Court of Aldermen
SBHB	St Bartholomew's Hospital
TNA	The National Archives
WA	Wardens' Accounts

PRINTED PRIMARY SOURCES

CSPD: Calendar of State Papers Domestic Series: Charles II.
  Originally published by His Majesty's Stationery Office, London. The dates covered by the volumes and the year of publication are: vol. 6 (1666–7) 1864; vol. 7 (1667) 1866; vol. 8 (November 1667–September 1668) 1893; vol. 9 (October 1668–December 1669) 1894.

CSPV: Calendar of State Papers Relating to English Affairs in the Archives of Venice (London, 1935).

Evelyn, J., *The Diary of John Evelyn*, ed. E.S. de Beer, 6 vols (Oxford, 1955).

Holme, R., *The Academy of Armory, or, A storehouse of armory and blazon: containing the several variety of created beings, and how born in coats of arms, both foreign and domestick. With the instruments used in all trades and sciences, together with their terms of art, also the etymologies, definitions, and historical observations on the same, explicated and explained according to our modern language* (Chester, 1688).

Pepys, S., *The Diary of Samuel Pepys: A New and Complete Transcription*, ed. Robert Latham and William Matthews, 10 vols (London, 1970–83).

INTRODUCTION

1. MC Depositions, LMA,CLA/024/06/016, 13 November 1666.
2. *Kurtze jedoch warhaffigeter Relation van dem erschrechkichen Feuer-Brunst welcher den 12, 13, 14, 15 and 16 Septembris die Stadt Londen getroffen. Gescrieben auss Londen, den 20 September, anno 1666*, Charles Purton Cooper pamphlet collection, vol. 194, item 4, Lincoln's Inn Library CPC 194.
3. E. Waterhouse, *A Short Narrative of the Dreadful Fire in London* (London, 1667), p. 48.
4. Compiled by a writer using the pseudonym Rege Sincera, a few weeks after the fire, but not published until the following year. The full title is: *Observations Both Historical and Moral Upon the Burning of London September 1666. With an Account of the Losses. And a Most Remarkable Parallel Between London and Mosco, both as to the Plague and Fire. Also an Essay Touching the Easterly-Winde* (London, 1667), p. 16.
5. T. Delaune, *The Present State of London: or, the Memorials comprehending a Full and Succinct Account of the Ancient and Modern State thereof* (London, 1681), p. 457.
6. CSPD: Charles II, 1666–7, 11 October 1666.
7. Clothworkers' Court Orders, CL/B/1/10 [1665–83], fol. 31, 13 September 1666.
8. Sincera, *Observations Both Historical and Moral*, p. 16.
9. S. Pepys, 2 September 1666, *Diary*, 10 vols (London, 1970–83), vol. VII, p. 268.
10. J. Evelyn, 2 September 1666, *Diary*, 6 vols (Oxford, 1955), vol. III, p. 452.
11. Barber-Surgeons' WA, MS 5255/2 [D/2/2], fol. 160.
12. Letter from Lady Anne Hobart to Sir Ralph Verney in Claydon, Claydon House Trust.
13. CSPD: Charles II, 1666–7, 4 September 1666.
14. From 1617 empty carts were kept at certain designated 'standings'. Laden carts or carts for hire could only enter Thames Street from the north and then to the centre. The laden carts had to follow a set route along five streets adjacent to Tower Wharf and the riverside markets of Billingsgate and Queenhithe. Empty carts crossing London Bridge were unable to turn east into Thames Street but had instead to follow a one-way system.
15. T. Brooks, *London's Lamentations: or, a serious Discourse concerning that late fiery Dispensation that turned our (once renowned) City into a ruinous Heap. Also the several Lessons that are incumbent upon those whose Houses have escaped the consuming flames* (London, 1670), p. 28.
16. Dr William Denton to his nephew Sir Ralph Verney in Claydon, 9 September 1666, Claydon House Trust.
17. E. Waterhouse, *A Short Narrative of the late Dreadful Fire in London* (London, 1667), pp. 28–9. Waterhouse actually says: 'ordinary House-keepers were put to 40 pound charge but to remove from the Fire, and some few of the more stored sort as I have been informed at near 400 pound.'
18. Broadside: 'Warhafftiger Bericht von der grossen Feuers-Brunst' on the great fire in London; with an engraving depicting a view of London burning, with three columns of letterpress underneath, engraved by Johann Hoffman, Nuremberg, 1666.
19. Tallow-Chandlers' CM, GL, MS 6153, vol. 3, 13 September and 28 November 1666.
20. J.M.S. Brooke and A.W.C. Hallen, *The Transcript of the Registers of the United Parishes of S.Mary Woolnoth and S.Mary Woolchurch Haw, in the City of London, from their commencement 1538 to 1760...* (London, 1886), p. 56.
21. CSPD: Charles II, 1666–7, n.d. [between 25 and 30 September 1666].
22. MC Interrogatories LMA, MC6/221B, 27 March 1668.
23. Skinners' Company CM, GL, MS 30708/5, fol. 10, 21 November 1667; fol. 15, 24 January 1668; fol. 29, 7 July 1668; fol. 31, 22 July 1668.
24. Royal College of Physicians, *A Collection of College Affaires left by Dr Goodall to the College of Physicians London*, MS 2189, fol. 1, February 1680.
25. Dr Merrett had a long-drawn-out dispute with the College. There is a paper note in Merrett's hand listing all 'such books as were preserved from the fire & belonging to the College of Physicians London delivered to the president 22 October 1667'; see Royal College of Physicians, MS 2189, fol. 15.
26. Merchant Taylors' Company CM, GL, MS 30101/8, fol. 161, 19 June 1668.
27. Goldsmiths' Company CB, MS 1548/B39, fols 90v and 91, 20 March 1667.
28. Letter from James Hicks to Williamson, CSPD: Charles II, 1666–7, 3 September 1666.
29. The location of the Letter Office is uncertain. Some authorities have suggested Cloak Lane, Dowgate, but there is no reference to this location in contemporary sources. According to *Leake's Survey of the City After the Great Fire of 1666*, it was located in Threadneedle Street.
30. Holograph letter from James Hicks, Postmaster of London ML, MS 42.39/4, 4 September 1666.

31. CH General Committee Minutes, LMA, CLC/210/B/001/MS 12806/06/0026, fols 31–2, 2–4 September 1666. Since the Hospital's foundation in 1552/3 the infant children were 'nursed' in Ware, Hoddesdon or Hertford, and only returned to London for schooling from the age of 10. See M. Barford, *Christ's Hospital Heritage Engravings* (Horsham, 2010).

32. The population of London at this time was around 400,000. How many people were actually affected and displaced by the fire is impossible to quantify.

33. Spectacle Makers' Company, CM, GL, Ms 5213/1, fol. 1v, 3 October 1666.

34. Grocers' Company Court of Assistants, GL, MS 11588/4, fol. 750, 29 November 1666.

35. Carpenters' Company, CM, GL, MS 4329/6 [not numbered], 23 March 1667 and 3 March 1668.

36. Clothworkers' Company Court Orders, CL/B/1/10 [1665–83], fol. 31, 13 September 1666.

37. CSPD: Charles II, 1666–7, 25–30 September 1666; 1667–8, March 1668.

38. 'Some Account of ye life of John Fryer & of severall of his Relations – written by himself 1715', GL, MS 12017/729.4. This holograph account covers 36 pages with notes and, notwithstanding the title, actually spans the period from *c.*1666 to 1724.

39. CSPD: Charles II, 1673–5, Entry Book 31, fol. 135, July 1674.

40. 'Extract wyt een Brief Van seeker particulier geode Vriendt, wyt London geschreven den 10–20 September, 1666', The Royal Library, The Hague; cited in Walter G. Bell, *The Great Fire of London* (London, 1920), pp. 318–20.

41. The Low Countries were ruled by Hapsburg Spain in this period. CSPD: Charles II, 1666–7, 7 September 1666.

42. CSPD: Charles II, 1666–7, 1–5 February 1667.

43. Pepys, 8 September 1666, *Diary*, vol. VII, pp. 281–2.

44. CSPD: Charles II, 1666–7, 25–30 September 1666.

45. CSPD: Charles II, 1666–7, 28–31 December 1666.

46. BBH, CM, LMA Ms 33011/12 [unfoliated], 5 October 1666.

47. Evelyn, 4 September 1666, *Diary*, vol. III, pp. 454–5.

48. Samuel Pepys, John Evelyn and William Taswell all mention the intense heat burning and scorching their shoe leather.

49. Pepys, 6 September 1666, *Diary*, vol. VII, p. 278.

50. S. De rennefort, *Relation du Premier Voyage de la Compagnie des Indes Orientales en l'Isle de Madegascar ou Dauphine* (Paris, 1668), pp. 326–8.

51. LMA, COL/CA/01/01/076 Rep. 71, fols 168v and 169, 6 September 1666.

52. LMA, COL/CA/01/01/076 Rep. 71, fols 169 and 170v, 8 September 1666.

53. HAC, CM, Book B [1661–92], fol. 89, 24 September 1666; fol. 89, 22 October 1666.

54. Stationers' Company CB, D TSC/1/B/01/02, fol. 124v, 2 October 1666. On 5 May 1668, Widow Warde was able to convert her shed to a permanent brick structure. The lease term was set at 61 years with annual rent of £14 payable quarterly. In view of her condition, the Company granted her a peppercorn rent for the next seven years; see fol. 143, 5 May 1668.

55. LMWB, vol. II, LMA, CLA/004/01/01/002, 18 September 1666.

56. Sheds were set up in the churchyards of St Katherine's Cree church in Leadenhall Street; St Martin's Outwich at the southern end of Bishopsgate; and St Edward's in Lombard Street.

57. 'An Account Book of money received and paid for sheds erected in Moorfields, Smithfield, and other places', Chamberlain's Office, 23 February 1667–7 May 1669/70, LMA, CLA/046/EM/01/015.

58. R. Johnson, *The Pleasant Walkes of Moore-fields* (London, 1607), n. pag.

59. LMA, CLA/046/EM/01/015, fol. 11 – taken by Richard Copson on 19 August 1667 for £5. His trade is not given.

60. REP, LMA, COL/CA/01/01/076, fols 19 and 55v.

61. REP, LMA, COL/CA/01/01/076, fols 56 and 56v, 4 December 1666.

62. REP, LMA, COL/CA/01/01/076, fol. 85, 26 March 1667.

63. LMA, CLA/046/EM/01/015, fols 8 and 11; Willson's fine was £60, and Smith's £10. Willson's occupation is not given.

64. Edmond Howes, 1607, quoted in W. Thornbury, *Smithfield and Bartholomew Fair, in Old and New London*, vol. 2 (London, 1878), ch. XLIII.

65. Thomas Pepys is given the label 'the turner' to differentiate him from Dr Thomas Pepys, another cousin, and Samuel Pepys's brother, also a Thomas. Thomas Pepys 'the turner' lived in St Paul's Churchyard before the fire. He became a prosperous merchant trading in the West Indies. Pepys, 14 September 1666, *Diary*, vol. VII, p. 286.

66. JCC, LMA, CLC/CC/01/01/044 JORS/46 [unfoliated], 14 November 1666.

67. JCC, LMA, CLC/CC/01/01/044 JORS/46, fol. 146v, 25 January 1667.

68. Pepys, 7 April 1667, *Diary*, vol. VIII, p. 155.

69. Goldsmiths' Company, CB, MS 1548/B39, fol. 215, 19 October 1668.

70. JCC, LMA, CLC/CC/01/01/044 JORS/46, 25 January 1667.

71. MC Interrogatories, LMA, MC6/224, 23 April 1668; see also MC Depositions, LMA/CLA/024/06/018.

72. J.G. White, *History of the ward of Walbrook in the city of London: together with an account of the aldermen of the ward and of the two remaining churches, S. Stephen, Walbrook, & St. Swithin, London Stone with their rectors* (London, 1904), 14 April 1670.

73. *Order of Court of Alderman for the removal of Sheds &c in Smithfield, Moorfields and other void places where they were allowed to be erected after the fire*, LMA, COL.SJ/27/372, 6 April 1673; LMA, COL.SJ/27/373, 17 March 1673.

74. E. Waterhouse, *A Short Narrative of the late Dreadful Fire in London* (London, 1667), p. 30.

75. Pepys, 7 September 1666, *Diary*, vol. VII, p. 279.

76. Haberdashers' Company CM, GL, MS 15,842/2, fol. 130, 24 July 1666.

77. CSPD: Charles II, 1666–7, 3 and 6 September 1666.

78. Evelyn, 4 September 1666, *Diary*, vol. III, p. 455. Evelyn had been appointed a commissioner for the care of sick and wounded seamen, soldiers and prisoners of war on 27 October 1664. Most of the wounded were treated outside London, but some were kept in 'Chelsey College and two other hospitals in the capital'. St Bartholomew's Hospital was probably one of them. See TNA, S.P.29/132, fols 23–4, 3 October 1665.

79. CSPD: Charles II, 1666–7, 6 September 1666.

80. CSPD: Charles II, 1666–7, Printed Proclamation Collection, 5 September 1666.

81. CSPD: Charles II, 1666–7, Entry Book 23, 6 September 1666.

82. CSPD: Charles II, 1666–7, 10 September 1666.

83. Holograph letter from Wind. Sandys to the Lord Scudamore, Homme Lacy, near Lincoln [*sic*], cited in W.G. Bell, *The Great Fire of London* (London, 1920), pp. 315–18.

84. *Autobiography and anecdotes by William Taswell, D.D., sometime Rector of Newington, Surrey, Rector of Bermondsey, and previously student of Christ Church, Oxford, A.D. 1651–1682*, in Camden miscellany, Camden Society, London, 1852, vol. 2.6, pp. 10–11.

85. *Middlesex County Records, Indictments, Recognizances, Coroners' Inquisitions-Post-Mortem, Orders, Memoranda and Certificates of convictions of conventiclers, temp. 1 Charles I. to 18 Charles II.*, vol. III, London, 1888, 4 September, 8 September and 20 November 1666.

86. Barber-Surgeons' Company WA, D/2/2 Ms 5255/2, fol. 187, 'Extraordinary Payments', 15 August 1667–20 August 1668.

87. Cutlers' Company CM, MS 7151/1 [unfoliated], 18 September 1666.

88. Drapers' Company 'Special Committees on Rebuilding of Drapers' Hall, Valued land &c', MS M.B./T.1 fo. 1, 18 March 1666.

89. Clothworkers' Company Court Orders, CL/B/1/10 [1665–83], fol. 32, 13 September 1666.

90. Apothecaries CM/B, MS GL8200/2, fols 471 and 465.

91. Barber-Surgeons' Company WA, D/2/2 MS 5255/2, fol. 160, 'Extraordinary Payments', 16 August 1666–15 August 1667.

92. Clothworkers' Company Renter & Quarter WA, CL/D/5/10 [1658–70], 'The Accompt of Mr John Child Quarterwarden ... ye Receipts of all Quarteridge & all other casuall Receipts & paymts from Midsomer 1666 untill Midsomer 1667', fol. 6.

93. Clothworkers' Company Renter & Quarter WA, CL/D/5/10 [1658–70] 'The Accompt of Mr John Child Quarterwarden ... ye Receipts of all Quarteridge & all other casuall Receipts & paymts from Midsomer 1666 untill Midsomer 1667', fols 8, 9v and 11v. 'Item paid for a Dogg to keepe ye Hall secure after the fire – 16s//Item paid for Collers and chaines for 2 doggs – 4s 10d//Item paid for another chaine for the greate dogg att the Hall – 5s//Item paid to the Constable of Cripplegate for the use of the watchman there for security of Lambs Chappell 3 nights after part of the lead was taken off ye same chappell – 4s 6d/11v – another payment of 5s//Item paid for a Mastiff dogg for the Companies use at the Hall – 12s//Item paid for provision for the dogs att ye hall for 42 weeks att 12d per week – £2 12s.'

94. LMWB, LMA, CLA/004/01/01/002, 31 December 1666.

95. CSPD: Charles II, 1666–7, Entry Book 23, 5 September 1667.

96. Holograph letter from Henry Griffith to his kinsman, ML, MS 42.39/1, 18 September 1666.

97. CSPV, vol. 35, 1666–68, pp. 62–80.

98. REP, LMA, COL/CA/01/01/071 no. 71, fol. 172, 8 September 1666.

99. JCC, LMA, CLC/CC/01/01/044 JORS/46, 19 September 1666; 22 September 1666.

100. JCC, LMA, CLC/CC/01/01/044 JORS/46, 3 November 1666.

101. CSPD: Charles II, 1666–7, 23 February 1667.

102. *Journal*, SBHB/HA1/6, fol. 16v, 15 September 1666.

103. *Journal*, SBHB/HA1/6, fols 16 and 16v, 3 September 1666.

104. *Ledger*, SBHB/HB/1/17 [1656–71], headed: 'The Rentall and Accompt of Peter Moulson Reviewer of all the Rents Quitt Rents and Annutys belongeinge to St Bartholomew hospital neare West Smithfeild London for one whole yeare vizt. From the Feast of Michael the Archangell Anno Dom. 1665 until the said feast Anno dom. 1666.'

105. *Journal*, SBHB/HA1/6, fol. 27v, 25 October 1666; fol. 21, 26 September 1666; fol. 16v, 15 September 1666.

106. *Journal*, SBHB/HA1/6, [unfoliated], 1 June 1657.

107. *Journal*, SBHB/HA1/6, fol. 17, 18 September 1666; fol. 19, 18 September 1666; fol. 238, 26 April 1669.

108. *Journal,* SBHB/HA1/6, fol. 19, 18 September 1666. Peter Mills was appointed a governor of St Bartholomew's Hospital on 10 December 1644. He rented a property from the hospital in Bartholomew Close and in his capacity as a bricklayer and surveyor offered much advice to the 'Shop Committee'.

109. *Journal*, SBHB/HA1/6, fol. 19v, 22 September 1666.

110. *Journal*, SBHB/HA1/6, fols 28 and 52, 25 October 1666 and 20 January 1669.

111. *Journal*, SBHB/HA1/6, fol. 33v, 3 November 1666.

112. *Journal*, SBHB/HA1/6, fols 21–22v, 28 September 1666; fol. 41v, 9 May 1667.

113. *Journal*, SBHB/HA1/6, fol. 28v, 28 September 1666; fols 30v and 34, 3 December 1666.

114. T. Vincent, *God's Terrible Voice in the City* (London, 1667), pp. 61–2.

115. REP, LMA, COL/CA/01/01/076, no. 71, fols 169v–170.

116. REP, LMA, COL/CA/01/01/076, no. 71, fol. 168, 6 September 1666; fol. 185, 10 September 1666.

117. REP, LMA, COL/CA/01/01/071, no. 71, fol. 172, 8 September 1666.

118. Mercers' Company GR [1629–69], fols 233, 234v and 235, 25 September 1666.

119. Mercers' Company GR [1629–69], fols 241–242, 25 September 1666.

120. Mercers' Company GR [1629–69], fols 243 and 247, 25–26 September 1666; fol. 249, 3 October 1666; fol. 245, 27 September 1666; fol. 238, 25 September 1666.

121. Mercers' Company GR [1629–69], fol. 259, 19 October 1666.

122. Mercers' Company GR [1629–69], fol. 251, 23 October 1666; fol. 289, 11 February 1667; fol. 245, 27 September 1666.

123. Mercers' Company Gresham Renter WA [1658–75] for the year 1666–67.

124. Goldsmiths' Company CB, MS 1549/B39, fol. 73, 26 November 1669.

125. Mercers' Company GR [1629–69], fols 254–266, 23 October–21 November 1666; fol. 289, 1 April 1667.

126. Mercers' Company GR [1629–69], fol. 246, 27 September 1666; fol. 282, 25 February 1667; fol. 279, 11 February 1667; fol. 273, 28 January 1668.

127. REP, LMA, COL/CA/01/01/076, no. 72, fol. 110, 21 May 1667.

128. Mercers' Company GR [1629–69], fol. 390, 12 June 1669.

129. Pepys, 9 September 1666, *Diary*, vol. VII, p. 283.

130. Brooks, *London's Lamentations*, p. 36.

131. Cited in R.R. Sharpe, *London and the Kingdom: A history derived mainly from the archives at Guildhall in the Custody of the Corporation of the City of London* (London and New York, 1894), p. 670.

132. This comment was reported by Marc Antonio Giustinian, the Venetian ambassador in France, to the Doge and Senate on 8 October 1666. See Calendar of State Papers Relating to English Affairs in the Archives of Venice (CSPV), vol. 35, 1666–68 (London, 1935).

133. CSPV, vol. 35, 1666–68, pp. 62–80.

134. *Relatione esattissima del' Incendio Calamitoso della citta di Londra*, Padua, 1666, printed in CSPD: Charles II, vol. 6, no. 164, 24 September 1666.

135. Brooks, *London's Lamentations*, pp. 23, 25.

136. JCC, LMA, COL/CC/01/01/044 JORS/46, [2?] October 1666.

137. CSPD: Charles II, vol. 6, no. 101, 25–30 September 1666.

138. Brooks, *London's Lamentations*, p. 36.

139. Letter from Dr William Denton to his nephew Sir Ralph Verney, 13 September 1666, Claydon House Trust.

140. CSPD: Charles II, vol. 6, no. 103, 1–11 November 1666; 25–30 September 1666; and vol. 177, no. 105, 1–11 November 1666.

141. Pewterers' CM, GL, MS 7090/6 [unfoliated], 13 December 1666.

142. REP, LMA, COL/CA/01/01/076, no. 71, fol. 168, 6 September 1666.

143. Carpenters' Company CM, GL, MS 4329/6 [unfoliated], 29 August 1667. William Walter Smyth appears on the Pudding Lane Hearth Tax in 1666. The property had three hearths.

144. REP, LMA, COL/CA/01/01/074, fol. 35v, 10 December 1667.

145. PEC, LMA, MS 19,504/10/23, 24 October 1667.

146. BBH, CM, LMA, MS 33011/12, 2 November 1666.
147. BBH, CM, LMA, MS 33011/12, 21 September 1666.
148. CH, CM, LMA, CLC/201/B/001/MS 12806/006, fol. 253, 5 October 1666.
149. CSPD: Charles II, 1666–7, 8 September 1666.
150. Brooks, *London's Lamentation*, pp. 23–4.

A–Z OF TRADES

1. T. Milles, *The Custumers Alphabet and Primer: Conteining, Their Creede or Beliefe in the True Doctrine of Christian Religion* (London, 1608), quoted in L.C. Knights, *Drama and Society in the Age of Jonson* (London, 1937; repr. New York, 1968), p. 138.
2. Letter from Robert Scrivener to James Hickes, CSPD: Charles II, 1666–7, vol. 6, no. 6, 17 September 1666.
3. 'Computation of the late losses per the fire' [c.1667?], in the hand of an unidentified amanuensis, but with autograph endorsement, BL, Add MS 72867, Petty Papers, vol. XVIII, fols 1–4v. Barber-Surgeons' WA, MS 5255/2 [D/2/2], fol. 159.
4. N. Culpeper, *The Complete Herbal: to which is now added upwards of one hundred additional herbs with a display of their medicinal and occult qualities physically applied to the cure of all disorders incident to mankind* (London, 1653).
5. Apothecaries were not permitted to prescribe or charge for consultations, which was the province of the physician. In practice the roles were often blurred, which proved a source of constant friction throughout the seventeenth century.
6. Apothecaries CMB [1651–80], MS GL8200/2, fol. 82v, 19 August 1663; fol. 90, 23 June 1664.
7. PEC, LMA, MS 19,504/09/12, 1663.
8. Culpeper, *The Complete Herbal*, sect. II, ch. I, 'Of Distilled Waters' (London, 1653).
9. CO, LMA, CLA/002/02/01/0292, fol. 30B, 6 July 1666.
10. I would like to thank Dr Derek Chadwick for his kind help.
11. MC Depositions LMA, CLA/024/06/018, 29 September 1668.
12. T. Nicholas, *Gemmarius Fidelius, or the Faithful Lapidary, Experimentally describing the richest Treasures of nature in an Historical Narration. Of the several Natures, Vertues and Qualities of all Pretious Stones. With an Accurate discovery of such as are Adulterate and Counterfeit* (London, 1659), p. 239.
13. MC Interrogatory LMA, MC6/239B, 6 September 1669.
14. T. Willis, *A Plain and Easie Method FOR Preserving [by God's Blessing] Those that are WELL from the Infection of the PLAGUE, AND For Curing such as are Infected With it. Written in the Year 1666 By Tho. Willis, M.D. late Sidney Professor in Oxford, and a Member of the Royal Society and College of Physicians in London* (London, 1691).
15. A. Boorde, *The Compendious Regiment, or, A Dyetary of Helth Made in Mountpyllier* (London, 1542), ch. XI, p. 261.
16. Bakers' Company CM, GL, MS 5177/5, [unfoliated], 7 August 1664.
17. R. Holinshed, *The Description and Historie of England written by W.H.*, vol. 1 (London, 1587), p. 168.
18. G. Markham, *The English Housewife* (London, 1615), 'Of Bread' no. 15, p. 209.
19. Cooks' Company CM, GL, MS 3111/1, fol. 105, 12 April 1670.
20. Hearth Tax Assessment, August 1666, TNA, E179/252/32pt4p6. The number of hearths is indicated alongside the names of the householder. Householders had to pay 1 shilling for each hearth and the tax was collected twice a year.
21. Bakers' Company CM, GL, MS 5177/4, fols 120 and 245; GL, MS 5185/1, fol. 39. St Margaret, New Fish Street GL, MS 1175/1; GL, MS 1176/1. See also W.B. Bannerman, ed., *The Registers of St Helen's, Bishopsgate*, Harleian Society, register section, 31 (London, 1904), p. 135.
22. ML, *London Gazette*, 10 September 1666.
23. Brooks, *London's Lamentations*, p. 31.
24. Last will and testament of Thomas Farriner, Citizen and Baker, TNA/PROB/11/384/174, fol. 362, 4 December 1670, probate inventory 23 December 1670.
25. CO inventories: Thomas Mitchell, LMA,CLA/002/02/01/07/0277, fol. 25; John Jasper, LMA,CLA/002/02/01/07/023, fol. 23; John Jarvis, LMA,CLA/002/02/01/0393, fol. 68B. PEC inventories: John Coleman, LMA,CLC/313/K/C/009 MS 19504/004/5/60; John Dawes, LMA, MS 19504/19/14; Richard Wood, LMA,MS 19504/16/13; William Bull, LMA, MS 19504/16/11; Christopher Hanch, LMA, MS 19504/20/18.
26. MC inventory for Thomas Poole, Whitebaker, LMA, CLA/024/02/106 MC1/68/205, July 1641.
27. R. Holme, *The academy of armory, or, A storehouse of armory and blazon containing the several variety of created beings, and how born in coats of arms, both foreign and domestick: with the instruments used in all trades and sciences, together with their their terms of art: also*

the etymologies, definitions, and historical observations on the same, explicated and explained according to our modern language: very usefel [sic] for all gentlemen, scholars, divines, and all such as desire any knowledge in arts and sciences (Chester, 1688), Book III, ch. 7, sect. 9.

28. CO inventory for Thomas Mitchell, Citizen and Fruiterer, LMA, CLA/002/02/01/0277, fol. 25, [no day] June 1666.

29. Holme, *The academy of armory*, Book III.

30. CO inventory for John Jarvis, LMA, CLA/002/02/01/0393, fol. 68B, 6 July 1668.

31. Mercers' Company Acts of Court [1663–69], fol. 100v, 19 August 1667; fol. 101v, 3 September 1667.

32. Clothworkers' Company Court Orders, CL/B/1/10, fols 62–3, 10 July 1668.

33. Coopers' Company CM, GL, MS 5602/5, fol. 46v, 18 October 1666.

34. Fishmongers' Company CM, GL, MS 5570/5, fol. 1, 13 September 1666.

35. *Journal,* SBHB/HA1/6, fol. 66, 17 August 1668.

36. Skinners' Company CM, GL, MS 30708/5, fol. 40, 3 November 1668.

37. Mercers' Company Acts of Court [1663–69], fol. 289, 11 February 1667.

38. Mercers' Company Gresham Renter WA [1658–75] 'Accompt of Thomas Papillon Renter Warden 1666–1667', Extraordinary Payments, fol. 7; see also fol. 5 under the heading 'In the Stone Walke' where Miles is listed as a tenant for a temporary shop for which he paid an annual rent of £1 2s 6d.

39. REP, LMA, COL/CA/01/01/076 no. 72, fol. 6v, 6 November 1666.

40. *Journal,* SBHB/HA1/6, fol. 51v, 14 December 1667.

41. REP, LMA, COL/CA/01/01/076, no. 72, fol. 6v, 6 November 1666.

42. Skinners' Company CM, GL, MS 30708/5, fol. 28, 1 July 1668; fol. 36, 30 September 1668.

43. Brewers' Company CM, GL, MS 5445/20, fol. 129, 16 February 1668; fol. 309, 25 January 1669; fol. 327, 22 April 1670.

44. Clothworkers' Company Court Orders, CL/B/1/10, fol. 54, 18 April 1667; fol. 57, 15 May 1667; fols 62–63, 10 July 1668; fol. 83, 29 January 1668. fol. 83, 26 February 1668.

45. A Royal Proclamation as to New Buildings in London and regulations as to the making and price of bricks, LMA,COL/SJ/27/037/01–06, 1630.

46. Clothworkers' Company Court Orders, CL/B/1/10, fol. 100, 18 May 1668; fol. 135, 23 September 1668; fol. 264, 5 May 1671; fol. 323, 17 March 1672.

47. *Journal,* SBHB/HA1/6, fol. 45v, 13 September 1667; fol. 50v, 9 December 1667; fol. 54v, 28 January 1668.

48. *Journal,* SBHB/HA1/6, fol. 69, 28 November 1668; fol. 71, 20 January 1668. See also '*Noate of ye severall orders of Mr Ridges*', SBHB/HC/4/46, which provides a chronological list of orders granted by the hospital in relation to his leasehold lands and property from 8 February 1661 to 1674/5.

49. Will proved 22 July 1670, TNA,PROB/11/334. The list of locations includes: St John's Street and St John's Lane; the Goat tavern in West Smithfield; Portingal Street, Lincoln's Inn Fields; Thames Street; Shere Lane; Carter Lane; Barbican; Aldersgate Street; Noble Street; Aldermanbury; Hatton Garden; Red Lyon Court between Golden Lane and Whitecross Street; and lands in Ireland.

50. CO inventory for William Ridges Esq, LMA,CLA/002/02/01/0692, 20 January 1670.

51. The destruction of the highway by the passage of brick carts was a general problem. See 'Recognizance taken before Sir Edmund Godfrey, knt, J.P. of Ralph Harwood, Leonard Sanders and Abott Nevill (alias Hunt) of St Martin's-in-the-Fields, all three brick-makers, in the sum of £40 each for "suffering their carts bound with iron-shod wheeles to pass along the street"', in Middlesex Sessions Rolls: *Middlesex County Records*, Volume 4: *1667–88*, ed. J.C Jeaffreson (London, 1892), pp. 1–6, 10 July 1667.

52. *Journal,* SBHB/HA1/6, fol. 59v, 29 January 1667 and 13 February 1667.

53. Goldsmiths' Company CB, MS 1548/B39, fol. 191v, 2 July 1668; see also further payment, 8 June 1670.

54. Mr Upton was the administrator of the Pest House and during the plague payments were made to him for treatment; see CO inventory for Thomas Dekker, blacksmith, LMA, CLA/102/02/01/0288, 8 December 1665.

55. *Journal,* SBHB/HA1/6, fol. 69, 28 November 1668.

56. *Journal,* SBHB/HA1/6, fol. 282v, 4 October 1675.

57. Coopers' Company CM, GL, MS 5602/5, fol. 55v, 2 April 1667.

58. Coopers' Company CM, GL, MS 5602/5, fol. 55v, 2 April 1667.

59. Coopers' Company CM, GL, MS 5602/5, fol. 232, 3 December 1672.

60. CSPD: Charles II, Charles II, 1666–7, vol. 7, no. 161, undated petition 1667.

61. MC Interrogatories LMA, MC6/208A and 208B, 9 July 1667.

62. PEC inventory, LMA, MS 19,504/7/119 [top of page missing], 1665.

63. PEC inventory, LMA, MS 19,504/05/61, 19 December 1664.

64. CO inventory, for John Wells Citizen and Cooper, LMA, CLA/002/02/01/0268, fol. 21, 31 October 1665.

65. CH, CB, LMA,CLC/210/B/005/MS 12811/003, fol. 159, 27 August 1667.

66. CH, CB, LMA,CLC/210/B/005/MS 12811/002, fol. 3, 25 July 1654.

67. CH, CB, LMA,CLC/210/B/005/MS 12811/002, fol. 5, 16 November 1654.

68. CH CB, LMA,CLC/210/B/005/MS 12811/002, fol. 12, 20 February 1654.

69. CH, Plan, LMA, CLC/201/4/181, c. 1660.

70. ML, trade token NN16694. Trade tokens in copper, brass or leather were issued between 1648 and 1672.

71. Inventory of Robert Whittaker, Cordwainer, St Giles without Cripplegate, PEC, LMA, MS19,504/10/16, 4 September 1667.

72. Inventory of Richard Wright, Cordwainer, St Giles without Cripplegate, PEC, LMA, MS 19,504/10/10, 20 September 1667.

73. Inventory of John Heath, Cordwainer, St Giles without Cripplegate, PEC, LMA, MS 19,504/3/03/11, 11 December 1661.

74. Inventory of John Blow, Cordwainer, St Giles Cripplegate, PEC, LMA, MS 19,504/16/15, 20 February 1671.

75. Inventory of Edward White, Cordwainer [no location given], CO, LMA/CLA/002/02/01/0583, 11 January 1669.

76. CH, CB, LMA, CLC/210/B/005/MS 12811/002, fol. 17, 8 May 1655.

77. CH,CB, LMA, CLC/210/B/005/MS 12811/002, fol. 293, 22 October 1661. The strained relationship with the Guppy family continued, and in 1661 Mr Guppy's widow complained to the Court about the abusive behaviour of Mrs Theame's daughter.

78. CH, CB, LMA, CLC/210/B/005/MS 12811/002, fol. 347, 1 September 1662.

79. CH, CB, LMA, CLC/210/B/005/MS 12811/002, fols 419, 424, 452, 459, 470 and 472.

80. CH, CB, LMA, CLC/210/B/005/MS 12811/003, fol. 93, 18 December 1666.

81. CH, CB, LMA, CLC/210/B/005/Ms 12811/003 fol. 159, 27 August 1667.

82. LMWB, LMA, CLA/004/01/01/002, 13 October 1666.

83. CH, CB, LMA, CLC/201/B/004/MS 12811/004, fol. 330, 22 January 1672.

84. CH, CB, LMA, CLC/201/B/005/MS 12811/002, fol. 100, 9 October 1657.

85. CH, CB, LMA, CLC/201/B/002/MS 12811/002, fol. 214, 12 August 1660.

86. CH, CB, LMA, CLC/201/B/005/MS 12811/003, fols 135–137, 25 June 1667.

87. Letter from Robert Scrivener to James Hickes, CSPD: Charles II, 1666–7, vol. 6, no. 6, 17 September 1666.

88. LMWB, LMA,CLA/004/01/01/002, 13 October 1666.

89. CH, CB, LMA, CLC/201/B/005/MS 12811/004, fol. 330, 22 January 1672.

90. CH, CB, LMA, CLC/201/B/005/MS 12811/003, fols 40 and 41, 26 September 1666.

91. CH, CB, LMA, CLC/201/B/005/MS 12811/003, fol. 234, 28 January 1668.

92. CH, CB, LMA, CLC/201/B/005/MS 12811/004, fol. 330, 22 January 1672.

93. Goldsmiths' Company CB, MS 1548/B39, fol. 79, 18 December 1666.

94. City of London Cash Book, LMA, COL/CHD/CT, fol. 209, 1 December 1667.

95. MC Interrogatory, LMA,6/111A and B, 1661.

96. Goldsmiths' Company CB, MS 1548/B39, fol. 79, 18 December 1666; fol. 86, 25 January 1667.

97. Mercers' Company Renter WA [1666–71], fol. 28, for the year 1666–67.

98. Journal, SBHB/HA1/6, fol. 102, 15 August 1670.

99. Letter from John Lord Berkeley to Sir Wm. Batten, CSPD: Charles II, 1666–7, vol. 6, no. 66, 3 September 1666.

100. Leathersellers' Company Rough CM, MS GOV/2/2 [unfoliated], 13 December 1666 and 21 May 1667.

101. Petition of Sir John Robinson, Lieutenant of the Tower to the King, CSPD: Charles II, 1666–7, vol. 6, no. 66, 8 November 1666. 300 buckets, 10 ladders and 12 hooks were also ordered.

102. Act of Common Council for the Prevention of Fires, 15 November 1667; see 'Fires' in Analytical Index to the Series of Records Known as the Remembrancia 1579–1664, ed. W.H. Overall and H.C. Overall (London, 1878), pp. 142–3.

103. EIC, BL, IOR/B/28, fol. 260, 8 February 1667.

104. Leathersellers' Company Rough CM, MS GOV/2/2 [unfoliated], 13 December 1666.

105. Leathersellers' Company Rough CM, MS ACC/1/3 [unfoliated]: payments of 1s 'to Mr Greene's men' for removal, 1667–68; 10s for mending, 1669–70; and another 9s 6d for mending, 1671–72.

106. Journal, SBHB/HA1/6, fol. 102, 15 August 1670; fol. 132, 3 February 1671.

107. *Journal*, SBHB/HA1/6, fol. 144v, 30 September 1672.
108. Plumbers' Company CM, GL, MS 2209/1, fol. 55, 2 February 1667.
109. J. Stow, *A Survey of London* [1598], ed. C.L. Kingsford (Oxford, 1908), p. 277.
110. S. Pepys, 4 September 1666, *Diary*, vol. VII, p .
111. Drapers' Company Minute Book, MS M.B./T.1, fol. 236v, 14 October 1659, fol. 237v, 17 October 1659.
112. Drapers' Company Minute Book, MS M.B.14, fol. 236v, 14 October 1659.
113. Drapers' Company Minute Book, MS M.B./T.1, fol. 317, 26 October 1666.
114. Carpenters' Company CM, GL, MS 4329/6 [unfoliated], 2 October 1666.
115. Drapers' Company WA, MS M.B.15, fol. 41v, 26 February 1671.
116. Drapers' Company CM, MS M.B.14, fol. 316, 10 September 1666; fol. 316v, 10 September 1666.
117. Carpenters' Company CM, GL, MS 4329/6 [unfoliated], 2 October 1666.
118. Grocers' Company Court Minutes, 'Orders of the Court of Assistants', vol. II, fol. 112.
119. Grocers' Company Court of Assistants, GL, MS 11571/5, Years 1665–1666, 1666–1667, 1668–9
120. JCC, LMA, COL/CC/01/01/044 JORS/46, [no day] February 1668.
121. Mercers' Company Renter WA [1666–71], fol. 44, Extraordinary Payments for the year 1666–1667.
122. Pepys, 2/3 September 1666, *Diary*, vol. VI, p. 272.
123. Drapers' Company Minute Book, MS M.B./T.1, fol. 217, 26 October 1666.
124. Merchant Taylors' Company CM, GL,MS 34010/8, fol. 116, 20 September 1666.
125. Grocers' Company Court of Assistants, GL, MS 11588/4, fols 749 and 750, 9 November 1666.
126. Grocers' Company Court of Assistant, GL, MS 11588/4, fol. 752, 4 December 1666.
127. Grocers' Company WA, GL, MS 11588/5 [1666–1667], 'Recd ye Extract from ye melted plate'.
128. Grocers' Company Court of Assistants. GL, MS 11588/4, fols 756 & 760, 1 and 4 February 1667.
129. Grocers' Company Court of Assistants, GL, MS 11588/4, fol. 765, 2 May 1667.
130. Drapers' Company Minute Book, MS M.B./T.1, fol. 213v, 2 August 1658. This pragmatism was nothing new. On 2 August 1658 the following entry appears in the minute book: 'New plate to be bought instead of plate sold – whereas this Company did about six yeeres paste in the times of extremity in the late Warres of this nacion for the raysinge of moneys for the Parliament sell away a greate parte of theyr plate which was lefte to them by benefactors and deceased members … to be kepte in memory of them for ever as pledged of theyr love to the company … ordered bought and provided such and the like peeces or parcells of plates as were soe given and sold as before said that the same shalbe made as neere as maybee made for quantity valew and fashion ansearable to the peeces or parcells of plate given by each respective person and sold as aforsaid.'
131. Cordwainers' Company CM, GL, MS 7353/2 [unfoliated], 18 October 1666. From the dates on the inscriptions, several items were gifted to the Company in the 1650s, and one item in 1662, so it is possible that some of the donors were still alive in 1666. Master Robert Botley died in 1669, and there is an entry in the minutes for the following year that he had retained in his possession six dozen silver spoons with 'Goatsheads not sold' belonging to the Company with an estimated valued of £60. An application was made to his executor for their return. Whether these came into Botley's care before, during or after the fire is unknown.
132. Coopers' Company CM, GL, MS 5602/5, fol. 43, 2 October 1666.
133. Coopers' Company CM, GL, MS, 5602/5, fol. 46, 18 October 1666.
134. Clothworkers' Company Renter & Quarter WA [1658–70] CL/D/5/10, fol. 5, 1666–67.
135. Mercers' Company Renter WA [1666–67], fol. 5, 'Received of Mr Rowland Worsop Mercer … £702.162.8' for 1,803¼ ounces of white plate and 850½ ounces of gilt plate, at the respective rates of 5s 1d and 5s 9d per ounce.
136. Mercer's Company GR [1629–69], fol. 242, 25 September 1666.
137. For further information, see D.M. Mitchell, '"Mr Fowle pray pay the washwoman": the trade of a London goldsmith-banker, 1660–1692', *Business and Economic History*, vol. 23, no. 1, London, 1994, pp. 27–38.
138. Clothworkers' Company Renter & Quarter WA, CL/D/5/10, fols 7, 8 and 10v, 'The Accompt of Mr John Child Quarterwarden … ye Receipts of all Quarteridge & all other casuall Receipts & paymts from Midsomer 1666 untill Midsomer 1667'.
139. Clothworkers' Company Renter & Quarter WA, CL/D/5/10, fol. 10v.
140. CSPD: Charles II, 1666–7, vol. 6, no. 106, 25–30 September 1666.
141. Goldsmiths' Company CB, MS 1548/B39, fol. 70, 26 October 1666.
142. Goldsmiths' Company CB, MS 1548/B39, fol. 75v, 30 November 1666. See also fols 175 and 177, 6 and 19 May 1668, for further references to molten silver 'taken out of the Rubish at Goldsmithes hall'.
143. Goldsmiths' Company CB, MS 1548/B39, fol. 92v, 16 February 1667; fol. 93v, 16 February 1667.

144. Goldsmiths' Company CB, MS 1548/B39, fols 118 and 118v, 5 July 1667. See also fol. 175, 6 May 1668, 'molten plate from the time of the fire weighing just over 50 ounces, with a parcel of other small wares, delivered to the goldsmith, Mr Mason to be reduced to standard'.

145. See Fire Court Decree G.C-120; B.M. 5070–42 28 February 1667/8 and 12 March 1667/8 in *The Fire Court: Calendar to the Judgments and Decrees of the Court of Judicature appointed to determine differences between landlords and tenants as to rebuilding after the Great Fire*, ed. P.E. Jones, vol. II (London, 1970). Maddox was a defendant with John Vaughan and others. By 18 December 1660, the messuage, the Golden Unicorn in Cheapside, parish of St Matthew, had been granted to Daniel Maddox for 23 years for a fine of £200 and a rent of £50 per annum. See also TNA, PCC PROB 11/333, 12 September 1670.

146. Goldsmiths' Company CB, MS 1548/B39, fol. 260, 9 March 1668.

147. CO inventory for Daniel Maddox, Citizen and Goldsmith, LMA,CLA/002/02/01/0674, fol. 251, 13 September 1670.

148. Goldsmiths' Company CB, MS 1548/B39, fol. 215, 19 October 1668.

149. Hearth Tax, TNA/E179/232/32, fol. 21v. Enodius [*sic*] Inman, gouldsmyth, parish of St Martin le Grand, Forster Lane, 3 hearths. Trade token: Museum of London, NN19193, Boyne reference London number 2862; obverse 'EUODIAS.INMAN.HIS.HALFE.PENY', reverse 'IN.SMITHFEILD.ROUNDS. GOULDSMITH'.

150. Goldsmiths' Company CB, MS 1548/B39, fols 257, 258 and 260v, 22 February–5 March 1668. Ann Terrett (sometimes spelt Terrell) was the wife of a goldsmith in Jewen Street.

151. Goldsmiths' Company CB, MS 1548/B39, fol. 266v, 23 March 1668. Inman continued to make substandard wares and was still living and working in Smithfield in 1672.

152. Hearth Tax Return, 45809, 1666 Cary Lane, in the parish of St Martin-le-Grand, 5 hearths. See also Gilbert Shepperd, last will and testament dated 6 August 1667, TNA,PROB/11/325, proved 18 November 1667. His name is variously spelt (see also Sheppard, Shepard).

153. Goldsmiths' Company CB, MS 1548/B39, fol. 202v; and MS 1549/B39, fols 49, 72 and 300.

154. Will of Abraham Wessell, TNA,PROB/11/388, 9 September 1689. Wessel was a Dutch merchant with properties in Bishopsgate Street, St Clement's Lane, in the parish of St George Southwark and, at the time of his death, in Chigwell, Essex. It is not clear from the rather scrappy and incomplete records for this case whether it was Wessel or Don Manuel Fero who had insured the stock – probably the latter.

155. MC Depositions, LMA,CLA/024/06/017, 25 February 1667.

156. J. Heywood, *The playe called the foure PP. A newe and a very mery enterlude of A palmer. A pardoner. A potycary. A pedler* (London, 1544), p. 36.

157. G. and C. Milne, with F. Pritchard, 'A Building in Pudding Lane Destroyed in the Great Fire of 1666: Excavations on the Peninsular House site, 1979–80', *Transactions of the London & Middlesex Archaeological Society* 36, 1985 (London), pp. 169–82.

158. Heath Tax Assessment 1666. Edward Baker and Edward Compton in Mitre Yard were also specialist hook-and-eye makers.

159. PEC inventory, LMA,CLC/313/K/C/009/MS 19,504/004, 9 February 1662.

160. CO inventories for John Bagnall LMA,CLA/002/02/01/0672, fol. 245B, 5 June 1671; and John Meadows, LMA,CLA/002/02/01/0442, fol. 92, 28 December 1668.

161. PEC inventory, LMA,CLC/313/K/C/009/MS 19,504/02/36, 4 September 1661.

162. CO inventories for Thomas Strong, LMA, CLA/002/02/01/0282, fol. 26B, 6 November 1666; Richard Eardley, LMA, CLA/002/02/01/0276, fol. 24B; Jeremiah Greene, LMA,CLA/002/02/01/0579, fol. 218, 21 March 1667; and PEC inventory for Roland Fleming, LMA, CLC/313/K/C/009/MS 19,504/004/5/17, 28 May 1663.

163. The New Exchange, founded by the Earl of Salisbury in 1608–09, was modelled on the Royal Exchange and specialized in selling luxury goods.

164. Court of Orphans' inventory for Herbert Allen, Citizen and Haberdasher, LMA/CLA/002/02/01/0570, fol. 215, 3 October 1668.

165. Letter form Commander Thomas Middleton to Samuel Pepys, CSPD: Charles II, 1666–7, vol. 6, no. 130, 23 September 1666.

166. BBH Court of Governors' Minutes, LMA,Ms 33011/12 [unpaginated], 25 October 1666.

167. Drapers' Company Minute Book MS M.B./T.1, fol. 6, 18 November 1668.

168. Fishmongers' CM, GL, MS 5570/5, fol. 8, 8 November 1666.

169. Plumbers' Company CM, GL, MS 2209/1, fol. 55, 2 February 1667.

170. Skinners' Company CM, GL, MS 30708/5 [1667–87], fol. 9, 7 November 1667.

171. Geoff Egan, in I. Blair and D. Sankey, *A Roman Drainage Culvert, Great Fire Destruction Debris and Other Evidence from Hillside Sites North-east of London Bridge: Excavations at Monument House and 13–21 Eastcheap, City of London*, MoLAS Archaeology Studies Series 17 (London, 2007), pp. 41–5.

172. CO inventory for Thomas Darker, LMA,CLA/002/02/01/0288, fol. 29, 8 December 1665.

173. CO inventory for Thomas Fowler, Citizen and Grocer (but ironmonger by trade in Bishopsgate Street) LMA, CLA/002/02/01/07/31, 6 February 1665. To the figure of 740,315 should be added thousands of (unspecified) pounds' weight of goods and various 'parcels'.

174. Pepys, 23 July 1666, *Diary*, vol. VII, p. 214. Thomas Simpson was master-joiner at the Deptford and Woolwich yards.

175. MC Depositions LMA,CLA/024/06/017, 13 and 14 May 1667. Brazilwood (often described in accounts simply as 'brazil') is a tropical hardwood of the family *Leguminosae*, whose core yields a brilliant red pigment ideal for dyeing cloth. The timber was also used for furniture inlays and veneers and by turners for all sorts of vessels and containers.

176. PEC inventory, LMA, MS 19,504/11/50, 5 October 1668. Carpenters' inventories for the period include references to ladders, working tools, toolboxes and grinding stones for sharpening tools; more rarely to stockpiles of timber in a yard, since most of the wood, nails and other construction materials were delivered directly to the place of work. See PEC inventories for: John Hawkins, LMA, MS 19,504/02/24; Thomas Casse LMA, MS 19,504/116/144; Thomas Lyon, LMA, MS 19,504/13/33; Thomas Woodroffe, LMA, MS 19,504/14/23; and Nicholas Bampton LMA, MS 19,504/18/24.

177. Pepys, 14 and 15 September 1666, *Diary*, vol. VII, pp. 285–6; see also 7 September for a reference to a bare bed in the house of Sir William Penn (p. 280).

178. PEC inventory, LMA, MS 19,504/09/20, 1 February 1667.

179. BBH Court of Governors' Minutes, LMA, MS 33011/12 [unfoliated], 12 June 1667.

180. *Journal*, SBHB/HA1/6, fol. 43, 4 August 1667.

181. PEC inventory, LMA, CLC/313/K/C/009/MS 19,504/19/76, 30 November 1674.

182. CO inventory for William Knight, Citizen and Skinner, LMA,CLA/002/02/01/0546, fol. 207, 21 November 1669.

183. Leathersellers' Company Rough CM, MS GOV/2/2 [unfoliated], 13 December 1666.

184. Act of the Court of Common Council, 29 April 1667, cited in John Noorthouck, 'Book 1, Ch. 15: From the Fire to the death of Charles II', in *A New History of London Including Westminster and Southwark* (London, 1773), pp. 230–55.

185. BBH Court of Governors' Minutes LMA, MS 33011/12 [unfoliated], 30 March 1671.

186. *Bills and orders for payment for supplying, repairing and painting leather buckets*, LMA,COL/SJ/27/044 Misc. MS 156.8.

187. Randle Holme, *The Academy of Armory* (Chester, 1688), Book 3, ch. 14, sect. Id, nos 58–9.

188. BL, Add. MS 12496, fol. 165.

189. Letters from John Greene to Allesio Morelli, glass-maker in Venice, BL, Sloane MS 857, no. 2, 28 August 1668.

190. BL, Sloane MS 857 no. 4, 10 February 1670.

191. Mercers' Company Acts of Court [1663–1669], fol. 247, 27 September 1666.

192. Court of Orphan's inventory for Samuel Soane, Citizen and Grocer, LMA/CLA/002/02/01/0787 fol. 288B, 20 April 1672. See also TNA/PROB/11/338, 28 March 1672. The name in the will is written 'Soanes'.

193. Leathersellers' Company CM, MS GOV/2/2, 20 October 1663.

194. BBH Court of Governors' Minutes, LMA, MS 33011/12, fol. 7, 14 September 1666. Edmond Silvester, Nicholas Hayes, John Lea, Jeremy Caslyn, Randall Jackson all received £7 per annum quarterly, and Richard Samon £5 per annum quarterly.

195. BBH Court of Governors' Minutes, LMA, MS 33011/12 [unpaginated], 15 and 27 February 1666. It is not quite clear whether this entry refers to Randall Jackson, silk weaver, or someone else. In one entry the name is given as Richard Jackson, and in another Leonard Jackson. To add to the confusion there are several entries for Randall Jennings, a shoemaker. I have not been able to find a Richard Jackson among the named artificers employed at Bridewell and so I have concluded, perhaps in error, that Randall, Richard and Leonard are one and the same, since the entries all relate to the use of the coal-hole space for a shed. On 15 September 1670 Benjamin Harrison and John Hew, the apprentices of Randall Jackson, complained that they did not have enough food to sustain themselves and had been forced to 'beg bread of the neighbours servnts and others and are immoderately beaten' by their master. The apprentices were removed from Jackson's care and he was summoned to account.

196. REP, LMA, COL/CA/01/01/076, no. 72, fols 77 and 77v, 4 December 1666; fol. 87, 28 March 1667.

197. PEC inventories, for Walter Wythes, LMA, MS 91,504/04/15, 7 March 1662; Arthur Nowell, LMA, MS 19,504/07/12, 9 August 1665; Anthony Holliman, CO inventory, LMA, CLA/002/02/01/0283, fol. 29, 26 November 1665.

198. Needlemakers' Company Extracts from Ordinances, GL, MS 2820, fol. 21 [date uncertain – 1674?].
199. PEC inventory for John Weaver, Citizen and Blacksmith, LMA, MS 19,504/4/16, 14 March 1662. See also Henrick Wilmore, Needlemaker, LMA, MS 19,504/12/10, 30 January 1668. Henrick's stock was not arranged in numbered packets, so the appraisers were forced to enter them as 'some thousand of needles – valued at £8'. His working tools were valued at £1 and the whole inventory was assessed at £19 13s 6d.
200. Needlemakers' Company Extracts from Ordinances, GL, MS 2820, fol. 37, March 1668/9.
201. Needlemakers' Company Extracts from Ordinances, GL, MS 2820, fol. 40, 7–14 May 1668; fols 18, 21, 29 and 36 [undated – 1674?].
202. Needlemakers' Company Extracts from Ordinances, GL, MS 2820, fol. 18 [n.d.; 1674?]; fol. 21 [n.d. – 1674?].
203. EIC, CB [1665–68], BL, IOR/B/28, fol. 188, 19 September 1666.
204. East India Company imports, in 'An Accompt of the exports from and imports into the City of London for the two years ending at Michaelmas 1663 and 1669; followed by an accompt of the revenue', BL, Add. MS 36785.
205. EIC, CB [1665–68], BL, IOR/B/29, 12 April 1667.
206. EIC, CB [1665–68], BL, IOR/B/28, fol. 186, 16 September 1666.
207. REP, LMA, COL/CA/01/01/076, no. 71, fol. 168, 6 September 1666.
208. EIC, CB [1665–68], BL, IOR/B/28, fol. 186, 16 September 1666; fol. 187, 14 September 1666; fols 188 and 189, 19 September 1666; fol. 190, 21 September 1666.
209. EIC, CB [1665–68], BL, IOR/B/28, fol. 210, 28 November 1666; fol. 233, 14 January 1667.
210. MC Interrogatory LMA, MC6/213, 20 November 1667.
211. Pepys, 11 April 1669, *Diary*, vol. IX, p. 515.
212. E. Waterhouse, *The Gentleman's Monitor*, London, 1665, p. 205.
213. CO inventory for John Brace, Citizen and Glazier, LMA, CLA/002/02/01/0946, 11 July 1674.
214. Samuel Peach's inventory, appraised on 27 December 1672, included 'one picture over the chimney of a fruitage' in the dining room, and in the chamber 'one old picture of a landskipp'; LMA, CLA/002/02/01/0833.
215. Pepys, 11 April 1669, *Diary*, vol. IX, pp. 514–15.
216. Barber-Surgeons' WA, MS 5255/2 [D/2/2], fol. 159, 16 August 1666–15 August 1667; fol. 162.
217. The Company officers had previous experience of moving the painting when it was taken to Whitehall at the behest of Charles I in 1627, an exercise that perhaps helped their disaster contingency planning in the first week of September 1666.
218. Barber-Surgeons' WA, MS 5255/2 [D/2/2], fol. 281, 8 March 1671. The nature of the work is unspecified, and it is quite possible that the payment for painting was actually for painting and decorating the fabric of the new Hall.
219. Pepys, 29 August 1668, *Diary*, vol. IX, pp. 292–3.
220. Plumbers' Company CM, GL, MS 2209/1, fol. 55, 2 February 1667.
221. Coopers' Company CM, GL, MS 5602/5, fol. 239, 4 March 1672.
222. The Royal College of Physicians, 'A Collection of College Affaires left by Dr Goodall to the College of Physicians London', February 1680, MS 2189, fol. 15, 10 October 1667. By tradition Harvey's portrait was reputedly scorched in the fire, but there is no surviving corroborative evidence.
223. PEC inventory for John Robinson, LMA, MS 19,054/16/14, 17 February 1671. John Robinson is recorded in the minutes of the Painter–Stainers' Company between 1668 and 1671. He was probably the father of Robert Robinson, a decorative painter and mezzotinter active from 1674 to 1691.
224. PEC inventory for Leonard Fryer, citizen and painter-stainer, LMA, MS 19,504/09/20, 1 February 1666. See also LMA, P69/GIS/A/002/MS 06419/006 and DCP/K/C/06/MS 25628/8.
225. Plumbers' Company CM, GL, MS 2208/4 [unfoliated], 18 September 1670.
226. *Bill for Worke done For the Honorable ye Citty of London* LMA, COL/SO/27/044 MISC MS 156/8, 1676.
227. Brewers' Company CM, GL, MS 5445/20, fol. 21, 2 May 1667.
228. John Fryer GL, MS 12017.
229. *Philosophical Transactions of the Royal Society*, vol. xii, no. 116, 26 July 1675.
230. Drapers' Company Minute Book, MS M.B./T.1, fol. 202, 14 October 1657; fol. 202v, 13 November 1657.
231. Drapers' Company Minute Book, MS M.B./T.1, fol. 247, 10 September 1660.
232. Pepys, 6 October 1663, *Diary*, vol. IV, p. 126.
233. H.R. Forsyth, *London Eats Out: 500 Years of Capital Dining* (London, 1999), chs 1 and 2.
234. J. Hatcher and T.C. Barker, *A History of British Pewter* (London, 1974), p. 131; 'the London

industry suffered less than those of the provinces [and] members of the London Company benefited from substantial supplies of tin at reduced prices form the monopolists, and the assurance of additional supplies at market rates.'

235. Clothworkers' Company Renter & Quarter WA, [1658–70] CL/D/5/10, fol. 7, for the year 1666–67.
236. Grocers' Company WA, [1665–66] GL, MS 11571/5.
237. Clothworkers' Company Court Orders, CL/B/1/10, fol. 79, 29 January 1668.
238. Pewterers' Company CM, GL, MS 7090/6 [unfoliated], 13 December 1666. Tin was purchased through individual subscriptions and distributed via an 'allottment' to members at an advantageous price.
239. CO inventory for John French, LMA, CLA/002/02/01/0575, fol. 216, 10 July 1669.
240. C. Ricketts, Pewterers of London 1600–1900 (Welshpool, 2001), p. 99.
241. Pewterers' Company CM, GL, MS 7090/6 [1662–76] [unfoliated], 20 June 1667.
242. LMA, CLA/046/EM/01/015.
243. Pewterers' Company CM, GL, MS 7090/6 [unfoliated], 22 August 1667.
244. PEC inventory, LMA, MS 19,504/18/25, 20 October 1673.
245. Clothworkers' Court Orders, CL/B/1/10 [1665–83], fol. 54, 18 April 1667.
246. Goldsmiths' Company CB, MS 1548/B39, fol. 74, 28 November 1666.
247. REP, LMA, COL/CA/01/01/076, no. 72, fol. 11v, 6 November 1666; fol. 52, 6 November 1666.
248. Chamberlain's Office, LMA, COL/CHD/CM/06/021, MS 359.
249. CSPD: Charles II, 1667–8, vol. 8, no. 162; also vol. 7, undated petitions for the year 1667.
250. Skinners' Company CM, GL, MS 30708/5, fol. 10, 21 November 1667.
251. Drapers' Company Minute Book, MS M.B./T.1, fol. 12, 9 June 1669.
252. Act of Common Council, cited in John Noorthouck, A New History of London Including Westminster and Southwark (London, 1773), Book 1, ch. 15, 'From the Fire to the death of Charles II', pp. 230–55.
253. PEC inventory for Daniel Fillops, LMA, MS 19,504/15/34, 10 June 1671.
254. CO inventory for Robert Tuckwell, Citizen and Plumber, LMA, CLA/002/02/01/0376, 25 July 1667.
255. CO inventory for Samuel Eames, Citizen and Plumber, LMA, CLA/002/02/01/0572, 20 September 1669.
256. CO inventory for Samuel Peach, Citizen and Plumber, LMA, CLA/002/02/01/0833, 27 December 1672.
257. Plumbers' Company CM, GL, MS 2209/1, fol. 39v, 3 November 1664. Lead cost about £1 per hundredweight; lead pipes cost £1 3s 4d per hundredweight. See the account for other prices. There are no other records for lead prices in the Company accounts before the fire.
258. BBBH Court of Governors' Minutes, LMA, MS 33011/12 [unfoliated], 5 October 1666.
259. Mercers' Company Acts of Court [1663–69], fol. 111v, 17 September 166.
260. Mercers' Company Renter WA [1666–7], fol. 5; fol. 28.
261. Fishmongers' Company CM, GL, MS 5570/5, fol. 8, 8 November 1666; 'Alsoe it is ordered by this Courte that the pewter and lead taken upp att this Companyes hall and belonging to this Company be melted by the plumber into piggs of lead of 300lb wt. att the least.'
262. Skinners' Company CM, GL, MS 30708/5, fol. 13, 28 November 1667.
263. JCC, LMA,COL/CC/01/01/044 JORS/46, fol. 122v, 2 October 1666.
264. Plumbers' Company CM, GL, MS 2209/1, fol. 58, 29 June 1667.
265. Plumbers' Company CM, GL, MS 2209/1, fols 72v and 73, 21 September 1668; [unfoliated], 29 September 1669.
266. Journal, SBHB/HA1/6, fol. 42, 17 June 1667.
267. CH, CB, LMA, CLC/201/B/005/MS 12811/003, fol. 81, 14 November 1666.
268. Clothworkers' Company Court Orders, CL/B/1/10, fol. 54, 18 April 1667.
269. Clothworkers' Company Renter and Quarter WA, CL/D/5/10, fols 10 and 11v, 18 April 1667.
270. Pepys, 4 November 1667, Diary, vol. VIII, p. 519.
271. Pepys, 24 December 1666, Diary, vol. VII, p. 420.
272. Spectacle Makers' Company CM, GL, MS 5213/1, fol. 1v, 3 October 1666.
273. Mercers' Company GR [1629–69], fol. 247, 27 September 1666.
274. 'An Accompt of the exports from, and imports into, the city of London for the two years ending at Michaelmas 1663 and 1669…', BL, Add. MS 36785 'Italie'.
275. Spectacle Makers' Company CM, GL, MS 5213/1, fol. 23, 15 May 1669; [unfoliated], 3 August 1671.
276. Spectacle Makers' Company CM, GL, MS 5213/1, fol. 2v, 10 January 1667, fol. 12, 20 June 1668.
277. Spectacle Makers' Company CM, GL, MS 5213/1, fol. 9, 20 April 1668; fol. 12, 20 June 1668.
278. CO inventory for John Clarke, Citizen and Spectacle-maker, LMA,CLA/002/02/01/0935, 14 May 1674. It is not entirely clear whether the John Clarke mentioned in the Company

accounts on 29 April 1669 at London Wall is the same person, as his first name is not supplied. The circumstantial evidence is strong.

279. Pepys, 3 February 1667, *Diary*, vol. VIII, pp. 42–3. Cranborne was Lady Carteret's house in Windsor Forest.

280. Grocers' Company Court of Assistants, GL, MS 11588/4, fols 790 and 791, 21 November 1667; Stationers' Company CM, TSC/1/B/01/02, fol. 155, 5 April 1669.

281. Chamberlain's Office LMA, COL/CHD/CM/O6/021, MS 359.

282. Weavers' Company CM, GL, MS 4655/4, fol. 99, 16 December 1667.

283. Skinners' Company CM, GL, MS 30708/4, fol. 167v, 27 September 1666. The first figure of the reward is very difficult to read – it could be 5 rather than 2 shillings.

284. PEC inventory for Thomas Driver, Bookbinder, LMA, MS 19,504/07/137, 27 November 1665.

285. PEC inventory for William Kendall, Stationer, LMA, MS 19,504/04/07, 13 February 1662.

286. Evelyn, 7 September 1666, *Diary*, vol. III, p. 459.

287. Thomas Vincent, *God's Terrible Voice in the City: Wherein are set Forth the Sound of the voice in a narration of the two dreadful Judgements of Plague and Fire inflicted upon the City of London in the Year 1665, and 1666* (London, 1667), p. 48.

288. CSPD: Charles II, 1666–7, vol. 6, 11 October 1666.

289. CSPD: Charles II, 1666–7, vol. 6, 12–21 November 1666.

290. CSPD: Charles II, 1666–7, vol. 6, no. 115, 29 September 1666.

291. Mercers' Company GR [1629–69], fols 235, 237, 244, 272 and 289.

292. CO inventory for Edward Greene, Citizen and Stationer, LMA, CLA/002/02/01/0452 A & B, fol. 96, 22 October 1668.

293. CSPD: Charles II, 1666–7, vol. 6, nos 109 and 110 [n.d. – September 1666?]; [n.d. – February 1667?].

294. Stationers' Company CM, TSC/1/B/01/02, fol. 124, 2 October 1666; see also fol. 162.

295. Stationers' Company WA, TSC/1/D/02/02, 6 July 1667–4 July 1668 'Item paid the Treasurer for the use of St Bartholomews hall for the yeare – £4'.

296. Pepys, 26 September 1666, *Diary*, vol. VII, pp. 297; 5 October 1666, pp. 297 and 309; Evelyn, 27 September 1666, *Diary*, vol. III, p. 459 n3.

297. CSPD: Charles II, 1667–8, vol. 8, [n.d.; July 1668].

298. CO inventory for George Hurlocke, LMA, CLA/002/02/01/0444 A & B, fol. 92B, 30 September 1668.

299. CO inventory for James Crumpe, Citizen and Stationer, LMA, CLA/002/02/01/044 A & B, fol. 94, 14 December 1668. Crumpe was the principal publisher for the writer Robert Younge of Roxwell, Essex, and he seems also to have had a contract with Alderman Owen for Welsh books. His 'separate debts' amounted to £1,229 9s 1s and his household goods and stock were valued at £408 7s 5d.

300. Stationers' Company English Stock, TSC/1/E/English Stock/D/01, 31 August 1666–1 September 1667.

301. 'Seasonable Advice for preventing the Mischief of Fire, that may come by Negligence, Treason, or otherwise. Ordered to be printed by the Lord-Mayor of London; and is thought very necessary to hang in every Man's House, especially in these dangerous Times. Invented by William Gosling, Engineer. Printed for H.B. at the Castle in Cornhill, London, 1645', in *Harleian miscellany: or, A collection of scarce, curious, and entertaining pamphlets and tracts, as well in manuscript as in print in the Earl of Oxford's Library…*, vol. 6 (London, 1810), pp. 399–401.

302. Pepys, 21 April 1662, *Diary*, vol. III, p. 69.

303. Pepys, 16 June 1662, *Diary*, vol. III, p. 111.

304. Pepys, 16 January 1666, *Diary*, vol. VII, p. 16.

305. Pepys, 5 September 1666, *Diary*, vol. VII, p. 277.

306. Pepys, 14 September 1666, *Diary*, vol. VII, p. 286.

307. *Journal*, SBHB/HA1/6, fol. 19, 22 September 1666.

308. *Ledger*, SBHB/HB/1/7 [1656–71]. Anthony and William Joyce appear in the Ledger accounts before the fire for two properties in Cow Lane: Anthony's name is listed for one property valued at 40s per annum; the other, under William's name, was valued at £7 per annum.

309. Pepys, 3 December 1666, *Diary*, vol. VII, p. 396.

310. Dead and live pigeons were used for a number of medical treatments.

311. Pepys, 21 January 1668, *Diary*, vol. IX, pp. 32–4.

312. *Journal*, SBHB/HA1/6, fol. 19, 22 September 1666.

313. *Ledger*, SBHB/HB/1/7 [1656–71], various payments for candles: 28 November 1665 – £37 3s; 28 October 1666 – £10; 3 November 1666 – £10; 8 December 1666 – £8 8s; 8 April 1667 – £5 5s; 30 April 1667 – £4.8s.

314. *Journal*, SBHB/HA1/6, fol. 17, 22 September 1666.

315. Brian Aliss (Aliffe) became liveryman of the Tallow Chandlers' Company on 26 August 1668; see Tallow Chandlers' CM, GL, MS 56153/3, fol. 10.

316. Tallow Chandlers' Livery CB, GL, MS 6153/3, fol. 274v, 18 May 1672.

317. Statutes of the Realm 1662 Act 14 Charles II, cap. 11, sect. XXIII. See also Lord Mayor's Proclamations Printed Mayoral Orders: 1593–1673, shelf mark 21, R.5, doc. 18.

318. Pepys, 2 March 1665, *Diary*, vol. VI, p. 49.

319. CO inventory for Mary Lee, Tallow-chandler, LMA, CLA/002/02/01/0706, 13 November 1669.

320. PEC inventories: James Jeater, LMA, MS 19,504/2, 1 March 1660; William Hieron, LMA, MS 19,504/3/35, 8 August 1662; Richard Mallett, LMA, MS 19,504/12/66, 15 November 1669; Thomas Williams, LMA, MS 19504/15/57; John Burnham, LMA, MS 19,504/18/13, 5 August 1673; John Thompson, LMA, MS 19,504/19/52, 16 June 1674. CO inventories: Andrew Patridge, LMA, CLA/002/02/01/0398, 7 November 1667; Henry Jordan, LMA, CLA/002/02/01/0410, 3 August 1668.

321. Carmen's Company CM, GL, MS 4907/1, fol. 62v, 3 February 1670.

322. Drapers' Company Minute Book, MS M.B./T.1, fol. 203v, 13 November 1657.

323. Cordwainers' Company CM, GL, MS 7353/2 [unfoliated], 18 July 1665.

324. N. Culpeper, *Culpeper's Family Physician; or Medical Herbal Enlarged*, vol. 2 (London, 1782), p. 134.

325. Pepys, 7 June 1665, *Diary*, vol. VI, p. 120.

326. Holme, *The Academy of Armory*, Book III, ch. 21, sect. 4.

327. PEC inventory, LMA, MS 19,504/19/70, 4 November 1674.

328. PEC, LMA, MS 19,504/08/18, 10 January 1666.

329. CO inventory for William Stackhouse, Citizen and Haberdasher, LMA, CLA/002/02/01/0286, fol. 28B, 27 April 1666.

330. CO inventory for Robert Travis, Citizen and Salter, LMA, CLA/002/02/01/0399, fol. 72B, 26 September 1667.

331. Goldsmiths' Company CB, MS 1548/B39, fol. 72v, 16 November 1666.

332. Leathersellers' Company Rough, CM, MS GOV/2/2 [unfoliated], 4 April 1665.

333. Fishmongers' Company CM, GL, MS 5570/5, fol. 2, 2 September 1666.

334. Cutlers' Company CM, GL, MS 7151/7 [unfoliated], 18 September 1666.

335. Pewterers' Company CM, GL, MS 7090/6 [unfoliated], 18 September 1666.

336. Skinners' Company CM, GL, MS 30708/5, fols 95 and 97, 2 and 7 June 1671.

337. Pepys, 4 September 1666, *Diary*, vol. VII, pp. 273–4.

338. Richard Howell was appointed Turner to the Navy Board in July 1660. Turners' Company CM, GL, MS 3295/2 [unfoliated], 3 October 1648. Richard Howell took on a new apprentice.

339. Pepys, 4 September 1661, *Diary*, vol. II, p. 171.

340. Pepys, 11 December 1661, *Diary*, vol. VII, pp. 231–2.

341. Pepys, 30 December 1662, *Diary*, vol. III, p. 298.

342. Pepys, 26 November 1665, *Diary*, vol. VI, p. 309.

343. Chamberlain's Office COL/CHD/CM/O6/021 MS 359, 1666–7.

344. Pepys, 4 June 1665, *Diary*, vol. VI, p. 117 and n1.

345. The last will and testament of Richard Howell, Turner, TNA, PROB/11/322 and PROB 11/322/96, 10 December 1666; proved 15 September 1666

346. Richard Howell's widow Sarah married Dr Edward Hickes, the rector of St Margaret Pattens, in 1668; see J.L. Chester-Foster, ed., *London Marriage Licences, 1521–1869* (London, 1887), p. 678.

347. Pepys' 'Navy White Book', TNA, Adm 2/1732, fol. 16v; Pepys' MS 'Navy White Book', PL 2581, 50.

348. Coopers' Company CM, GL, MS 5602/5, fol. 152v, 29 September 1670.

349. CO inventory for Edward Greene, Citizen and Stationer, LMA, CLA/002/02/01/0452 A and B, 22 October 1668.

350. These names were given by the appraisers to differentiate one chamber from another. They may not have been labels used by the householder.

351. CO inventory for William Lane, Citizen and Clothworker, LMA, CLA/002/02/01/0544, fol. 206, 13 July 1668.

352. CO inventory for George Browne, Citizen and Merchant Taylor, LMA, CLA/002/02/01/0544, fol. 212B, 24 December 1667.

353. Pepys, 11 October 1663, *Diary*, vol. IV, p. 329.

354. BL, 165/622/8, 1689, Petition *'For the Consumption of the Woollen Manufacture in this Kingdom…'*

355. BL, Add. MS 36785, 'An Accompt of the exports from, and imports into, the City of London for the two years ending at Michaelmas 1663 and 1669'; followed (fol. 59b) by 'an accompt of the revenue'.

356. Grocers' Company WA [1669–70], 'Particular Payments', GL, MS 11571/15.

357. Mercers' Company Renter WA [1666–71], fol. 44, for the year 1667–68.

358. Coopers' Company CM, GL, MS 5602/5, fol. 152v, 29 September 1670.

359. Goldsmiths' Company CB, MS 1549/B39, fol. 101, 1 April 1670.

360. Pewterers' Company CM, GL, MS 7090/6 [unfoliated], 30 April 1672.

361. CO inventory for John Young, Citizen and Draper, LMA, CLA/002/02/01/0671, fol. 245B, 1 October 1670.

362. CO inventory for William Ridges, Citizen and Skinner, LMA, CLA/002/02/01/0692, fol. 251B, 20 January 1670.

363. PEC inventory, LMA, MS 19,504/10/33, 24 October 1667.

364. CO Inventory for William Soule, LMA, CLA/002/02/01/0715, 17 September 1671.

365. Pepys, 2 September 1666, *Diary*, vol. VII, p. 271.

366. Sir William Petty, *The advice of W.P. to Mr. Samuel Hartlib for the advancement of some particular parts of learning* (Oxford, 1648), p. 5.

367. R. North, *Roger North on Music: Being a Selection from His Essays Written during the Years c. 1695–1728*, ed. J. Wilson (London, 1959), p. 294.

368. Pepys, 10 November 1666, *Diary*, vol. VII, p. 364.

369. Hearth Tax: City of London 1666, St Olave Old Jewry'. James White is listed as having six hearths.

370. I would like to thank Dr Darryl Martin for his technical advice, pers. comm. January 2016.

371. J. Boeringer, *Organa Britannica: Organs in Great Britain 1660–1860* (London, 1983), p. 99.

372. J. Playford, *Musicks Hand-maid: New Lessons and Instructions for the Virginals or Harpsichord* (London, 1663).

373. PEC inventory of Thomas White, LMA,CLC/313/K/C/009 MS 19504/004/5/16, 2 March 1664.

374. PEC inventory of John Haward, LMA, CLC/313/K/C/009 MS 19504/2/15, 26 April 1661.

375. Pepys, 4 April 1668, *Diary*, vol. IX, pp. 148–9.

376. Pepys, 13 May 1665, *Diary*, vol. VI, p. 101.

377. Pepys, 22 September 1666, *Diary*, vol. VII, p. 293.

378. Plumbers' Company CM, GL, MS 2209/1, fol. 55, 2 February 1667.

379. Mercers' Company GR [1629–69], fols 247 and 266, 27 September 1666. Benjamin Wolverton was living in Broad Street Ward in a house with three hearths in 1663. See Hearth Tax, TNA/E179/367/8, fol. 12. See also LMA, CLA/046/EM/01/015.

380. CO inventory for Benjamin Wolverton, Citizen and Clockmaker, LMA, CLA/002/02/01/0534, fol. 203, 6 November 1669.

381. Clockmakers' Company CM, GL, MS 2710/1, 30 November 1640.

382. St Dunstan's-in-the-West Parish Register, GL, MS 10,346.

383. Hearth Tax Assessment, GL, MS 2962/2.

384. From the inventory evidence this property had four hearths, possibly five (there is no reference to hearth equipment in the workshop).

385. Churchwardens' Accounts, St Dunstan's-in-the-West, GL, MS 2968/5.

386. TNA/PROB 11/333, quire 120, 10 September 1670.

387. CO inventory for Benjamin Hill, Citizen and Clockmaker, LMA, CLA/002/02/01/0673, fol. 245B, 21 October 1670.

388. ML, *London Gazette*, 15–18 December 1684

FURTHER READING

Bell, W.G., *The Great Fire of London in 1666* (London, 1920).

Haydon, C., *The Great Fire of London: Myths and Realities* (Winchester, 2007).

Milne, G., *The Great Fire of London* (London, 1986).

Porter, S., *The Great Fire of London* (Stroud, 2009).

Reddaway, T.F., *The Rebuilding of London after the Great Fire* (London, 1940).

Schofield, J., *The Building of London: From the Conquest to the Great Fire* (London, 1984).

Tinniswood, A., *By Permission of Heaven: The Story of the Great Fire of London* (London, 2003).

Acknowledgements

Most of the research for this book was undertaken at the London Metropolitan Archives and the Guildhall Library, and I am grateful to the staff of these institutions for their guidance and help. For allowing me to consult their records I wish to thank the Society of Apothecaries and the companies of Bakers, Barber-Surgeons, Brewers, Carpenters, Clockmakers, Clothworkers, Cooks, Coopers, Cordwainers, Cutlers, Distillers, Drapers, Fishmongers, Founders, Goldsmiths, Grocers, Haberdashers, Ironmongers, Joiners, Leather-sellers, Mercers, Merchant Taylors, Needlemakers, Painter-Stainers, Pewterers, Plumbers, Salters, Spectacle-Makers, Stationers, Tallow Chandlers, Turners, Tylers and Bricklayers and Wax Chandlers. Some records are retained by individual institutions and for their many kindnesses I would like to thank: Janet Payne (Society of Apothecaries); Victoria West (Worshipful Company of Barber-Surgeons); Mike Barford (Christ's Hospital); Hannah Dunmow (Worshipful Company of Clothworkers); Penny Fussell (Worshipful Company of Drapers); David Beasley, Eleni Bide and Sophia Tobin (Worshipful Company of Goldsmiths); Justine Taylor (Honourable Artillery Company); Jerome Farrell (Worshipful Company of Leathersellers); Jane Ruddell, Donna Marshall and Charlotte Dew (Worshipful Company of Mercers); Pamela Ford, Emma Shepley, Beth Wilkey (Royal College of Physicians); Kate Jarman (St Bartholomew's Hospital); Katie George (Worshipful Company of Salters) and Sue Hurley (Worshipful Company of Stationers). I would also like to thank Dr Stephen Freeth, Dorian Gerhold, Professor Vanessa Harding, Valerie Hart, Dr Peter Ross and Jo Wisdom.

I am most grateful to my colleagues Beatrice Behlen, Sally Brooks, Natasha Fenner, Meriel Jeater, Melina Plottu, Roy Stephenson and Sean Waterman for their help and support. Warmest thanks are due to Nikki Braunton in the picture library and to the museum photographers Richard Stroud and John Chase, the quality of whose work speaks for itself. I would also like to thank Clare Martelli and Anne Jackson at Philip Wilson Press for their enthusiasm and support in seeing this book through to press. Above all, I owe a great personal debt of gratitude to Robin Gable for punctilious and thoughtful copy-editing, and to Lucy Morton for such sensitive and beautiful design.

Lastly, my thanks to Roy and Audrey for their love and support.

Image sources

Index

References to images are in *italics*.